CTIC OCEAN

Svalbard

Norwegian Sea

Franz Josef Land

Novaya Zemlya

Kara Sea

Severnaya Zemlya

New Siberian Is.

Barents Sea

L. Taymyr

Laptev Sea

Kola Pen.

NORWAY SWEDEN

Scandinavia

FINLAND

L. Onega

L. Ladoga

EST.
LAT.
LITH.

Moscow

Ural Mountains

Ob

Yenisey

RUSSIA

Central Siberian Plateau

Lena

Verkhoyansk Mts.

Kolyma

Kolyma Mts.

North Sea

DOM

DEN.

Baltic Sea

BELARUS

West Siberian Plain

Irtysh

Angara

Lena

Stanovoy Range

Aldan

Amur

Kamchatka Peninsula

Sea of Okhotsk

London

NETH.

GERMANY
BELG. LUX.
SWITZ. CZECH.

POLAND

UKRAINE

MOLDOVA

Don

Volga

KAZAKHSTAN

L. Balkhash

Aral Sea

L. Baikal

Altay Mts.

MONGOLIA

GOBI

Sakhalin

Hokkaido

FRANCE

ALPS

AUST.
SLOV.
HUNG.
CROA.
BOSN. & HERZ.
SERB. & MONT.
ALB.

ROMANIA

BULG.

Caspian Sea

Caucasus Mts.

GEORGIA

UZBEKISTAN

Tien Shan

KYRG.

Tarim Basin

Kunlun Shan

Beijing

Tianjin

N. KOREA

S. KOREA

Sea of Japan

JAPAN

Honshu

Tokyo

Shikoku

Kyushu

SPAIN

GAL

Sardinia

ITALY

MAC.

GREECE

Sicily

Istanbul

Black Sea

TURKEY

ARM.

AZERB.

TURKMENISTAN

TAJIK.

Hindu Kush

Plateau of Tibet

CHINA

Huang He

Yangtze

Shanghai

Chongqing

East China Sea

Kyushu

CO

Atlas Mts.

TUNISIA

Mediterranean Sea

CYPRUS
LEBANON
ISRAEL

SYRIA

Tehran

IRAN

AFGHANI-
STAN

Indus

HIMALAYAS

NEPAL

BHUTAN

Xi

Hong Kong

TAIWAN

Hainan

Luzon

PACIFIC OCEAN

ALGERIA

LIBYA

EGYPT

JORDAN

KUWAIT

Cairo

IRAQ

Zagros Mts.

Persian Gulf

SAUDI ARABIA

QATAR

U.A.E.

PAKISTAN

Delhi

Karachi

Ganges

INDIA

BANGLADESH

MYANMAR

Irrawaddy

LAOS

VIETNAM

South China Sea

PHILIPPINES

Mindanao

SANIA

MALI

SAHARA

NIGER

CHAD

Sahel

L. Chad

Nile

Red Sea

Arabian Desert

OMAN

ERITREA

YEMEN

DJIBOUTI

Arabian Sea

Deccan Plateau

Bay of Bengal

Bangkok

THAILAND

CAMBODIA

Mekong

BRUNEI

MALAYSIA

Celebes

New Guinea

NEA

BURKINA FASO

Niger

GHANA

NIGERIA

BENIN

TOGO

CAMEROON

CEN. AFRICAN REP.

Congo

UGANDA

ETHIOPIA

SOMALIA

SRI LANKA

SINGAPORE

Sumatra

Borneo

INDONESIA

Java

Jakarta

PAPUA NEW GUINEA

RE

EQ. GUINEA

GABON

REP. OF THE CONGO

DEM. REP. OF THE CONGO

L. Victoria

L. Tanganyika

KENYA

TANZANIA

EAST TIMOR

Timor

SOLOMON ISLANDS

ANGOLA

MALAWI

L. Malawi

INDIAN OCEAN

ZAMBIA

Zambeze

MADAGASCAR

Great Sandy Desert

Great Dividing Range

NAMIBIA

ZIMBABWE

BOTSWANA

Kalahari Desert

SWAZILAND

SOUTH AFRICA

LESOTHO

AUSTRALIA

Great Victoria Desert

Darling

NTIC

AN

Kerguélen Is.

Tasmania

ICA

Junior
Worldmark
Encyclopedia of
Physical
Geography

Junior Worldmark Encyclopedia of
Physical Geography

VOLUME 1

Afghanistan to Comoros

Karen Ellicott and Susan B. Gall,
Editors

Detroit • New York • San Diego • San Francisco • Cleveland • New Haven, Conn. • Waterville, Maine • London • Munich

THOMSON
✦
GALE ™

JUNIOR WORLDMARK ENCYCLOPEDIA OF PHYSICAL GEOGRAPHY

Editors
Karen Ellicott and Susan Bevan Gall

Associate Editors
Robert J. Groelsema, Ph.D.,
Jeneen Hobby, Ph.D., Maura Malone,
and Rosalie Wieder

Graphics and Layout
Steven Ollay

Project Editor
Allison McNeill

Imaging and Multimedia
Christine O'Bryan

Cover Design
Cynthia Baldwin

Composition
Evi Seoud

Manufacturing
Rita Wimberley

Library of Congress Cataloging-in-Publication Data

Junior worldmark encyclopedia of physical geography / Karen Ellicott and Susan Bevan Gall, editors.
  v. cm.
Includes bibliographical references.
Contents: v. 1. Afghanistan to Comoros -- v. 2. Congo, Democratic Republic of the to India -- v. 3. Indonesia to Mongolia -- v. 4. Morocco to Slovakia -- v. 5. Slovenia to Zimbabwe.
  ISBN 0-7876-6265-8 (set : hardcover) -- ISBN 0-7876-6266-6 (v. 1) -- ISBN 0-7876-6267-4 (v. 2) -- ISBN 0-7876-6268-2 (v. 3) -- ISBN 0-7876-6269-0 (v. 4) -- ISBN 0-7876-6633-5 (v. 5)
  1. Physical geography--Encyclopedias, Juvenile. [1. Physical geography--Encyclopedias.] I. Ellicott, Karen. II. Gall, Susan B.
  GB58.J86 2003
  910'.02'03--dc21
                              2003009019

Printed in the United States of America
1 0 9 8 7 6 5

Contents
Volume 1

Cumulative Contents vi
Countries by Continent.......................... viii
Reader's Guide..................................... x
Words to Know...................................... xv

Afghanistan 1
Albania 6
Algeria 10
Andorra 15
Angola 18
Antarctica 22
Antigua and Barbuda 30
Argentina 33
Armenia 40
Australia 44
Austria 54
Azerbaijan 58
Bahamas, The 62
Bahrain 65
Bangladesh..68
Barbados 72
Belarus 75
Belgium 78
Belize 82
Benin 86
Bhutan 89
Bolivia...92
Bosnia and Herzegovina 97
Botswana...101
Brazil 105
Brunei 111
Bulgaria 114

Burkina Faso 119
Burundi..123
Cambodia 126
Cameroon 130
Canada 135
Cape Verde 145
Central African Republic 148
Chad 152
Chile 157
China 162
Colombia 172
Comoros 180

Appendixes......................................xxvii
    A. Continents by Area xxvii
    B. Countries by Area xxvii
    C. Countries by Population xxxiii
    D. Oceans and Seas by Area xxxix
    E. Oceans by Depth............................ xli
    F. Islands by Area xlii
    G. Deserts by Area............................ xlv
    H. Mountains by Height........................ xlvi
    I. Volcanoes by Height li
    J. Rivers over 1,000 Miles (1,600 Kilometers) ... liv
    K. Waterfalls by Height lvii
    L. Lakes by Area.............................. lix
    M. Lakes by Depth............................. lxi
    N. Seven Wonders of the Ancient World lxiii
    O. Seven Wonders of the Natural World lxiv

Selected Sources for Further Study lxv

Cumulative Contents

Volume 1

Afghanistan 1
Albania 6
Algeria 10
Andorra 15
Angola 18
Antarctica 22
Antigua and Barbuda 30
Argentina..33
Armenia 40
Australia...44
Austria 54
Azerbaijan..58
Bahamas, The 62
Bahrain 65
Bangladesh 68
Barbados 72
Belarus...75
Belgium 78
Belize...82
Benin 86
Bhutan...89
Bolivia..92
Bosnia and Herzegovina.......................................97
Botswana..101
Brazil 105
Brunei 111
Bulgaria 114
Burkina Faso 119
Burundi 123
Cambodia..126
Cameroon 130
Canada..135
Cape Verde 145
Central African Republic......................................148
Chad 152
Chile...157
China..162
Colombia...172
Comoros..180

Volume 2

Congo (DROC) 1
Congo (ROC) 6
Costa Rica 10
Côte d'Ivoire 15
Croatia 19
Cuba 23

Cyprus..27
Czech Republic 31
Denmark..34
Djibouti 39
Dominica..42
Dominican Republic...45
East Timor..51
Ecuador..54
Egypt...59
El Salvador 66
Equatorial Guinea 72
Eritrea..76
Estonia...80
Ethiopia 85
Fiji 92
Finland...95
France 100
Gabon 107
Gambia, The 111
Georgia 114
Germany 118
Ghana 125
Greece..130
Grenada 135
Guatemala...138
Guinea 142
Guinea-Bissau 146
Guyana 150
Haiti 154
Honduras...158
Hungary 162
Iceland..166
India...172

Volume 3

Indonesia..1
Iran..7
Iraq..15
Ireland..19
Israel..23
Italy...28
Jamaica..34
Japan...37
Jordan..46
Kazakhstan 50
Kenya 55
Kiribati 62
Korea, North 65
Korea, South...70

CUMULATIVE CONTENTS

Kuwait 74
Kyrgyzstan 77
Laos 81
Latvia 85
Lebanon 88
Lesotho 91
Liberia 94
Libya 97
Liechtenstein 102
Lithuania 104
Luxembourg 108
Macedonia 111
Madagascar 115
Malawi 119
Malaysia 123
Maldives 129
Mali 132
Malta 136
Marshall Islands 138
Mauritania 141
Mauritius 145
Mexico 149
Micronesia, Federated States of 155
Moldova 159
Monaco 162
Mongolia 165

Volume 4

Morocco 1
Mozambique 7
Myanmar 13
Namibia 18
Nauru 24
Nepal 26
Netherlands 31
New Zealand 36
Nicaragua 42
Niger 48
Nigeria 51
Norway 57
Oman 63
Pakistan 67
Palau 72
Panama 76
Papua New Guinea 82
Paraguay 88
Peru 92
Philippines 99
Poland 106
Portugal 110
Puerto Rico 115
Qatar 119
Romania 122
Russia 128

Rwanda 139
Saint Kitts and Nevis 142
Saint Lucia 145
Saint Vincent and the Grenadines 148
Samoa 152
San Marino 156
Sao Tome and Principe 158
Saudi Arabia 161
Senegal 166
Serbia and Montenegro 171
Seychelles 176
Sierra Leone 180
Singapore 184
Slovakia 187

Volume 5

Slovenia 1
Solomon Islands 5
Somalia 9
South Africa 14
Spain 20
Sri Lanka 27
Sudan 32
Suriname 39
Swaziland 43
Sweden 46
Switzerland 52
Syria 57
Taiwan 62
Tajikistan 66
Tanzania 70
Thailand 77
Togo 83
Tonga 86
Trinidad and Tobago 89
Tunisia 93
Turkey 97
Turkmenistan 105
Tuvalu 109
Uganda 112
Ukraine 117
United Arab Emirates 123
United Kingdom 126
United States 133
Uruguay 141
Uzbekistan 144
Vanuatu 148
Vatican 152
Venezuela 155
Vietnam 162
Yemen 166
Zambia 171
Zimbabwe 175

Countries of the World, by Continent

Africa
Algeria
Angola
Benin
Botswana
Burkina Faso
Burundi
Cameroon
Cape Verde
Chad
Comoros
Congo, Democratic Republic of the
Congo, Republic of
Côte d'Ivoire
Djibouti
Egypt
Equatorial Guinea
Eritrea
Ethiopia
Gabon
Gambia, The
Ghana
Guinea
Guinea-Bissau
Guyana
Kenya
Lesotho
Liberia
Libya
Madagascar
Malawi
Mali
Mauritania
Mauritius
Morocco
Mozambique
Namibia
Niger
Nigeria
Rwanda
São Tomé and Príncipe
Senegal
Seychelles
Sierra Leone
Somalia
South Africa
Sudan
Swaziland
Tanzania

Togo
Tunisia
Uganda
Zambia
Zimbabwe

Asia
Afghanistan
Armenia
Azerbaijan
Bahrain
Bangladesh
Bhutan
Brunei
Cambodia
China
Cyprus
East Timor
Georgia
India
Indonesia
Iran
Iraq
Israel
Japan
Jordan
Kazakhstan
Korea, North (Democratic People's Republic of)
Korea, South (Republic of)
Kuwait
Kyrgyzstan
Laos
Lebanon
Malaysia
Mongolia
Myanmar
Nepal
Oman
Pakistan
Philippines
Qatar
Russia
Saudi Arabia
Singapore
Sri Lanka
Syria
Taiwan
Tajikistan
Thailand

Turkey
Turkmenistan
United Arab Emirates
Uzbekistan
Vietnam
Yemen

Australia

Australia

Europe

Albania
Andorra
Austria
Belarus
Belgium
Bosnia and Herzegovina
Bulgaria
Croatia
Czech Republic
Denmark
Estonia
Finland
France
Germany
Greece
Hungary
Iceland
Ireland
Italy
Latvia
Liechtenstein
Lithuania
Luxembourg
Macedonia
Malta
Moldova
Monaco
Netherlands
Norway
Poland
Portugal
Romania
Russia
San Marino
Serbia and Montenegro
Slovakia
Slovenia
Spain
Sweden
Switzerland
Ukraine
United Kingdom
Vatican City

North America

Antigua and Barbuda
Bahamas
Barbados
Belize
Canada
Costa Rica
Cuba
Dominica
Dominican Republic
Ecuador
El Salvador
Guatemala
Haiti
Honduras
Jamaica
Mexico
Nicaragua
Panama
Puerto Rico
Saint Kitts and Nevis
Saint Lucia
Saint Vincent and the Grenadines
United States of America

Oceania

Note: The island nations lying in the Pacific Ocean are not part of any continent.

Fiji
Kiribati
Marshall Islands
Micronesia
Nauru
New Zealand
Palau
Papua New Guinea
Samoa
Solomon Islands
Tonga
Tuvalu
Vanuatu

South America

Argentina
Bolivia
Brazil
Chile
Colombia
Paraguay
Peru
Suriname
Trinidad and Tobago
Uruguay
Venezuela

Reader's Guide

Junior Worldmark Encyclopedia of Physical Geography presents a comprehensive survey of the physical geography of 192 countries of the world plus Taiwan, Antarctica, and Puerto Rico.

The entries are arranged alphabetically by country in five volumes. Following the format of other popular titles in the *Junior Worldmark* series, information in each entry is presented in a consistent format, allowing student researchers to find information and compare countries quickly and easily.

A topographic map—with notable mountain ranges and peaks, lakes, rivers, deserts, and coastal areas labeled—accompanies each entry. In addition, more than 200 photographs illustrate the varied landscapes found in the countries of the world. Adding further interest are the "Did You Know?" boxes appearing in the entries, noting interesting or unusual geographic features or facts or explaining regional geographic references.

Organization

Each volume begins with the contents listed for that volume, followed by a cumulative table of contents for all five volumes in the set. To help researchers who wish to identify a country within one of the world's continents, a finder table—Countries of the World by Continent—appears at the front of each volume. Words to Know, a glossary of terms related to geography, completes the front matter. Entries for individual countries follow. Although all numbered rubrics are included in every entry, entries vary in length depending primarily on the geographic complexity of the country's land area.

Each entry begins with a list of key facts about the physical characteristics of the country; measurements are provided in both metric and English units. Student researchers should be reminded that geography is an imprecise science, and measurements of geographical features may vary from source to source.

Key Facts

■ **Official name**

The countries of the world are referred to by a common name; the more formal official name is listed here.

■ **Area**

The country's area, usually including islands, is provided in square kilometers and square miles.

■ **Highest point on mainland**

The height, in meters and feet, is given for the highest point on the mainland portion of the country. For most countries, this is also the highest point anywhere in the country.

■ **Highest point in territory**

For some countries with islands and territories, the highest point not on the mainland is provided in meters and feet.

■ **Lowest point on land**

The elevation, in meters and feet, for the lowest point on the mainland portion of the country is provided.

Hemispheres

The country's hemispheres (Northern, Southern, Eastern, and Western) help the researcher locate the country on the globe.

Time zone

The time zone of the country's capital is provided, with the time related to Greenwich Mean Time (GMT). For some large countries, more than one time zone may be listed.

Longest distances

Measurements in kilometers and miles of the country's widest points from north to south and east to west are given. For some countries, longest distances may be measured on a slight diagonal (northwest to southeast, for example).

Land boundaries

The total distance making up the country's borders with other nations is provided in kilometers and miles, followed by the border distances with the individual neighboring countries.

Coastline

Coastline measurements, in kilometers and miles, are approximate. Coastline measurements are likely to vary from source to source.

Territorial sea limits

The territory extending into the ocean over which the country claims control or jurisdiction. Territorial sea limits are given in kilometers and nautical miles, and generally govern activities such as fishing and mineral rights.

The first four numbered rubrics offer a general overview of the country.

1 ⊕ LOCATION AND SIZE

This section gives the reader an overview of where the country lies and provides its relation to the bodies of water around it. Also included is information about whether the country is divided into states, provinces, or other internal administrative units.

2 ⊕ TERRITORIES AND DEPENDENCIES

Many countries exercise jurisdiction over territories—often islands—that are not part of the mainland. This section lists any such territories and dependencies.

3 ⊕ CLIMATE

The general climate of the country is described, with a table providing seasonal temperature ranges included for many countries. General information about rainfall and snow patterns is also included here.

4 ⊕ TOPOGRAPHIC REGIONS

An overview of the general topography (shape of the country's land surface) is provided, with key features (mountain ranges, plateaus, deserts, valleys, lakes, rivers) noted.

The next eight numbered rubrics—5 through 12—describe specific geographic features. All entries include all eight headings. Since all countries do not include every geographic feature, individual entries note the absence of specific features.

5 ⊕ OCEANS AND SEAS

The oceans and seas bounding the country are listed. Subheadings describe specific features of the country and its coastal areas. Subheads are used in entries as appropriate and may include:

Seacoast and Undersea Features

Includes discussion of nearby undersea features of note, such as deep ocean trenches or coral reefs.

Sea Inlets and Straits

Includes major bays, gulfs, sounds, channels, straits, and other sea inlets that characterize the coastal areas.

Islands and Archipelagos

Major islands and island chains are described here.

Other Coastal Features

Includes notable peninsulas, isthmuses, and describes the type and quality of the coastal areas.

6 ⊕ INLAND LAKES

Major and significant lakes are included. When a lake straddles a border between two countries, it is covered in both entries. Major man-made reservoirs are also included in this section in some entries.

7 ⊕ RIVERS AND WATERFALLS

Describes important rivers, giving length and general characteristics. Also includes major waterfalls.

8 ⊕ DESERTS

Arid and semi-arid flatland regions are described.

9 ⊕ FLAT AND ROLLING TERRAIN

Areas that range from flat and treeless to rounded terrain are described.

10 ⊕ MOUNTAINS AND VOLCANOES

Mountain peaks, including volcanoes, are described here, typically in the context of a mountain range.

11 ⊕ CANYONS AND CAVES

Notable canyons and cave systems are described.

12 ⊕ PLATEAUS AND MONOLITHS

Regions of high elevation but with relatively flat terrain and monoliths (huge stone outcroppings) are described here.

The final two numbered rubrics describe notable man-made features, and provide resources for further study. Supplementing the Further Reading suggestions provided in each entry is the Selected Sources for Further Study that appears in the back of each volume.

13 ⊕ MAN-MADE FEATURES

Notable man-made features—such as dams, canals, major bridges, tunnels, and other structures—that affect a country's geography are described.

14 ⊕ FURTHER READING

This section lists selected books and Web sites that provide more information on the country's geography.

Additional Features

Additional reference materials appear at the back of each volume. Researchers looking for comparative information on some of the world's key geographic features can refer to a series of Appendixes. These provide the following rankings: continents by area;

countries by area; countries by population; oceans and seas by area; oceans by depth; islands by area; deserts by area; mountain peaks by height; volcanoes by height; rivers by length; waterfalls by height; lakes by area; and lakes by depth. The seven wonders of the ancient world and seven wonders of the natural world are described in the final two appendixes. Lastly, a listing of selected references for the further study of physical geography completes the backmatter. Volume 5 contains a cumulative general index to all five volumes. Topographic world maps appear on each volume's endsheets.

Photographs

The photographs in *Junior Worldmark Encyclopedia of Physical Geography* were assembled with assistance from ARAMCO; Raoul Russo, UNESCO imaging; Marcia L. Schiff, AP/Wide World Photos; Maura Malone, EPD Photos; and Mimi Dornack, National Geographic Imaging.

Comments and Suggestions

We welcome your comments and suggestions for features to be included in future editions. Please write: Editors, *Junior Worldmark Encyclopedia of Physical Geography*, U•X•L, 27500 Drake Road, Farmington Hills, Michigan 48331-3535; call toll-free: 1-800-877-4253; fax to (248) 699-8097; or send e-mail via http://www.gale.com.

Words to Know

A

aboriginal ⊕ Something that is the first or earliest known of its type in a country or region, such as an aboriginal forest.

aborigines ⊕ The first known inhabitants of a country and their descendents.

acid rain ⊕ Rain (or snow) that has become slightly acidic by mixing with industrial air pollution.

alluvial plain ⊕ Flatlands containing deposits of alluvium.

alluvium ⊕ Clay, silt, sand, or gravel deposited by running water, such as a stream or river.

Antarctic Circle ⊕ (also called South **Frigid Zone**) The parallel of latitude approximately 66°33′ south and the region that lies between this latitude and the south pole; the region surrounding Antarctica.

aquatic ⊕ Of or relating to the water, particularly the animals and plants that live there.

aqueduct ⊕ A pipe or channel, usually man-made, that carries water from a remote source. Also, a bridge-like structure that carries water over obstacles.

aquifer ⊕ An underground layer of porous rock, sand, or gravel that holds water.

arable land ⊕ Land that is naturally suitable for cultivation by plowing and is used for growing crops.

archipelago ⊕ A group of islands or a body of water containing many islands.

Arctic ⊕ Relating to the northernmost part of the Earth that lies within and around the Arctic Circle. Also, **arctic**: anything that is frigidly and invariably cold.

Arctic Circle ⊕ (also called the North **Frigid Zone**) The parallel of latitude approximately 66°33′ north and the region that lies between this latitude and the north pole.

arid ⊕ Extremely dry, particularly applied to regions of low rainfall where there is little natural vegetation and agriculture is difficult.

artesian well ⊕ A type of well where underground pressure forces water to overflow up to the surface.

atmosphere ⊕ The air surrounding the Earth's surface.

atoll ⊕ An island consisting of a strip or ring of coral surrounding a central lagoon.

avalanche ⊕ A swift sliding of snow or ice down a mountain.

B

badlands ⊕ Eroded and barren land.

Balkan Peninsula ⊕ The southernmost peninsula of Europe, which is surrounded by the Adriatic, Ionian, Aegean, and Black seas

Balkan States ⊕ (also called The Balkans) Those countries that lie on or near the Balkan Peninsula; includes Albania, Bulgaria, continental Greece, southeast Romania, European Turkey, Serbia and Montenegro, Slovenia, Croatia, Bosnia and Herzegovina, and Macedonia.

Baltic States ⊕ The countries of Estonia, Latvia, and Lithuania. These independent countries were once provinces of Russia and all border on the Baltic Sea.

barren land ⊕ Unproductive land that is partly or entirely treeless.

barrier island ⊕ An island parallel to the shore that was formed by wave and tidal action and protects the shore from rough ocean waves.

barrier reef ⊕ A coral reef that lies parallel to the coast, often forming a lagoon along the shore.

basalt ⊕ Black or nearly black dense rock, usually formed by the solidification of magma or from some other high-temperature geological event.

basin ⊕ A depression on land or on the ocean floor. Usually relatively broad and gently sloped, as compared to a trench, canyon, or crater.

bay ⊕ A wide inlet of a sea or a lake.

bayou ⊕ A stagnant or slow-moving body of water.

beach ⊕ An area of sediment deposited along the shoreline of a large body of water through the action of waves and the process of erosion.

bedrock ⊕ Solid rock lying under loose earth.

bight ⊕ A bend in a coastline that forms an open bay.

bluff ⊕ Elevated area with a broad, steep cliff face.

bog ⊕ Wet, soft, and spongy ground where the soil is composed mainly of decayed or decaying vegetable matter.

bora ⊕ A very cold wind blowing from the north in the Adriatic Sea region.

broadleaf forest ⊕ A forest composed mainly of broadleaf (deciduous) trees, as opposed to a coniferous forest.

butte ⊕ An elevated, flat-topped area, similar to but smaller than a plateau or mesa.

C

caldera ⊕ A crater formed by the eruption of a volcano.

canal ⊕ An artificial waterway constructed to connect two bodies of water or for irrigation of farmland.

canyon ⊕ A deep gorge cut by a river, usually found in arid regions and often surrounded by plateaus.

cape ⊕ A part of the coast that protrudes into a body of water.

Caribbean ⊕ The region that includes the Caribbean Sea, its islands, and the Central or South American coastal areas of the sea.

catchment ⊕ Area that collects water.

cave ⊕ Hollow man-made or natural passages in the Earth with an opening to the surface.

cay (or key) ⊕ A small, low-lying island or reef formed by coral or sand.

Caucasus ⊕ Region between the Black and Caspian seas that forms the traditional boundary between Europe and Asia; includes the countries of Georgia, Azerbaijan, and Armenia, as well as parts of southwestern Russia.

Central America ⊕ A region of southern North America that extends from the southern border of Mexico to the northern border of Colombia; includes the countries of Belize, Guatemala, Honduras, El Salvador, Nicaragua, Costa Rica, and Panama

channel ⊕ A narrow body of water that connects two larger areas of water; an area where water flows through a narrow restricted path.

cliff ⊕ A high, vertical face of rock.

climate ⊕ Weather conditions pertaining to a specific area.

cloud forest ⊕ A tropical forest that is covered in clouds throughout most of the year, usually located on mountain peaks.

coast ⊕ Typically, the land that borders an ocean or sea.

coastal ⊕ Relating to the area along the coast.

coastal plain ⊕ A fairly level area of land along the coast of a land mass.

coniferous forest ⊕ A forest consisting mainly of evergreen trees such as pine, fir, and cypress trees.

conifers ⊕ Trees and plants that have needle-like, or scale-like, leaves and also produce cones; evergreens.

contiguous ⊕ Sharing an edge or boundary or connected without any breaks, as in *the 48 contiguous states*.

continent ⊕ One of the seven major land masses of Earth.

continental climate ⊕ A climate typical of the interior of a continent. Particulars can vary widely depending on the region, but in general, areas with a continental climate have greater variations in daily and seasonal temperatures than areas with a maritime climate.

continental divide ⊕ An extensive elevated region of land that separates the drainage basins of a continent so that the rivers on either side of the divide flow in opposite directions.

continental shelf ⊕ A shallow submarine plain extending from the coast of a continent into the sea and varying in width; typically the shelf ends in a steep slope to the ocean floor.

coral reef ⊕ A ridge in warm water areas of the ocean made up of the limestone and calcium deposits of coral animals.

cordillera ⊕ A continuous ridge, range, or chain of mountains; part of the principal mountain system of a continent or country.

crater ⊕ A bowl-shaped depression on the surface of the Earth, generally with relatively deep, steep, sides. The most common type of crater is a caldera, formed by volcanic eruption. Other craters are created by explosions or by impact, such as from a meteoroid.

cyclone ⊕ A violent rotating wind storm, particularly one that originates in the southwestern Pacific or the Indian Ocean. Cyclones rotate counterclockwise in the northern hemisphere and clockwise in the southern hemisphere.

WORDS TO KNOW

D

dam ⊕ A structure built across a river that restricts its flow, causing a reservoir to form behind it. Dams are often used to generate hydropower.

deciduous ⊕ Relates to trees or shrubs that shed their leaves on a regular basis, as opposed to those that retain them (coniferous).

deforestation ⊕ The removal or clearing of a forest, usually to enable the land to be used for another purpose, such as agriculture or settlements.

delta ⊕ Triangular-shaped deposits of soil formed at the mouths of large rivers. They are formed out of the silt carried by the river and have the effect of forcing the river to split into distributary channels, sometimes over a very wide area.

depression ⊕ Any place where the Earth's surface is lower than the surrounding terrain.

desert ⊕ Any dry land area with little precipitation and sparse vegetation; often a sandy region but also includes areas of permanent cold that are generally lacking plant life.

desertification ⊕ The process where land that supports vegetation gradually becomes desert as a result of climatic changes, land mismanagement, or both.

dike ⊕ An artificial riverbank built up to control the flow of water.

discontiguous ⊕ Not connected to or sharing a boundary with.

distributary ⊕ A stream that branches off from a river and never rejoins it, flowing independently into another body of water.

doldrums ⊕ An area near the equator characterized by variable winds and periods of calm.

dormant volcano ⊕ A volcano that has not exhibited any signs of activity for an extended period of time.

dune ⊕ A mound or ridge of loose, wind-blown sand.

E

Earth ⊕ Fifth-largest planet in the solar system; its orbit is third from the sun, its circumference is 40,064 kilometers (24,900 miles) at the equator and 40,000 kilometers (24,860 miles) when measured around the poles. The diameter at the equator is 12,753 kilometers (7,926 miles) and, from pole to pole, 12,711 kilometers (7,900 miles).

earthquake ⊕ Shaking or other movement of the earth that is caused by tectonic shifts or volcanic activity.

East Asia ⊕ A subregion of Asia that includes the countries of China, Mongolia, Korea, and the islands of Taiwan and Japan.

easterlies ⊕ Winds or air currents blowing more or less consistently from east to west.

Eastern Europe ⊕ A geopolitical term that usually refers to those countries in the east of Europe that were once allied with the Soviet Union under the Warsaw Pact (1955-1991). Today, the independent countries of the region include: Albania, Bulgaria, Czech Republic, Slovakia, Hungary, Croatia, Slovenia, Bosnia and Herzegovina, Poland, Romania, Serbia and Montenegro, and Macedonia.

Eastern Hemisphere ⊕ The half of the Earth's surface that extends east of the Prime Meridian to the 180th meridian.

eddy ⊕ An air or water current that follows a course different from that of the main flow and usually has a swirling circular motion.

El Niño ⊕ The warming of the ocean off the west coast of South America that causes a change in climate elsewhere in the world, especially in North America. El Niño conditions have occurred about every four to twelve years.

enclave ⊕ A country or portion of a country that lies entirely within the boundaries of one other country. Also, a culturally distinct community within a country.

endangered species ⊕ A plant or animal species that is at risk of becoming extinct.

endemic ⊕ Anything that is native to, unique to, or characteristic of a specific place or region.

equator ⊕ An imaginary line running around the middle of the Earth halfway between the North and South Poles. Identified as 0° latitude, it divides the Northern and Southern Hemispheres.

erosion ⊕ Changes in the shape of the Earth's surface as a result of damage from wind, water, or ice.

escarpment ⊕ (also called scarp land) A steep slope that separates areas of different elevations.

estuary ⊕ The region where a river and a large lake or sea meet so that their waters gradually blend into each other.

Eurasia ⊕ The land mass that contains the continents of Europe and Asia.

exclave ⊕ Part of a country that is separated from the larger, main portion of the country by foreign territory.

F

Far East ⊕ Traditionally, those countries that are a part of East Asia and the easternmost portion of Siberia. Often, the term includes the countries of Southeast Asia as well.

fault ⊕ (also called a fault line) A fracture in the Earth's crust where the rock formation splits, allowing the opposing sides to shift. Most commonly found along the boundaries between tectonic plates, the shifting sometimes causes earthquakes.

fen ⊕ Wet, soft, and spongy ground where the soil is composed mainly of decayed or decaying vegetable matter and is fed by surrounding soils and groundwater. Fens are similar to bogs but have higher nutrient levels.

fjord ⊕ A relatively narrow arm of the sea that indents deeply into the land, with generally steep slopes or cliffs on each side.

flood ⊕ The flow of excessive quantities of water over land that is generally above water.

flood plain ⊕ An area of low-lying land bordering a stream of water where floods, and the resulting deposits of alluvium, occur frequently.

Frigid Zone ⊕ Either of the extreme north and south latitude zones of the Earth. The North Frigid Zone lies between the North Pole and the Arctic Circle. The South Frigid Zone lies between the South Pole and the Antarctic Circle. The climate of these regions is characterized by extreme cold throughout the year.

G

game reserve ⊕ An area of land reserved for wild animals that are hunted for sport or for food.

geopolitical ⊕ Refers to the relationship between geographic, political (or governmental), and cultural aspects of a nation or region.

geothermal energy ⊕ Energy derived from the heat that constantly and naturally radiates out from the center of the Earth. Also used to describe the radiation itself.

geyser ⊕ A hot spring that periodically erupts through an opening in the surface of the Earth, spewing boiling water and steam.

glacier ⊕ A large body of ice that moves along the Earth's surface.

gorge ⊕ A deep, narrow passage with steep, rocky walls.

grassland ⊕ An area where the vegetation is mostly grasses and other grass-like plants, often providing a transition between forests and deserts.

Greenwich Mean Time ⊕ The time at Greenwich, England, in the United Kingdom. This time is used as a basis for calculating time throughout most of the world. It is also called universal time, and is abbreviated GMT.

groundwater ⊕ Water located below the earth's surface, providing a source for wells and springs.

gulf ⊕ A large inlet of a sea or ocean that is partially enclosed by land, such as by capes or peninsulas.

Gulf Stream ⊕ Warm ocean current flowing from roughly the Gulf of Mexico northeast along the coast of North America, then east toward Europe.

H

harbor ⊕ A protected inlet along the shore of a sea or lake that is deep enough for ships to anchor.

hardpan ⊕ A layer of hardened clay soil, usually underlying a thin layer of topsoil.

hardwoods ⊕ Deciduous trees, such as cherry, oak, maple, and mahogany, that produce very hard, durable, and valuable lumber.

harmattan ⊕ An intensely dry, dusty wind felt along the coast of Africa between Cape Verde and Cape Lopez. It prevails at intervals during the months of December, January, and February.

headland ⊕ Slightly elevated land lying along or jutting into a body of water.

headstream ⊕ Stream that forms the source of a river.

headwater ⊕ Source of a stream or river.

heath ⊕ Uncultivated land with low shrubs.

hemisphere ⊕ Any half of the globe. The Northern and Southern Hemispheres are divided by the equator while the Eastern and Western Hemispheres are divided by the Prime Meridian and 180° longitude.

hill ⊕ A rounded area of elevation rising more or less prominently above the surrounding, flatter landscape. Hills are generally no more than 300 meters (1,000 feet) high.

Humboldt Current ⊕ A cold ocean current that runs north from Antarctica along the west coast of South America, primarily from June to November.

hurricane ⊕ A tropical storm originating in the Atlantic or Pacific Oceans, generally with winds over 74 miles per hour.

hydropower ⊕ (also called hydroelectric power) Electricity generated by the flow of water through the turbines of river dams.

I

iceberg ⊕ A massive block of floating ice that has broken off of a glacier or an ice shelf through a process known as calving.

ice caps ⊕ Ice sheets covering less than 50,000 square kilometers (19,000 square miles). They form primarily in polar and sub-polar regions, generally occupying high and relatively flat regions.

ice shelves ⊕ Sheets of ice that extend from the edge of a continent over the surface of the ocean, with ocean water flowing beneath them. They typically range from approximately 200–1000 meters (500–3,500 feet) thick. The Arctic Ocean is partly covered by ice shelves and the continent of Antarctica is almost completely surrounded by them.

indigenous ⊕ A native species; vegetation that originates from or occurs naturally within a particular region.

Indochina ⊕ A subregion that includes the peninsular countries of southeast Asia that lie between India and China, including: Vietnam, Laos, Cambodia, Thailand, Myanmar (Burma), and the mainland territory of Malaysia. The term indicates that the culture in these countries has been influenced by both Indian and Chinese traditions.

inlet ⊕ Any water filled indentation along a coast or shore, such as a bay or gulf; a narrow passage through which water from an ocean or other large body of water passes, usually into a bay or lagoon.

International Date Line ⊕ An arbitrary, imaginary line at about 180° longitude that designates where one day begins and another ends.

island ⊕ A land mass entirely surrounded by water.

isthmus ⊕ A narrow strip of land that connects two larger bodies of land such as two continents, a continent and a peninsula, or two parts of an island. An isthmus is bordered by water on two sides.

K

karst ⊕ An area of limestone characterized by caverns and rock formations that are caused by erosion and underground streams.

key. *See* **cay.**

L

Labrador Current ⊕ A North Atlantic current that flows southward from polar waters along the east coast of Canada.

lagoon ⊕ A shallow body of water, often connected with or barely separated from a nearby ocean or sea by coral reefs or sandbars.

lake ⊕ A large inland body of standing water.

landlocked country ⊕ A country that does not have direct access to an ocean; a country that is completely surrounded by other countries.

landslide ⊕ A flow of muddy soil or loose rock that is usually triggered by heavy rainfall in areas where the terrain is steep.

Latin America ⊕ A geopolitical term that relates to the countries that are south of the United States in the Western Hemisphere, particularly countries where the Latin-based languages (or Romance languages) of Spanish, Portuguese, and French are spoken.

latitude ⊕ (also called parallel) An imaginary line running around the Earth parallel to the equator. The equator is at 0° latitude and divides the Earth into two sets of lines of latitude, north and south. Each set covers 90°.

lava ⊕ Molten rock (magma) that has been poured out on the Earth's surface, usually through a volcano.

leeward ⊕ The direction identical to that of the prevailing wind.

littoral ⊕ A coastal region or shore; or, the area between the high water and low water marks of a shore or coastal region.

loam ⊕ Light soil consisting of clay, silt, and sand.

loess ⊕ A windblown accumulation of fine yellow clay or silt.

longitude ⊕ (also called meridian) An imaginary line that extends along the surface of the Earth directly from one pole to another. The Earth is divided into 360 degrees of longitude, with 0° being designated as the Prime Meridian.

M

Maghreb ⊕ Region in northwest Africa made up of Algeria, Morocco, and Tunisia.

magma ⊕ Molten rock beneath the Earth's surface that has been melted by the heat of the Earth's interior. When magma breaches the Earth's surface it is known as lava.

mangrove ⊕ A tree that abounds on tropical shores in both hemispheres. It is characterized by its numerous roots that arch out from its trunk and descend from its branches. Mangroves form thick, dense growths along the tidal mud, covering areas that are hundreds of miles long.

marine life ⊕ The life that exists in or is formed by the seas and oceans.

maritime climate ⊕ The climate and weather conditions typical of areas bordering large bodies of water. Generally, areas close to water have more even temperatures than areas with a continental climate.

marsh ⊕ An area of soggy land, usually covered wholly or in part by shallow water and containing aquatic vegetation.

massif ⊕ The central part of a mountain or the dominant part of a range of mountains.

mean temperature ⊕ The air temperature unit measured by adding the maximum and minimum daily temperatures together and diving the sum by two; an average temperature.

Mediterranean ⊕ The region surrounding the Mediterranean Sea.

Mediterranean climate ⊕ A wet-winter, dry-summer climate with a moderate annual temperature range, as is typically experienced by countries along the Mediterranean Sea.

meridian. *See* **longitude.**

mesa ⊕ An isolated, elevated, flat-topped area of land, typically larger than a butte but smaller than a plateau.

Mesopotamia ⊕ The name means, "between rivers," and refers to the territory between and around the Tigris and Euphrates rivers (currently a part of Iraq). This area has been nicknamed "The Cradle of Civilization" because it was home to the ancient empires of Babylon, Sumer, and Assyria, among others. The Tigris and Euphrates are also two of the four rivers mentioned in the Biblical story of Eden.

Middle East ⊕ A geopolitical term that designates those countries of southwest Asia and northeast Africa that stretch from the Mediterranean Sea to the borders of Pakistan and Afghanistan, including the Arabian Peninsula. This area was considered to be the midpoint between Europe and East Asia, usually called the Far East. The term is sometimes used to include all the countries of that general region that are primarily Islamic.

mistral ⊕ In southern France, a cold, dry, northerly wind.

moist tropical climate ⊕ A weather pattern typical to the tropics, known for year-round high temperatures and large amounts of rainfall.

monolith ⊕ A large, natural rock formation, usually one that is isolated from other areas of high elevations; a large, stone block, column, or figure.

monsoon ⊕ Seasonal change in the wind direction of Southeastern Asia, leading to wet and dry seasons. A monsoon develops when there is a significant difference in air temperatures over the ocean and the land.

moor ⊕ A poorly drained open area containing peat and heath.

moraine ⊕ A deposit of rocky earth deposited by a glacier.

mountain ⊕ A lofty elevation of land, generally higher than 300 meters (1,000 feet), but varying greatly depending on the surrounding terrain, with little surface area at its peak; commonly formed in a series of ridges or in a single ridge known as a mountain range.

N

nature preserve ⊕ An area (often a park) where one or more specific species of plants and/or animals are protected from harm, injury, or destruction.

Northern Hemisphere ⊕ The northern half of the Earth's surface, as measured from the equator to the North Pole.

O

oasis ⊕ Originally, a fertile spot in the Libyan Desert where there is a natural spring or well and vegetation; now refers to any fertile tract in the midst of a wasteland.

ocean ⊕ The entire body of saltwater that covers almost three-fourths of the Earth's surface; any of the five principal divisions of the ocean.

Oceania ⊕ Oceania is a term that refers to the islands in the region that covers the central and south Pacific and its adjacent seas; sometimes includes Australia, New Zealand, and the Malay Archipelago (an large group of islands off the southeast coast of Asia).

P

pampas ⊕ Grass-covered plain of South America.

panhandle ⊕ A long narrow strip of land projecting like the handle of a frying pan.

parallel. *See* **latitude.**

peneplain ⊕ A flat land surface that has been subjected to severe erosion.

peninsula ⊕ A body of land surrounded by water on three sides.

permafrost ⊕ A frozen layer of soil that never thaws.

petroglyph ⊕ Ancient carvings or line drawings created on the surface of rocks by prehistoric peoples; often found in caves.

plain ⊕ An expansive area free of major elevations and depressions.

plateau ⊕ A relatively flat area of an elevated area of land.

plate tectonics ⊕ A set of theories about the Earth's structure used by many geologists to explain why land masses and oceans are arranged as they are and why seismic activity occurs. According to plate tectonics the Earth's surface, including the bottom of the oceans, rests on a number of large tectonic plates. These plates are slowly moving over the interior layers of the Earth. Where they grind against each other, earthquakes and other seismic activity occurs, and the shape of the land gradually changes.

polar circle ⊕ (also called the polar region) A circular region around the North and South Poles that separates the frigid polar zones from the temperate zones. The Earth has two polar circles, the Arctic Circle in the north and the Antarctic Circle in the south.

polar climate ⊕ A humid, severely cold climate controlled by arctic-like air masses, with no warm or summer season.

polder ⊕ A low land area reclaimed from a body of water and protected by dikes or embankments.

pole (geographic pole) ⊕ The extreme northern and southern points of the Earth's axis, where the axis intersects the spherical surface. The geographic North Pole is located at 90°N latitude/0° longitude. The geographic South Pole is located at 90°S latitude/0° longitude.

pole (magnetic pole) ⊕ Either of two points on the Earth's surface, close to the geographic North Pole and South Pole, where the magnetic field is most intense. The North Magnetic Pole is located at 78°N latitude/104°W longitude in the Queen Elizabeth Islands of northern Canada. The South Magnetic Pole is located at 66°S latitude/139°E longitude on the Adélie Coast of Antarctica.

pond ⊕ A small body of still, shallow water.

prairie ⊕ An area of level grassland that occurs in temperate climate zones.

Prime Meridian ⊕ The meridian designated as 0° longitude that runs through Greenwich, England, site of the Royal Observatory. All other longitudes are measured from this point.

R

rainforest ⊕ A dense forest of tall trees with a high, leafy canopy where the annual rainfall is at least 254 centimeters (100 inches) per year.

rain shadow ⊕ An area that receives very little precipitation due to natural barriers, such as mountains, which keep rain clouds from covering the region.

Ramsar ⊕ The Ramsar Convention on Wetlands of International Importance is an international organization concerned with the preservation and protection of major wetland environments throughout the world.

ravine ⊕ A steep, narrow valley or gorge, usually containing the channel for a stream.

reef ⊕ String of rocks or coral formations, usually on a sandy bottom, that are barely submerged.

reforestation ⊕ Systematically replacing forest trees that were lost due to fire or logging.

reservoir ⊕ A lake that was formed artificially by a dam.

Ring of Fire ⊕ The region of seismic activity roughly outlined by a string of volcanoes that encircles the Pacific Ocean.

river ⊕ A substantial stream of water following a clear channel as it flows over the land.

riverine ⊕ Related to a river or the banks of a river.

S

Sahel ⊕ Sahel is an Arabic word meaning "shore." It refers to the 5,000 kilometer (3,125 mile) stretch of savanna that is the shore or edge of the Sahara desert. The Sahel spreads west to east from Mauritania and Senegal to Somalia.

salinization ⊕ An accumulation of soluble salts in soil. This condition is common in irrigated areas with desert climates, where water evaporates quickly in poorly drained soil due to high temperatures. Severe salinization renders soil poisonous to most plants.

salt pan ⊕ (also salt flat) An area of land in a sunny region that is periodically submerged in shallow water, usually due to tides or seasonal floods. The sun causes the shallow water to evaporate and leave the salt it contained behind on the ground.

sand bar ⊕ A deposit of sedimentary material that lies in the shallow water of a river, lake, or sea.

savanna ⊕ (also spelled savannah) A treeless or near treeless plain of a tropical or subtropical region dominated by drought-resistant grasses.

Scandinavia ⊕ The region of northwestern Europe that lies on the peninsula bordered by the Atlantic Ocean, the Baltic Sea, and the Gulf of Bothnia. Even though Norway and Sweden are the only two countries that lie directly on this peninsula, the countries of Denmark, Iceland and Finland are usually considered to be Scandinavian countries in a cultural context.

sea ⊕ A body of salt water that is connected to (and therefore a part of) the ocean; sometimes, a name given to a large lake.

sea level ⊕ The level of the ocean's surface, specifically the average between the levels at high tide and low tide. Sea level is often designated as 0 meters (0 feet) and is used as the baseline for measuring elevations and depressions on land and on the ocean floor.

seasonal ⊕ Dependant on the season. The flow of rivers and volume of lakes often varies greatly between seasons, as can vegetation.

seasons ⊕ Regular variations in weather patterns that occur at the same times every year.

sedimentary rock ⊕ Rock, such as sandstone, shale, and limestone, formed from the hardening of material deposits.

seismic activity ⊕ Relating to or connected with an earthquake or earthquakes in general.

semiarid ⊕ A climate where water and rainfall is relatively scarce but not so rare as to prohibit the growth of modest vegetation. Semiarid areas are often found around arid deserts and semiarid land is sometimes called a desert itself.

shoal ⊕ A shallow area in a stream, lake, or sea, especially a sand bank that lies above water at low tide or during dry periods.

shore ⊕ Typically, the land that borders a lake or river; may also be used to designate the land bordering an ocean or sea.

sierra ⊕ A rugged, jagged, irregular chain of hills or mountain.

silt ⊕ Fine, gravel-like, inorganic material, usually sand and coarse clay particles, that is carried by the flow of a river and deposited along its banks. Silt is generally very fertile soil.

skerry ⊕ A rocky island.

slough ⊕ A marshy pond that occurs in a river inlet.

softwoods ⊕ Coniferous trees with a wood density that is relatively softer than the wood of those trees referred to as hardwoods.

sound ⊕ A wide expanse of water, usually separating a mainland from islands or connecting two large bodies of water; often lies parallel to the coastline.

South Asia ⊕ A subregion of Asia that includes the countries of Afghanistan, Pakistan, India, Bangladesh, and Nepal.

Southeast Asia ⊕ A subregion of Asia that lies between India on the west, China to the north, and the Pacific Ocean to the east. The region includes the Indochina Peninsula of the South China Sea, the Malay Peninsula, and the Indonesian and Philippine Archipelagos The countries of Southeast Asia are: Brunei, Cambodia, Indonesia, Laos, Malaysia, Myanmar, the Philippines, Singapore, Thailand, and Vietnam.

Southern Hemisphere ⊕ The southern half of the Earth's surface between the equator and the South Pole.

Southwest Asia ⊕ A subregion of Asia that includes Turkey and extends southward through the Arabian Peninsula. Iran can also be included in the region.

spring ⊕ Water flowing from the ground through a natural opening.

stalactites ⊕ Deposits of calcium carbonate formed in a cavern or cave that hang down from the ceiling like icicles.

stalagmites ⊕ Deposits of calcium carbonate formed in a cavern or cave that rise up from the floor like cones or columns.

steppe ⊕ A flat, mostly treeless, semiarid grassland, marked by extreme seasonal and daily temperature variations. Although sometimes used to describe other areas, the term applies primarily to the plains of southeastern Europe and Central Asia.

strait ⊕ Narrow body of water connecting two larger bodies of water.

stream ⊕ Any flowing water that moves generally downhill from elevated areas towards sea level.

subarctic climate ⊕ A high latitude climate. The continental subarctic climate has very cold winters; short, cool summers; light precipitation; and moist air. The marine subarctic climate is a coastal and island climate with polar air masses causing high levels of precipitation and extreme cold.

subcontinent ⊕ A land mass of great size, but smaller than any of the continents; a large subdivision of a continent.

subtropical climate ⊕ A middle latitude climate dominated by humid, warm temperatures and heavy rainfall in summer, with cool winters and frequent cyclonic storms.

T

taiga ⊕ An area of open forest made up of coniferous trees.

tectonic ⊕ Relating to the structure of the Earth's crust.

tectonic plate ⊕ According to the theory of plate tectonics, the outer layer of the Earth consists of a series of large plates of rock called tectonic plates. The largest plates have entire oceans or continents on their surface.

Temperate Zone ⊕ The parts of the Earth lying between the Tropics and the polar circles. The North Temperate Zone is the area between the Tropic of Cancer and the Arctic Circle. The South Temperate Zone is the area between the Tropic of Capricorn and the Antarctic Circle. Temperate zones are marked by the greatest seasonal variations in temperature; however, temperatures and rainfall tend to stay within a moderate range, without extremes.

terraces ⊕ Successive areas of flat lands.

terrain ⊕ General characteristics of the Earth's surface in a region, including its characteristic vegetation.

tidal bore ⊕ A distinctive type of wave that travels up a shallow river or estuary on the incoming tide. It is a dramatic phenomenon that occurs in few places in the world; the incoming tidal waters flow against the river's current.

tidal wave. *See* **tsunami**.

tide ⊕ The rise and fall of the surface of a body of water caused by the gravitational attraction of the sun and moon.

timber line ⊕ The point of high elevation on a mountain above which the climate is too severe to support trees.

topography ⊕ The surface features of a region; also, the study of such features.

tornado ⊕ A violent, whirling wind storm that forms a funnel-shaped cloud and moves in a path over the surface of the Earth.

Torrid Zone ⊕ The part of the Earth's surface that lies between the Tropic lines, so named for the warm, humid, character of its climate.

trade winds ⊕ Winds that consistently blow from the northeast and southeast toward the equator.

trench ⊕ A steep-sided depression in the ocean floor where the water is very deep.

tributary ⊕ Any stream that flows into another larger stream.

tropical monsoon climate ⊕ One of the tropical rainy climates; it is sufficiently warm and rainy to produce tropical rainforest vegetation, but also has a winter dry season.

Tropic of Cancer ⊕ A latitudinal line located 23°27′ north of the equator, the highest point on the globe at which the sun can shine directly overhead.

Tropic of Capricorn ⊕ A latitudinal line located 23°27′ south of the equator, the lowest point on the globe at which the sun can shine directly overhead.

tsunami ⊕ A powerful, massive, and destructive ocean wave caused by an undersea earthquake or volcanic eruption.

tundra ⊕ A nearly level, treeless area whose climate and vegetation are characteristically arctic due to its position near one of the poles; the subsoil is permanently frozen.

typhoon ⊕ Violent hurricane occurring in the region of the South China Sea, usually in the period from July through October.

U

UNESCO ⊕ The United Nations Educational, Scientific, and Cultural Organization. An international organization promoting peace and security around the world through education, science, culture, and communication.

V

valley ⊕ An elongated depression through which a stream of water usually flows, typically an area that lies between mountains, hills, and/or other uplands.

vegetation ⊕ Plants, including trees, shrubs, grasses, and other plants.

volcano ⊕ A hole or opening through which molten rock and superheated steam erupt from the interior of the Earth. Also, a mountain created by the accumulation of these ejected materials.

W

wadi ⊕ Dry stream bed, usually in a desert region in southwest Asia or north Africa.

waterfall ⊕ A steep, natural descent of water flowing over a cliff or precipice to a lower level.

watershed ⊕ An area of shared water drainage, where all the rainfall drains into a common river or lake system.

waves ⊕ The alternate rise and fall of ridges of water, generally produced by the action between the wind and the surface of a body of water.

weather ⊕ Atmospheric conditions at a given place and time.

Western Europe ⊕ A geopolitical term that usually refers to those countries of Europe that are allies of the United States and Canada under the North Atlantic Treaty Organization (NATO, established 1949). The original European countries in NATO were Belgium, France, Great Britain, Italy, Luxembourg, the Netherlands, and Portugal. Today, Western European countries also include Germany, Spain, Ireland, amd Austria. Though Denmark is geographically part of Europe, it is culturally considered as part of Scandinavia.

Western Hemisphere ⊕ The half of the Earth's surface that lies west of the Prime Meridian to 180° longitude.

West Indies ⊕ The islands lying between North America and South America made up of the Greater Antilles (Cuba, Haiti, Dominican Republic, Jamaica, and Puerto Rico), the Lesser Antilles (Virgin Islands, Trinidad and Tobago, Barbados), and the Bahamas.

wildlife sanctuary ⊕ An area of land set aside for the protection and preservation of animals and plants.

windward ⊕ Facing into the prevailing wind, or lying closest to the direction from which the wind is blowing.

Junior
Worldmark
Encyclopedia of
Physical
Geography

Afghanistan

- **Official name:** Islamic Republic of Afghanistan

- **Area:** 647,500 square kilometers (250,001 square miles)

- **Highest point on mainland**: Mount Nowshak (7,485 meters/24,558 feet)

- **Lowest point on land:** Amu Darya River (258 meters/846 feet)

- **Hemispheres**: Northern and Eastern

- **Time zone:** 4:30 P.M. = noon GMT

- **Longest distances:** 1,240 kilometers (770 miles) from northeast to southwest; 560 kilometers (350 miles) from northwest to southeast

- **Land boundaries**: 5,529 kilometers (3,436 miles) total boundary length; China, 76 kilometers (47 miles); Iran, 936 kilometers (582 miles); Pakistan, 2,430 kilometers (1,511 miles); Tajikistan, 1,206 kilometers (750 miles); Turkmenistan, 744 kilometers (463 miles); Uzbekistan, 137 kilometers (85 miles)

- **Coastline:** None

- **Territorial sea limits**: None

1 ⊕ LOCATION AND SIZE

Afghanistan is a landlocked nation (does not have access to the sea) in south-central Asia. At the crossroads of north-south and east-west trade routes, the country has been invaded many times, by Alexander the Great in the fourth century B.C., and by the Soviet Union in the twentieth century A.D. Almost as large as the state of Texas, Afghanistan is bounded by six different countries. Afghanistan's longest border—accounting for its entire southern boundary and most of its eastern one—is with Pakistan. The shortest one, bordering China's Xinjiang province, is only 76 kilometers (47 miles), at the end of the Wakhan corridor.

2 ⊕ TERRITORIES AND DEPENDENCIES

Afghanistan has no territories or dependencies.

3 ⊕ CLIMATE

The climate of Afghanistan ranges from semi-arid (light annual rainfall) to arid (almost no annual rainfall), with wide variations in temperature, both between seasons and between different times of day. Its summers are hot and dry, but its winters are bitterly cold. Recorded temperatures have ranged as high as 53°C (128°F) and as low as -26°C (-15°F) in the central highlands, which have a subarctic climate. (Subarctic climate features long, very cold winters with short, cool summers, and little rainfall.) Summertime temperatures in Kabul, the capital of Afghanistan, can vary from 16°C (61°F) at sunrise to 38°C (100°F) by noon. Summer highs in Jalalabad average 46°C (115°F). The mean January temperature in Kabul is 0°C (32°F). Strong winds that blow between June and September (called the "Winds

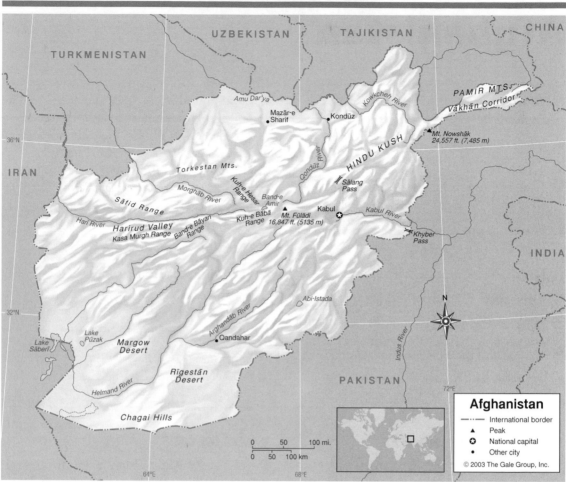

of 120 Days") can have a velocity of up to 180 kilometers per hour (108 miles per hour).

In much of the country, rainfall is sparse and irregular, averaging 25 to 30 centimeters (10 to 12 inches) and mostly occurring between October and April. Rainfall is generally heavier in the eastern part of the country than in the western regions. Afghan summers are generally dry, cloudless, and hot. Humid air from the Persian Gulf (body of water lying west of Afghanistan between Saudi Arabia and Iran) sometimes produces summer showers and thunderstorms in the southwest. Most of the precipitation in the mountains falls in the form of snow—and sometimes as hail. During the Soviet Union's occupation of Afghanistan in the 1980s, the Afghan resistance fighters called *mujahideen* referred to the heavy hail that fell in the mountains as "Allah's mine-sweepers" because its force was sometimes strong enough to set off land mines.

SEASON	MONTHS	AVERAGE TEMPERATURE
Summer	June to September	16 to 33°C (61 to 91°F)
Winter	November to March	-8 to 2°C (18 to 36°F)

4 ⊕ TOPOGRAPHIC REGIONS

From northeast to southwest, the Hindu Kush Mountains divide Afghanistan into three major regions: 1) the central highlands, which form part of the Himalaya Mountains and

© UNESCO/Dominique Roger

The northern plains contain Afghanistan's most fertile soil.

comprise roughly two-thirds of the country's area; 2) the southwestern plateau, which accounts for one-fourth of the land; and 3) the smaller northern plains area, which contains the country's most fertile soil. The Wakhan corridor, lying between Tajikistan and Pakistan, is a narrow panhandle in the northeast Hindu Kush.

5 ⊕ OCEANS AND SEAS

Afghanistan is landlocked. The nearest seacoast is roughly 483 kilometers (300 miles) south in Pakistan on the shores of the Arabian Sea.

6 ⊕ INLAND LAKES

There are few lakes in Afghanistan, and the largest of them are along the country's southwestern border. The Daryacheh-e Namakzar and the Hamun-e Sāberī (also called Lake Helmand) have most of their surface area in Iran. Lake Zorkul is located in the Wakhan corridor near the border with Tajikistan. Abi-Istada, about 193 kilometers (120 miles) northeast of Qandahar, is a salt lake. Five small lakes in the central highlands, collectively called Band-e Amir, are known for their unusual colors, which range from a filmy white to a deep green.

7 ⊕ RIVERS AND WATERFALLS

Afghanistan's drainage system is landlocked. Most of its rivers and streams end in shallow desert lakes or oases (plural of oasis; any fertile tract in the midst of a wasteland) inside or outside the country's boundaries. A few rivers in the eastern part of the country, however, eventually reach the Arabian Sea after first emptying into the Indus River in Pakistan.

In the western part of the northern plains many rivers disappear underground before emptying into the Amu Darya River (also called the Oxus River). In the west, the sandy deserts along the Iranian frontier (border) have no watercourses (natural flowing water).

The Amu Darya River, at 2,661 kilometers (1,654 miles) long, is the country's longest river. About 965 kilometers (600 miles) of its upper course separates Afghanistan from its neighbors Turkmenistan, Uzbekistan, and Tajikistan. The Helmand is the principal river in the southwest, bisecting (crossing through) the entire region. The Helmand is approximately 1,400 kilometers (870 miles) long. The Kabul River, 515 kilometers (320 miles) long, is a vital source of water in the Kuh-e Baba Mountains.

8 ⊕ DESERTS

The Rigestan Desert, along the country's southern border, occupies roughly one-quarter of the southwestern plateau. Sand ridges and dunes alternate with wide desert plains devoid of vegetation. West of the Rigestan Desert lies the Dasht-e Margo, a desolate region with salt flats. A flat strip of desert and grassy steppe (treeless flat land) extends along the banks of the Amu Darya River. Desert areas are also found along the foothills of the central Hindu Kush and west of Mazar-e Sharif.

DID YOU KN⊕W?

The city of Mazar-e Sharif is famous throughout the Islamic world as the place where Ali, the son-in-law of the Muslim prophet Muhammad, is buried.

9 ⊕ FLAT AND ROLLING TERRAIN

North of the mountainous central highlands are the northern plains, Afghanistan's smallest natural region, with an area of approximately 103,600 square kilometers (40,000 square miles). They stretch from the Iranian border in the west to the foothills of the Pamir mountains in the east. The eastern half of this region, which forms a part of the Central Asia steppe, is bounded by the Amu Darya River. The northern plains have an average elevation of 609 meters (2,000 feet), except for the Amu Darya valley floor, which drops to as low as 183 meters (600 feet).

10 ⊕ MOUNTAINS AND VOLCANOES

The mountainous central highlands formed by the Hindu Kush and its subsidiary ranges (the ranges that branch from the Hindu Kush) are extensions of the Himalayas. Crossing the country for 965 kilometers (600 miles) from east to west and covering an area of approximately 414,400 square kilometers (160,000 square miles), this area contains towering peaks alternating with steep gorges and barren slopes.

This mountain system—Afghanistan's dominant physical feature—is composed of three high ridges. The main ridge begins in China and runs southwestward as the eastern Hindu Kush, with summits over 6,400 meters (21,000 feet) high. The highest mountains are in the Wakhan corridor, including the country's highest peak, Mount Nowshak. At the Anjuman Pass, the eastern Hindu Kush becomes the central Hindu Kush. The Kuh-e Baba range runs parallel to and south of the central Hindu Kush. Other important mountain ranges include the Kuh-e Hisar, the Firoz Kuh, and the Paropamisus.

A similar series of ranges runs parallel to the Paropamisus and Hindu Kush at lower altitudes along the southern rim of the northern plains. In addition, several mountain chains fan out to the southwest. In the southeast, several lower ridges enclose long valleys that run parallel to the boundary with Pakistan. The valley region that is home to the capital city of Kabul is bounded by this range system.

11 ⊕ CANYONS AND CAVES

The caves that have been used for military purposes since the 1970s are largely man-made (see below). Afghanistan has few natural caves; limestone, from which most natural caves are formed, is found only in isolated areas of the country. Afghanistan's largest natural cave is the 1,120-meter-long (1,120-foot-long) Ab Bar Amada northwest of Kabul.

12 ⊕ PLATEAUS AND MONOLITHS

The southwestern plateau southwest of the central highlands is an arid region of desert and semidesert extending into Pakistan to the south and into Iran to the west. From an altitude of about 914 meters (3,000 feet) at its highest point, it slopes gently to the southwest. A few large rivers traverse this plateau, including the Helmand and its major tributary the Arghandab. The southwestern plateau region covers approximately 129,500 square kilometers (50,000 square miles) and includes the Rigestan Desert.

13 ⊕ MAN-MADE FEATURES

Afghanistan's so-called "caves" are actually man-made dugouts built into the mountains by *mujahideen* rebels fighting the Soviet Union during the 1970s and 1980s. Al Qaeda Muslim extremists also used the caves for military purposes in 2001 and 2002. The dugouts are between 3 and 9 meters (10 to 30 feet) deep.

14 ⊕ FURTHER READING

Books

Elliot, Jason. *An Unexpected Light: Travels in Afghanistan*. London: Picador, 1999.

Ellis, Deborah. *Women of the Afghan War*. Westport, CT.: Praeger, 2000.

Ewans, Martin. *Afghanistan: A New History*. Richmond: Curzon, 2001.

Periodicals

"The Most Dangerous Place on Earth: A Look Inside Afghanistan." Special report. *Current Events*. Nov. 30, 2001, pp.S1-5.

Web Sites

Afghanistan Online. http://www.afghan-web.com/ (accessed February 14, 2003).

National Geographic. http://www.nationalgeographic.com/popups/popunder.html (accessed June 21, 2003).

Albania

- **Official name:** Republic of Albania
- **Area:** 28,748 square kilometers (17,864 square miles)
- **Highest point on mainland:** Mount Korabit (2,753 meters/9,033 feet)
- **Lowest point on land:** Sea level
- **Hemispheres:** Northern and Eastern
- **Time zone:** 6 P.M. = noon GMT; has Daylight Savings Time
- **Longest distances:** 148 kilometers (92 miles) from east to west; 340 kilometers (211 miles) from north to south

- **Land boundaries:** Total: 720 kilometers (447 miles); Former Yugoslav Republic of Macedonia, 151 kilometers (94 miles); Serbia and Montenegro, 287 kilometers (179 miles); [Serbia 114 kilometers (71 miles), Montenegro 173 kilometers (108 miles)]; Greece, 282 kilometers (175 miles)
- **Coastline:** 362 kilometers (225 miles)
- **Territorial sea limits:** 22 kilometers (12 nautical miles)

1 ⊕ LOCATION AND SIZE

Albania is one of the smallest countries in Europe. It is located in southeastern Europe on the west coast of the Balkan peninsula (the peninsula surrounded by, from west to east, the Adriatic, Ionian, Aegean, and Black Seas) along the Strait of Otranto, which connects the Adriatic and Ionian Seas. Albania covers 28,748 square kilometers (17,864 square miles), or slightly more area than the state of Maryland.

2 ⊕ TERRITORIES AND DEPENDENCIES

Albania has no territories or dependencies.

3 ⊕ CLIMATE

Albania has a coastal Mediterranean climate (hot, dry summers and rainy winters) in the western regions and a continental climate (hot summers and cold winters) in the east. The coastal plain has mild, rainy winters and hot, dry summers. In the mountains, air masses moving south across the European continent produce warm to hot summers and very cold winters with heavy snowfall; summer rainfall is also heavier in this region than on the coast. Albania's average annual temperature is 15°C (59°F). Average annual rainfall ranges from about 100 centimeters (40 inches) on the coastal plain to more than 250 centimeters (100 inches) in the mountains.

4 ⊕ TOPOGRAPHIC REGIONS

More than 70 percent of Albania's terrain is rugged and mountainous, with mountains running the length of the country from north to south. The remainder consists mostly of coastal lowlands. These lowlands stretch from the northern border to Vlorë, covering 200 kilometers (124 miles) from north to south and extending as much as 50 kilometers (31 miles) inland. A large part of this region is former marshland (soft, wet land; also called wetlands) that was reclaimed during the Communist era (1944–90). (Reclaimed land is an area in which

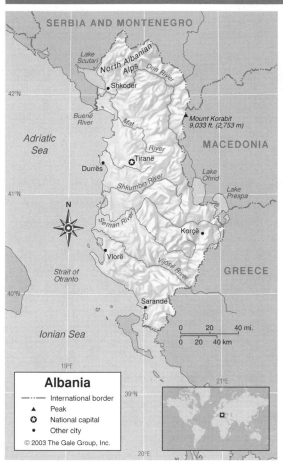

Albania
- – – – – International border
- ▲ Peak
- ✪ National capital
- • Other city

© 2003 The Gale Group, Inc.

the natural conditions have been changed, usually by building dams or dikes, to redirect the water.) The reclaimed land in Albania is now used for agriculture.

5 ⊕ OCEANS AND SEAS

Albania lies on the southeastern shore of the Adriatic Sea and is also bordered by the Ionian Sea to the south.

Seacoast and Undersea Features

Albania has no significant undersea features.

Sea Inlets and Straits

Albania has no good natural harbors. The Strait of Otranto, which connects the Adriatic Sea with the Ionian Sea, borders Albania on the southwest, separating it from the "heel" on the southeastern tip of the Italian peninsula.

Islands and Archipelagos

The island of Sazan lies off the coast of Albania, west of Vlorë. The islands in the Ionian Sea off the south coast of Albania belong to Greece.

Coastal Features

Albania's Ionian Sea coastal area is known for its rugged natural beauty, with rocky highlands extending right to the edge of the beach; the area between Vlorë and Sarandë is called the "Riviera of Flowers." The beaches along the Adriatic coast stretch about 300 kilometers (188 miles), with sandy beaches and shallow coastal waters.

6 ⊕ INLAND LAKES

Albania has three large lakes, which it shares with several neighboring countries: Lake Scutari (Skadarsko Jezero) with Serbia and Montenegro, Lake Ohrid (Ohridsko Jezero) with Macedonia, and Lake Prespa (Prespansko Jezero) with Greece. Lake Ohrid is the deepest lake, not only in Albania but also in the Balkans, with a depth of 294 meters (965 feet).

7 ⊕ RIVERS AND WATERFALLS

Albania's major rivers are the Drin, the Mat, the Buenë, the Seman, the Shkumbin, and the Vijosë. They all empty into the Adriatic Sea. The Buenë is Albania's only navigable river. (A navigable river is one that can be used by boats.)

8 ⊕ DESERTS

There are no desert regions in Albania.

9 ⊕ FLAT AND ROLLING TERRAIN

Citrus fruits, maize, and wheat are grown in Albania's coastal lowlands. Although the former marshland in the region was drained

EPD/Miguel Torres Curado

Albania's rural landscape.

to create productive agricultural land, flooding still occurs.

10 ⊕ MOUNTAINS AND VOLCANOES

Albania's mountains are located to the north, east, and south of the coastal lowlands. They can be divided into three groups. The northernmost range, the North Albanian Alps, is an extension of both the Montenegrin limestone plateau and the Dinaric Alps, which run parallel to the Adriatic coast in Croatia and in Montenegro. Some of the mountains in this region reach heights greater than 2,700 meters (8,800 feet). These limestone peaks are the country's most rugged. Albanians call them "the accursed mountains," because they present a barrier to travel.

The central uplands extend south along the Macedonian border, from the Drin River valley to the southern mountains. The central uplands are generally lower than the North Albanian Alps. However, Albania's highest peak, Mount Korabit, is located in these mountains. The southern highlands are lower and more rounded than the mountains to the north. At the southernmost end of Albania, south of Vlorë, the mountains reach all the way across the country, meeting the Ionian Sea.

11 ⊕ CANYONS AND CAVES

There are a few caves with stalactites in Albania in the eastern region near the largest lakes.

12 ⊕ PLATEAUS AND MONOLITHS

There are no significant plateaus in Albania.

13 ⊕ MAN-MADE FEATURES

Several dams, the first of which was built in the early 1960s, generate hydroelectric energy. The Drin River has been dammed to produce hydroelectric energy, and marshland has been reclaimed for agriculture.

14 ⊕ FURTHER READING

Books

Carver, Robert. *The Accursed Mountains: Journeys in Albania.* London: John Murray, 1998.

Dawson, Peter, and Andrea Dawson. *Albania: A Guide and Illustrated Journal.* Old Saybrook, CT: Globe Pequot Press, 1995.

Sherer, Stan. *Long Life to Your Children! A Portrait of High Albania.* Amherst: University of Massachusetts Press, 1997.

Web Sites

CARE International in Albania Web site. http://www.care.org.al/mission.htm (accessed January 27, 2003).

Geography of Albania, Land of the Eagles. http://www.albania.co.uk/geography/index.html/ (accessed June 17, 2003).

Algeria

- **Official name:** Democratic and Popular Republic of Algeria

- **Area:** 2,381,740 square kilometers (919,590 square miles)

- **Highest point on mainland:** Mount Tahat (3,003 meters/9,853 feet)

- **Lowest point on land:** Chott Melrhir (40 meters/131 feet below sea level)

- **Hemispheres:** Northern and Eastern

- **Time zone:** 1 P.M. = noon GMT

- **Longest distances:** 2,400 kilometers (1,500 miles) from east to west; 2,100 kilometers (1,300 miles) from north to south

- **Land boundaries:** 7,341 kilometers (4,561 miles) total boundary length; Tunisia, 958 kilometers (595 miles); Libya, 982 kilometers (610 miles); Niger, 956 kilometers (594 miles); Mali, 1,376 kilometers (855 miles); Mauritania, 463 kilometers (288 miles); Morocco, 1,637 kilometers (1,017 miles)

- **Coastline:** 998 kilometers (620 miles)

- **Territorial sea limits:** 22 kilometers (12 nautical miles)

1 ⊕ LOCATION AND SIZE

Algeria is the largest of the three countries that form the Maghreb region of northwest Africa. (The Maghreb region is made up of Algeria, Morocco, and Tunisia.) Algeria is the second-largest country in Africa; only Sudan is larger. Algeria is a little less than three-and-a-half times the size of Texas, and it is as large as the whole of Western Europe.

2 ⊕ TERRITORIES AND DEPENDENCIES

Algeria has no territories or dependencies.

3 ⊕ CLIMATE

Algeria's geographical diversity produces a range of climatic conditions. The northern part of the country has a Mediterranean climate with mild, wet winters and hot, dry summers. The plateau region has a semiarid (having light annual rainfall) climate, with greater contrasts between summer and winter. Temperatures vary the most in the Sahara Desert region, which has an arid climate with almost no annual rainfall. Summer temperatures average about 25°C (77°F) in the northern coastal region, 27°C (81°F) on the plateau, and 34°C (93°F) in the desert, where readings as high as 49°C (120°F) have been recorded. Average winter temperatures range from about 5°C (41°F) on the plateau to about 11°C (52°F) in the north; winter lows in the desert can plummet to as low as -10°C (14°F). The hot, dusty wind known as the sirocco often blows in the summer.

Just as its temperatures vary, Algeria's rainfall also differs by region. Fewer than 10 centimeters (4 inches) of rain fall annually in the Sahara Desert, but as many as 100 centimeters (40 inches) may fall in the easternmost section of the mountainous Tell region in the north. Precipitation is heaviest between September and December, tapering off in January. Very little rainfall occurs in the

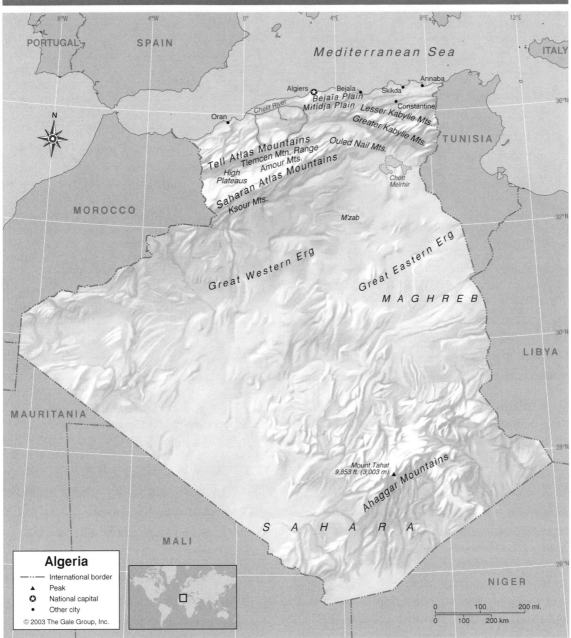

summer months. Drought occurs frequently in the Saharan region.

4 ⊕ TOPOGRAPHIC REGIONS

The southern 80 percent of Algeria's land is in the Sahara Desert and almost completely uninhabited. The northern half of the desert is less arid than the southern half, and most of the region's oases (any fertile tract in the midst of a wasteland) are found here. The southern zone of the Sahara is almost totally arid and consists mostly of barren rock.

EPD/RAMSAR/Ammar Boumezbeur

This fouggara, lying in approximately the center of Algeria, is a partially underground system of channels to distribute water from the oasis, Ouled Saïd, to families living in the surrounding area.

Its most prominent feature is the Ahaggar mountain range, which rises in the southeast.

To the north of the Sahara lies the Tell region, made up of consecutive belts of land extending west to east, roughly parallel to the Mediterranean border. The region consists of a narrow strip of coastal plains and the two Algerian sections of the Atlas Mountains (Tell Atlas and Saharan Atlas), as well as a plateau that separates them. In contrast to the Tell region, the prominent topographic features (mountains, plains, and basins) in the northeastern corner of Algeria do not parallel the coast.

5 ⊕ OCEANS AND SEAS

The Mediterranean Sea borders Algeria to the north. The Mediterranean Sea is an almost completely landlocked sea that lies between southern Europe, northern Africa, and southwest Asia. It links to the Atlantic Ocean in the west through the Strait of Gibraltar, and to the Red Sea in the southeast through the Suez Canal. It also connects to the Black Sea to the northeast through the Dardanelles, the Sea of Marmara, and the Bosporus.

Sea Inlets and Straits

Algeria's Mediterranean coastline is relatively smooth, especially in the center. The shallow Gulf of Bejaïa is the only indentation of any size. There are several smaller bays at the eastern and western ends of the coast.

Coastal Features

Coastal plains alternate with steep uplands along much of the coast, except for the easternmost section, where the coast is mostly mountainous.

6 ⊕ INLAND LAKES

There are shallow salt lakes and salt marshes (soft, wet lands) in the high plateaus.

7 ⊕ RIVERS AND WATERFALLS

Because its rainfall is scanty and irregular, Algeria has few permanent inland bodies of water and no navigable rivers (rivers that can be used for boating). Almost all of the Algerian rivers flow only seasonally (during rainy periods) or irregularly. The longest and best known of these is the Chelif, which wanders for 230 kilometers (143 miles) from its source in the Tell Atlas to the Mediterranean Sea. Most of the Tell streams diminish to trickles or go dry in summer. In the western part of the country, reservoirs have been developed for irrigation in the Chelif and Hamiz river basins (area drained by a river). The land in the southernmost Saharan region is largely arid but contains some date-palm oases.

DID YOU KN⊕W?

Chott Ech Chergui, lying southwest of Algiers near the border with Morocco, is the second largest chott (or shatt, salt-water lake) in North Africa. (Only Chott Djerid in Tunisia is larger.) The chott features marshy, stagnant water, while the region around Chott Ech Chergui is barren. In winter, migrating waterfowl nest around Chott Ech Chergui.

8 ⊕ DESERTS

South of the Saharan Atlas, the Algerian portion of the Sahara Desert extends southward 1,500 kilometers (931 miles) to the country's borders with Niger and Mali. Its average elevation is about 460 meters (1,500 feet). Immense areas of sand dunes, called ergs, occupy about one-fourth of the desert. The two major ergs are the Grand Erg Occidental (Great Western Erg) and the larger Grand Erg Oriental (Great Eastern Erg), where enormous dunes 2 to 5 meters (7 to 16 feet) high are spaced about 40 meters (130 feet) apart. Much of the remainder of the desert is covered by bare, rocky platforms called hamada that are elevated above the sand dunes. Almost the entire southeastern quarter of the desert is taken up by the Ahaggar Mountains. They are surrounded by sandstone plateaus cut by deep gorges and, to the west, a flat, pebble-covered expanse that stretches to the Mali frontier (border).

The Sahara is the world's largest desert. It spans the width of the African continent from the Atlantic Ocean to the Red Sea, extending over parts of Algeria, Morocco, Tunisia, Mali, Chad, Niger, and Sudan. The Sahara covers a vast area of around 8,547,000 square kilometers (3,300,000 square miles).

9 ⊕ FLAT AND ROLLING TERRAIN

The major cities of Algiers, Oran, and Annaba are located on Algeria's narrow coastal plains. The port cities of Bejaia and Skikda also are situated along the coast. The country's most fertile agricultural areas are in these northern plains, including the gentle hills that extend 100 kilometers (62 miles) westward from Algiers.

10 ⊕ MOUNTAINS AND VOLCANOES

The Atlas Mountains cover much of Morocco and extend eastward into Tunisia. Within Algeria, they are known as the Tell Atlas and

Saharan Atlas ranges. The Tell Atlas, farther to the north, extends from the Moroccan frontier in the west to Bejaia in the east. Its peaks, some of which rise to heights of over 1,830 meters (6,000 feet), include the Greater and Lesser Kabylie, as well as the Tlemcen and Madjera summits.

The Saharan Atlas Mountains separate the Maghreb desert region from the Sahara Desert to the south. They are higher and more continuous than the Tell Atlas Mountains, and they consist of three ranges: the Ksour near the Moroccan border, the Amour, and the Ouled Nail south of Algiers. Dominating the southeast area of the country are the Ahaggar Mountains, with irregular heights reaching above 2,000 meters (6,561 feet). Algeria's highest peak, Mount Tahat (3,003 meters/9,853 feet), rises from in this range.

11 ⊕ CANYONS AND CAVES

About 50 miles (80 kilometers) east of Algiers, there are a few limestone caves as well as near Tlemcen in the northwest.

12 ⊕ PLATEAUS AND MONOLITHS

The High Plateaus stretch for more than 600 kilometers (372 miles) eastward from the Moroccan border. They consist of a steppe-like (treeless) tableland lying between the Tell and Saharan Atlas ranges. Averaging between 1,100 and 1,300 meters (3,609 and 4,265 feet) in elevation in the west, the plateaus drop to 400 meters (1,312 feet) in the east. They are so dry that they are sometimes considered part of the Sahara.

13 ⊕ MAN-MADE FEATURES

Most of the Tell streams diminish to trickles or go dry in summer, but in the west, reservoirs have been developed in the Chelif and Hamiz river basins for irrigation purposes.

14 ⊕ FURTHER READING

Books

Fromentin, Eughne. *Between Sea and Sahara: An Algerian Journa*l. Athens: Ohio University Press, 1999.

McLaughlan, Anne, and Keith McLaughlin. *Morocco & Tunisia Handbook, 1996; With Algeria, Libya, and Mauritania.* Lincolnwood, IL: Passport Books, 1995.

Ruedy, John. *Modern Algeria: The Origins and Development of a Nation.* Bloomington: Indiana University Press, 1992.

Web Sites

ArabNet. http://www.arab.net/algeria/algeria_contents.html (accessed February, 3, 2003).

Miftah Shamali Web site. http://i-cias.com/m.s/algeria/ (accessed June 19, 2003).

Andorra

- **Official name:** Principality of Andorra

- **Area:** 468 square kilometers (180 square miles)

- **Highest point on mainland:** Coma Pedrosa Peak (Pic de Coma Pedrosa) (2,946 meters/9,665 feet)

- **Lowest point on land:** Runer River (Riu Runer) (840 meters/2,755 feet)

- **Hemispheres:** Eastern and Northern

- **Time zone:** 1 P.M. = noon GMT

- **Longest distances:** 30.1 kilometers (18.7 miles) from east to west; 25.4 kilometers (15.8 miles) from north to south

- **Land boundaries:** 120.3 kilometers (74.6 miles) total boundary length; France, 56.6 kilometers (35.1 miles); Spain, 63.7 kilometers (39.5 miles)

- **Coastline:** None

- **Territorial sea limits:** None

1 ⊕ LOCATION AND SIZE

Andorra is one of the smallest independent countries on earth. It is a landlocked nation (does not have access to the sea) located on the southern slopes of the Pyrenees Mountains between Spain and France.

With a total land area of 468 square kilometers (180 square miles), Andorra is about two-and-one-half times the size of Washington, D.C. The country is divided into seven parishes.

2 ⊕ TERRITORIES AND DEPENDENCIES

Andorra has no territories or dependencies.

3 ⊕ CLIMATE

Andorra has a temperate (moderate) climate, but the winters are severe because of the high elevation. Snow completely fills the northern valleys for several months. Summers are generally warm and dry. Most of the country's rainfall occurs from October to May.

4 ⊕ TOPOGRAPHIC REGIONS

Andorra's terrain (land) is rough and mountainous. Surrounding the mountain peaks, which often rise higher than 2,900 meters (9,500 feet), there are many narrow gorges and valleys.

There is very little level ground. All the valleys are at least 900 meters (3,000 feet) above sea level, and the mean (midpoint between highest and lowest) elevation is over 1,800 meters (6,000 feet).

5 ⊕ OCEANS AND SEAS

Andorra is a landlocked nation.

6 ⊕ INLAND LAKES

Andorra has several small mountain lakes that are usually named after the highest nearby peak. For instance, the Tristaina Lakes are located near the Tristaina Peak (Pic de Tristaina) and Lake Estanyó (Estany de l'Estanyó) is located near the Estanyó Peak (Pic de l'Estanyó). The Circle of Pessons is a series of small glacial pools linked together and set in the largest

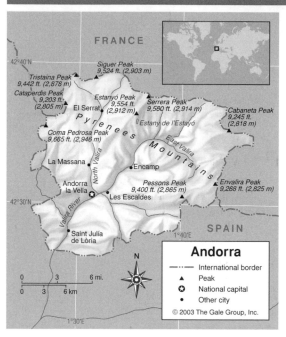

FRANCE

Siguer Peak
9,524 ft. (2,903 m)

Tristaina Peak
9,442 ft. (2,878 m)

Cataperdis Peak
9,203 ft.
(2,805 m)

El Serrat

Estanyó Peak
9,554 ft.
(2,912 m)

Serrera Peak
9,560 ft. (2,914 m)

Cabaneta Peak
9,245 ft.
(2,818 m)

Pyrenees

Estany de l'Estayó

Coma Pedrosa Peak
9,665 ft. (2,946 m)

Mountains

East Valira

North Valira

La Massana

Encamp

Andorra
la Vella

Pessons Peak
9,400 ft. (2,865 m)

Envalira Peak
9,268 ft. (2,825 m)

Les Escaldes

Valira River

Saint Julià
de Lòria

SPAIN

Andorra

— · — · — International border
▲ Peak
✪ National capital
• Other city

© 2003 The Gale Group, Inc.

N

0   3   6 mi.
0   3   6 km

glacial granite circle in Andorra. It is located near the Pessons Peak (Pic dels Pessons).

7 ⊕ RIVERS AND WATERFALLS

The Valira River (Riu Valira) is Andorra's main river. It has two branches and leads to six small open basins (areas drained by rivers).

The North Valira (Valira del Norte) is the northwest branch of the main river, flowing through the cities of La Massana, Ordino, and El Serrat. The East Valira (Valira d'Orient) is the northeast branch, flowing through Les Escaldes, Encamp, Canillo, Soldeu, and Pas de la Casa.

8 ⊕ DESERTS

There are no desert regions in Andorra.

9 ⊕ FLAT AND ROLLING TERRAIN

Since most of Andorra is mountainous, there are no significant areas of plains, or flat land.

10 ⊕ MOUNTAINS AND VOLCANOES

Andorra is located in the chain of mountains known as the Pyrenees. Because of its mountainous terrain it is a very popular site for winter skiing.

The highest mountain peak is Coma Pedrosa Peak (Pic de Coma Pedrosa), which rises to 2,946 meters (9,665 feet). It is located near the western point where the borders between Andorra, France, and Spain meet.

Further north along the border with France are the Cataperdis Peak (Pic de Cataperdis), which rises to 2,805 meters (9,203 feet), and Tristaina Peak (Pic de Tristaina), which rises to 2,878 meters (9,442 feet). To the east are the Siguer Peak (Pic de Siguer), with an elevation of 2,903 meters (9,524 feet), Serrera Peak (Pic de Serrera), 2,814 meters (9,232 feet), and Nerassol Peak (Pic de Nerassol), 2,533 meters (8,310 feet).

Near the southern border is Cabaneta Peak (Pic de Cabaneta), with an elevation of 2,818 meters (9,245 feet).

11 ⊕ CANYONS AND CAVES

Archeological excavations have shown that the first inhabitants of Andorra were cave dwellers. The oldest known cave site in Andorra is the Balma de La Margineda, a rock shelter found near Andorra la Vella on the Valira River.

Archeologists believe that groups of Mesolithic hunter-gatherers lived here between the 10,500 B.C. and 5,500 B.C. Arrow tips, flint stones, bone tools, ceramic fragments, and human remains have been found here.

12 ⊕ PLATEAUS AND MONOLITHS

There are no significant plateau regions in Andorra.

EPD/Saxifraga/Jan van der Straaten

Andorra's landscape is mountainous.

13 ⊕ MAN-MADE FEATURES

There are no major man-made structures affecting the geography of Andorra.

14 ⊕ FURTHER READING

Books

De Cugnac, Pascal. *Pyrenees & Gascony: Including Andorra*. London: Hachette UK, 2000.

Morgan, Bryan. *Andorra, the Country in Between*. Nottingham: Palmer, 1964.

Taylor, Barry. *Andorra*. Santa Barbara, CA: Clio Press, 1993.

Web Sites

Andorra, the Pyrenean Country. http://www.andorra.ad/angles/index.htm (accessed June 17, 2003).

Angola

- **Official name**: Republic of Angola
- **Area:** 1,246,700 square kilometers (481,226 square miles)
- **Highest point on mainland:** Mount Moco (Morro de Moco) (2,620 meters/8,596 feet)
- **Lowest point on land:** Sea level
- **Hemispheres:** Southern and Eastern
- **Time zone:** 1 P.M. = noon GMT
- **Longest distances:** 1,758 kilometers (1,092 miles) from southeast to northwest; 1,491 kilometers (926 miles) from northeast to southwest; the Cabinda Province extends 166 kilometers (103 miles) north-northeast to south-southwest and 62 kilometers (39 miles) east-southeast to west-northwest

- **Land boundaries:** Total land boundaries 5,198 kilometers (4,812 miles); Democratic Republic of the Congo, 2,511 kilometers (1,557 miles), of which 220 kilometers (85 miles) is the boundary of the discontiguous Cabinda Province; Republic of the Congo, 201 kilometers (77.5 miles); Namibia, 1,376 kilometers (531 miles); and Zambia, 1,110 kilometers (428.5 miles)
- **Coastline:** 1,600 kilometers (992 miles)
- **Territorial sea limits:** 22 kilometers (12 nautical miles)

1 ⊕ LOCATION AND SIZE

Angola is located on the west coast of the African continent, south of the equator. Angola is south and southeast of the Democratic Republic of Congo (DROC), northwest of Zambia, north of Namibia, and east of the Atlantic Ocean. Cabinda Province is separated from the rest of Angola by the DROC and is completely surrounded by that country and the Republic of the Congo. With a total land area of 1,246,700 square kilometers (481,226 square miles), including the exclave (area separate from the main part of a country) of Cabinda, Angola is slightly less than twice the size of Texas. Angola is divided into eighteen provinces.

2 ⊕ TERRITORIES AND DEPENDENCIES

Angola has no territories or dependencies.

3 ⊕ CLIMATE

Angola's temperatures and climates vary from region to region. The north has a wet, tropical (supports plant growth year round) climate; the east has a moderate tropical climate; and the southern central strip near the border with Namibia has hot, dry desert conditions. There are two seasons in Angola: a dry, cool winter and a hot, rainy summer. The average temperature is about 20°C (68°F); however, temperatures are warmer along the coast and cooler on the central plateau. The annual average rainfall is 5 centimeters (2 inches) near the southern coast (Namibe); 34 centimeters (13 inches) at the northern coast (Luanda); and as high as 150 centimeters (59 inches) in the northeast. Regions of Angola do suffer from occasional drought.

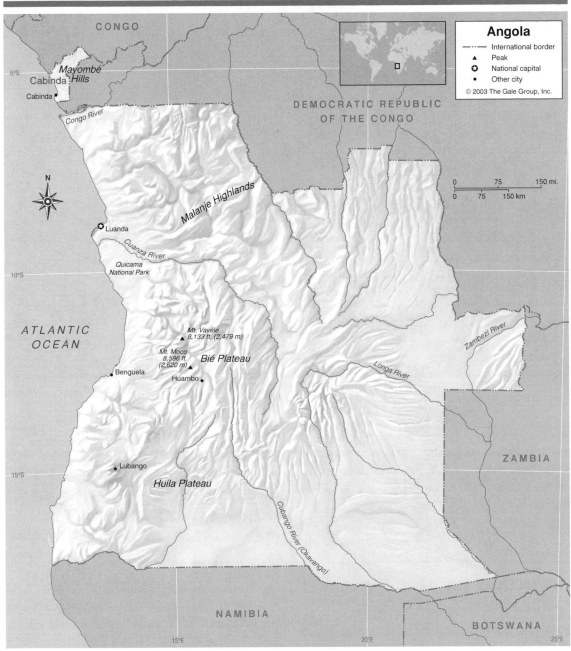

4 ⊕ TOPOGRAPHIC REGIONS

Most of Angola is covered with broad table-lands (broad areas that are higher in elevation than their surroundings) that are greater than 1,000 meters (3,300 feet) high. Angola also has high plateaus in the central and south-ern regions as high as 2,400 meters (7,920 feet). There are many rivers in Angola, but only a few of them are navigable (suitable for boating). The Cabinda region, which lies between DROC and Republic of the Congo just north of the Angolan mainland, is also a part of Angola. The wet regions of the north

EPD/Cynthia Bassett

The zebra still finds habitat in Angola.

and northwest, including Cabinda, are covered with thick forests, while the drier areas in the center of the country support sparse savanna-like grassy vegetation. Land abuse, such as desertification (land losing its ability to support plant life), forest loss, and water impurity are significant environmental problems.

5 ⊕ OCEANS AND SEAS

Seacoast and Undersea Features

Angola's western coast borders on the Atlantic Ocean. The waters off the coast support a fishing industry that contributes to export income.

Coastal Features

The Atlantic coastland is an arid (almost no annual rainfall) strip that is well irrigated by the western-flowing rivers. The coastal lowlands vary in width from approximately 25 kilometers (15 miles) to more than 150 kilometers (93 miles).

6 ⊕ INLAND LAKES

There are no major lakes within Angola.

7 ⊕ RIVERS AND WATERFALLS

Most rivers originate in central Angola. Several rivers flow toward the Atlantic coast and provide both hydroelectric power and irrigation for the normally dry coastal strip. Only two rivers are navigable by any but the very smallest boats.

The Cuanza (Kuanza or Kwanza) River, located in the central portion of the country, is the longest river at 966 kilometers (600 miles), but only 200 kilometers (126 miles) of its length is navigable. The Cuanza drains into the Atlantic Ocean. The Cuango (Kwango) River, located in the northern region, is a fairly navigable waterway that drains into the Congo River system. The Cuando (Kwando) and Cubango Rivers both drain southeast to the Okavango (Cubango) Swamp.

The southernmost rivers in Angola, which flow to the Atlantic, are seasonal and thus are completely dry during much of the year.

8 ⊕ DESERTS

The southern desert-steppe is sandy and dry and has sparse vegetation, except along the major rivers. Inconsistent precipitation keeps the far south somewhat dry. The area is marked by sand dunes, which give way to dry scrub (low shrubby plants) in the central portions.

9 ⊕ FLAT AND ROLLING TERRAIN

The coastal grasslands are well irrigated because of the drainage of the rivers from the higher central plateaus. Elephant grass and scrubby forest cover the surface of the sandy floodplains. Meadows and pastures constitute about 23 percent of the total land area.

The Mayombé Hills in northeast Cabinda were once covered by rain forest. As of 2002, much of the rain forest trees had been cut down.

10 ⊕ MOUNTAINS AND VOLCANOES

The highest peak in Angola is Mount Moco (Morro de Moco) with an elevation of 2,620 meters (8,596 feet). It is located just northwest of Huambo.

Other major peaks rising from the coastal lowlands are Mount Mejo (Morro de Mejo) at 2,583 meters (8,474 feet) in the Benguela region and Mount Vavéle (Morro de Vavéle) at 2,479 meters (8,133 feet) in Kuanza Sul. Running through the center of the country (and into Zambia) is the Lunda Divide, a set of low ridges marking the divisions between west- and east-flowing rivers.

11 ⊕ CANYONS AND CAVES

There are no significant caves or canyons in Angola.

12 ⊕ PLATEAUS AND MONOLITHS

The Bié Plateau, also known as the Great Central Plateau, covers most of Angola. Precipitation at the highest points in the central plateau permits the growth of deciduous forest (trees that lose their leaves), although much of the forest has been cut down for timber and fuel. The climate and soils of these central plateaus support a variety of vegetation. Most of the eastern half of Angola is a relatively flat and open plateau characterized by sandy soils.

13 ⊕ MAN-MADE FEATURES

The country has six dams, but as of 2002, only three were functioning. The Cambembe Dam on the Cuanza River provides power to Luanda.

14 ⊕ FURTHER READING

Books

Black, Richard. *Angola*. Santa Barbara, CA: Clio Press, 1992.

Broadhead, Susan H. *Historical Dictionary of Angola*. 2nd ed. Metuchen, NJ: Scarecrow Press, 1992.

Cushman, Mary Floyd. *Missionary Doctor, The Story of Twenty Years in Africa*. New York: Harper & Brothers, 1944.

Lauré, J. *Angola*. Chicago: Children's Press, 1990.

U.S. Department of State. *Angola, 1996 Post Report*. Washington, DC: The Department of State, 1996.

Web Sites

Welcome to the Republic of Angola. http://www. angola.org/ (accessed June 17, 2003).

Antarctica

- **Official name**: Antarctica
- **Area:** 14,000,000 square kilometers (5,405,430 square miles)
- **Highest point on mainland:** Vinson Massif (5,140 meters/16,864 feet)
- **Lowest point on land:** Bentley Subglacial Trench (2,540 meters/8,333 feet below sea level)
- **Hemispheres:** Southern, Eastern, and Western
- **Time zone:** Each research station chooses its own time zone (usually based on its home country)

- **Longest distances:** Longest distance traversing the South Pole 5,339 kilometers (3,337 miles); shortest distance traversing the South Pole 1,234 kilometers (771 miles)
- **Land boundaries:** None
- **Coastline:** 17,968 kilometers (11,164 miles)
- **Territorial sea limits:** None

1 ⊕ LOCATION AND SIZE

The continent of Antarctica is almost entirely south of the Antarctic Circle (66.5°S), surrounded by the Southern Ocean. Both the geographic and magnetic South Poles are located on the continent. With a total area of about 14,000,000 square kilometers (5,405,430 square miles), Antarctica ranks fifth in size among the world's continents, larger than Australia or Europe. It is slightly less than one-and-one-half times the size of the United States.

2 ⊕ TERRITORIES AND DEPENDENCIES

Antarctica is unique. It is a continent, but it has no native population or government. It does not belong to any one nation, but parts of Antarctica are claimed by seven different countries: Argentina, Australia, Chile, France, New Zealand, Norway, and the United Kingdom. The international community, however, does not recognize their claims, and they cannot enforce them under the terms of the Antarctic Treaty, which has been signed by forty-five nations of the world. First signed in 1961 by twelve nations, the treaty specifies that "Antarctica shall be used for peaceful purposes only." As of 2002, twenty-seven nations held consulting member status in the international treaty agreements protecting Antarctica.

3 ⊕ CLIMATE

The average annual temperature in the interior is a frigid -57°C (-71°F), with a mean summer temperature of -40°C (-40°F) and an average winter temperature of -68°C (-90°F). In the coastal areas, the mean summer temperature is 0°C (32°F). McMurdo Station near the Ross Ice Shelf in East Antarctica has the most moderate climate, with a mean winter temperature of -9°C (16°F). The lowest temperature ever recorded on Earth was at Vostok, East Antarctica, where the mercury dipped to -89°C (-129°F) in 1983.

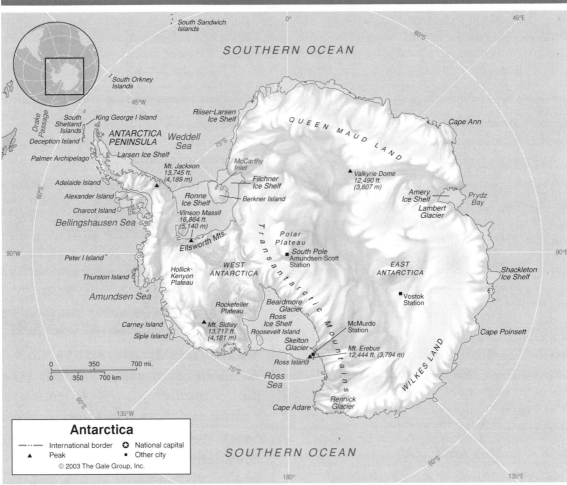

Antarctica

- – – – International border
- ▲ Peak
- ⊙ National capital
- ▢ Other city

© 2003 The Gale Group, Inc.

Since the 1950s, scientists have recorded an overall increase in temperature on Antarctica of about 2°C (4°F), which is much more than the increase in overall temperature elsewhere in the world. Five of the largest ice shelves have shrunk in size during this time period. Some scientists speculate that this is an early sign of global warming caused by human activity, but this theory has not been proven.

Antarctica has continuous daylight from mid-September to mid-March and six months of continuous darkness from mid-March to mid-September. During the daylight months, the continent receives more solar radiation than equatorial regions. Observation has

shown that the layer of high-atmosphere ozone that helps reflect harmful solar radiation away from Earth's surface is thin to nonexistent over Antarctica. The ozone hole varies in size from season to season, but it appears to be expanding. Many blame human activity for this hole in the ozone, but the exact causes are unknown.

Most of the continent receives less than 5 centimeters (2 inches) of precipitation annually, in the form of snow.

4 ⊕ TOPOGRAPHIC REGIONS

Antarctica is generally described as having two parts, West Antarctica and East Antarctica. West Antarctica lies directly south of the South American continent and includes the Antarctic Peninsula, which extends farther north than any other part of the continent. East Antarctica is the larger region; it lies south of the southern tips of Africa and Australia. East and West Antarctica are separated by the Transantarctic Mountains.

About 98 percent of the land area is permanently covered with ice. The remainder is exposed barren rock. Antarctica is generally mountainous, with elevations typically ranging from 2,000 to 4,000 meters (6,600 to 13,200 feet). Mountain peaks rise to heights in excess of 5,000 meters (16,500 feet).

There are no native vertebrate animals on Antarctica. The ocean waters surrounding Antarctica support several species of whale, seals (including the crabeater, elephant, and leopard seal), and about a dozen species of birds, the best-known of which are two varieties of penguin, the Adélie and Emperor. Penguins are birds, but they cannot fly.

5 ⊕ OCEANS AND SEAS

Seacoast and Undersea Features

In 2000, the International Hydrographic Association drew boundaries for a new ocean, called the Southern Ocean, that encompasses all of the water south of 60° latitude. Since this decision, the ocean surrounding Antarctica has been called the Southern Ocean. Due to the great temperature differences between the ice and the open ocean, as well as the lack of any land to impede them, powerful winds blow across the Southern Ocean and the southernmost parts of the surrounding oceans.

The Southern Ocean is home to the Antarctic Circumpolar Current. This ocean current flows east completely around the earth in a great circle just to the north of Antarctica. The current is the most powerful on earth, and it is unique in that it is unimpeded by landforms as it travels around the globe. The current tends to keep cold water to the south, near Antarctica, and holds warmer water back to the north, with a relatively sharp boundary flowing down the middle of the current known as the Antarctic Convergence.

Sea Inlets and Straits

All of the Antarctic seas are inlets of the Southern Ocean. The Bellingshausen Sea lies off the western coast of the Antarctic Peninsula. It is named for Russian explorer Fabian von Bellingshausen, the first person to sail completely around Antarctica in 1819–21. His expedition also gave names to Queen Maud

DID YOU KN⊕W?

Both the geographic and magnetic south poles are located on the continent of Antarctica. Earth's two geographic poles are designated as 90°N latitude/0° longitude (North Pole) and 90°S latitude/0° longitude (South Pole).

Earth's magnetic poles represent the two nearly opposite ends of the planet where the earth's magnetic intensity is the greatest. These locations are different than the geographic poles. The South Magnetic Pole is located at 66°S latitude and 139°E longitude on the Adélie Coast of Antarctica. The North Magnetic Pole is located at 78°N latitude and 104°W longitude in the Queen Elizabeth Islands of northern Canada.

Land and Peter I Island. Off of West Antarctica is the Amundsen Sea, named for the Norwegian explorer Roald Amundsen, who was the first explorer to reach the South Pole.

The Ross Sea lies off the coast of the Ross Ice Shelf directly south of New Zealand. Both are named for Sir James C. Ross, an explorer in the region in 1839–43 from the United Kingdom. The Weddell Sea is named for the British explorer James Weddell, who conducted an exploration in 1823. It is the body of water east of the Antarctic Peninsula.

The Drake Passage lies between Antarctica and South America, which is located hundreds of miles to the north of Antarctica.

Islands and Archipelagos

Antarctica's largest island, Alexander Island (43,200 square kilometers/16,700 square miles), is separated from the Antarctic Peninsula by the George VI Sound, although thick ice sheets connect the two land masses. There are dozens of smaller islands in the Bellingshausen Sea and Amundsen Seas, including Thurston, Siple, Carney, and Charcot Islands. Further north along the Antarctic Peninsula is Adelaide Island and the Palmer Archipelago. Most of these islands are connected to the mainland mass by ice.

Berkner Island (3,880 square kilometers/ 1,500 square miles), covered by the Ronne and Filchner Ice Shelves, lies in the McCarthy Inlet of the Weddell Sea. Roosevelt Island is the largest land mass found within the Ross Sea, but it is completely covered by the Ross Ice Shelf. Ross Island is smaller, but it has access to the ocean in the summer months.

The South Shetland Islands, situated between Antarctica and the southern tip of South America, include Deception Island and King George I Island, among others. Deception Island lies in an active volcanic field

known as the Branfield Rift. It is a horseshoe-shaped island with a central caldera (a crater formed by the eruption of a volcano) that has a surface area of about 26 square kilometers (10 square miles) and is breached at one end to be accessible from the open sea. The water of the caldera is heated by underground volcanic activity and has at times reached the boiling point. Also lying in the ocean between Antarctica and South America are the South Orkney Islands, South Georgia, and the South Sandwich Islands. Zavadovski Island in the South Sandwich Islands is home to one of the largest penguin colonies in the world—with a population estimated at two million penguins.

Coastal Features

Even during the summer, only a few coastal areas are ever free of ice, including parts of Wilkes Land in East Antarctica and parts of the Antarctic Peninsula. During the winter, the ocean around Antarctica freezes, surrounding the continent with ice that expands far out to sea. As winter proceeds, the ice surrounding the Antarctic land mass grows at the rate of about 103,600 square kilometers (40,000 square miles) per day. By the heart of winter, it is roughly six times larger than normal, expanding the effective size of the continent to 33,000,000 square kilometers (13,000,000 square miles).

Almost half of the coastal regions are covered by ice shelves, which are formed as thick fields of ice branch out into the ocean. The ice shelves meet the bottom of the ocean near the shores but narrow into surface ice sheets (with water beneath them) as they stretch away from the land. The shelves extend out into the water for hundreds of kilometers.

The Ross Sea and the Weddell Sea both contain enormous ice shelves. The Ross Ice Shelf in the sea of the same name is the larger of the two, with an area of roughly 336,770 square kilometers (130,100 square miles). The Ronne, Filchner, Larsen, and Riiser-Larsen Ice Shelves are all found in the Weddell Sea.

West Antarctica has a highly irregular coastline, with many small peninsulas and inlets, most of them ice-covered. The S-shaped Antarctic Peninsula extends far to the northeast. It comes closer to another continent (South America) than any other part of Antarctica. Away from the Weddell and Ross Seas, East Antarctica has a much more regular coastline than the western part of the continent. It arcs in a rough half circle from one sea to the other. Since this coast is much closer to the Antarctic Circle than that of West Antarctica, its ice shelves are smaller. The Amery Ice Shelf, along the East Antarctic coast, envelops most of Prydz Bay, that coastline's only significant indentation. East Antarctica extends north slightly beyond the Antarctic Circle at both Cape Ann and Cape Poinsett. The Shackleton Ice Shelf lies not far from the second of these capes. Cape Adare marks the point where the East Antarctic coast curves sharply inwards to form one side of the Ross Sea.

6 ⊕ INLAND LAKES

While a large portion of the world's fresh water is located on Antarctica, it is present mostly in the form of ice. Non-frozen water does exist, however, in the lakes beneath the ice. These lakes are believed to be at least 30 meters (100 feet) deep. Scientists are studying these lakes to determine whether they support any marine life. To conduct their experiments, they must use exceptionally sterile methods to collect specimens in order to avoid contaminating the glacial environment.

Antarctica's largest known lake, Lake Vostok (26,000 square kilometers/10,000 square miles), is approximately the same size as North America's Lake Erie, but it is buried under 3.5 kilometers (2.8 miles) of ice. Other lakes found in the McMurdo Dry Valleys include Lake Vanda, Lake Brownworth, Lake Fryxell, Lake Bonney, and Lake Hoare. These lakes are fed by runoff from the glaciers that lie in the deepest mountain valleys. During the summer, the air temperatures warm to about the freezing point (0°C/32°F), causing the glaciers to melt slightly and to send water flowing

DID YOU KN⊕W?

The discovery of the geographic South Pole is a story of one of the most famous exploration "races" in history. British adventurer Robert F. Scott set out to be the first person to reach the South Pole in 1909. At the same time, unbeknownst to Scott, Norwegian explorer Roald Amundsen was making secret plans to try the trip himself. When Amundsen set sail in 1910, he told his crew and government that he was on his way to the North Pole. Shortly after setting off, he switched directions and the race began. Amundsen reached the pole first, on December 14, 1911, and he set up a small tent and a flag to mark the occasion. This is what Scott saw when he arrived only a few weeks later on January 18, 1912. Unlike Amundsen, Scott and his crew did not survive the trip back from the South Pole. Today, the research station located at the South Pole is named in honor of these two explorers.

The stark landscape of the Skelton Glacier, which lies near McMurdo Research Station.

into small streams for a few weeks before the temperature again drops below freezing. The stream flow feeds the lakes, which lie beneath 3 meters (10 feet) of permanent ice cover.

7 ⊕ RIVERS AND WATERFALLS

The only river of any significance in Antarctica is the Onyx River. With a length of about 25 kilometers (20 miles), it is the largest of the streams that flow during the summer months. The Onyx River flows into Lake Vanda.

8 ⊕ DESERTS

Due to the lack of precipitation, the entire continent is technically considered a desert, despite the fact that it holds more than two-thirds of the world's fresh water. By definition, a desert is any barren land with very little rainfall, extreme temperatures (both hot and cold), and sparse vegetation. This definition can include a permanently cold region, such as Antarctica.

9 ⊕ FLAT AND ROLLING TERRAIN

In Antarctica, glaciers (a large body of ice that moves over Earth's surface) completely cover the land beneath them, allowing only the most dramatic mountain peaks to poke through. Antarctica contains 90 percent of the world's natural ice total. Over land, it averages 2 kilometers (1.5 miles) thick, and is about 3.5 kilometers (3 miles) deep at its widest point. The East Antarctic glaciers are slightly larger than the West Antarctic glaciers. Some coastal areas support a few lichens during the summer months, but the ice sheets are otherwise barren.

Glaciers move over the land at a slow and steady pace. Dramatic formations and striations (stripes, believed to be remnants of volcanic ash) may be observed in the glaciers. The advancing edge of the glacier becomes a high sheer cliff as the top levels of ice push forward. The Antarctic polar ice cap moves an average of 10 meters (33 feet) each year.

In East Antarctica, the continent's largest valley glacier, the Lambert Glacier, lies over several mountain peaks that rise to 1,017 meters (3,355 feet). Massive sections of ice discharge from the Lambert Glacier to become part of the floating Amery Ice Shelf each year. Other noteworthy glaciers include the Skelton Glacier, Rennick Glacier, Recovery Glacier, and Beardmore Glacier.

Lying between the mountain peaks of the Transantarctic Mountains are Victoria Valley, Wright Valley, and Taylor Valley. These large, relatively ice-free territories are known collectively as the McMurdo Dry Valleys. They account for about 4,800 square kilometers (1,733 square miles) of dry land in an area measuring approximately 60 by 75 kilometers (48 by 60 miles). The valleys are ice-free because the mountains impede the flow of the sheet of ice that covers most of the rest of the continent. The valleys are filled with sandy, spongy gravel.

10 ⊕ MOUNTAINS AND VOLCANOES

Dividing Antarctica into two regions, East Antarctica (Greater Antarctica) and West Antarctica (Lesser Antarctica), is the continent's major mountain range, the Transantarctic Mountains.

The Antarctic Peninsula, a finger of land jutting into the ocean from the mainland of West Antarctica, is also mountainous, with underlying volcanic activity. The Ellsworth Mountains of West Antarctica include the territory's highest point, the Vinson Massif (5,140 meters/16,864 feet). Other notable peaks in West Antarctica are Mount Sidley (4,181 meters/13,717 feet), Mount Jackson (4,189 meters/13,745 feet), and Mount Berlin (3,518 meters/11,543 feet).

East Antarctica features at least two active volcanoes, and scientists believe they will likely discover more that have peaks buried beneath the ice. Mount Erebus (3,794 meters/ 12,444 feet), one of the active volcanoes, is on Ross Island. Other notable peaks in East Antarctica are Mount Melbourne at 2,732 meters (9,016 feet) and the Gamgurtsev Subglacial Mountains at 4,030 meters (13,300 feet).

11 ⊕ CANYONS AND CAVES

The Bentley Subglacial Trench, a canyon extending 2,540 meters (8,333 feet) below sea level, is covered by solid ice, making it the lowest point on Earth that is not underwater.

12 ⊕ PLATEAUS AND MONOLITHS

Even where it is not mountainous, Antarctica's elevations are high. Its average elevation of roughly 2,440 meters (8,000 feet) is greater than that of any other continent. As a consequence, most of the land areas outside of the mountain ranges can be considered to be plateaus. Covered by thick ice, most of these plateaus have no names. A few exceptions are the Hollick-Kenyon and Rockefeller Plateaus in West Antarctica, and the Polar Plateau over the South Pole in East Antarctica. The elevation of the South Pole is 2,835 meters (9,355 feet).

13 ⊕ MAN-MADE FEATURES

There are about seventy research stations on Antarctica that are operated by scientists from around the world. Only about half of these centers are used year-round; the others are occupied only during the summer months. Researchers come to Antarctica from many different fields of study, including astrophysics and astronomy, biology, meteorology, geology, oceanography, and biomedicine, among others. The largest research community is at McMurdo Station, governed by the United States and located on Hut Point Peninsula of Ross Island, which is the southernmost point of solid ground that is accessible by ship. There are more than one hundred structures in the complex, including a harbor, a landing strip, and the DASI (Degree Angular Scale Interferometer) telescope observation point for the study of cosmic microwave background radiation. Resident scientists number about twelve hundred people in the summer months and two hundred people in the winter.

14 ⊕ FURTHER READING

Books

Campbell, David G. *The Crystal Desert: Summers in Antarctica*. Boston: Houghton Mifflin, 1992.

Mastro, Jim. *Antarctica: A Year at the Bottom of the World*. Boston: Little, Brown and Company, 2002.

Stewart, John. *Antarctica: An Encyclopedia*. Jefferson, NC: McFarland, 1990.

Wheeler, Sara. *Terra Incognita: Travels in Antarctica*. London: Vintage, 1997.

Web Sites

Antarctic Connection. http://www.antarctic connection.com/antarctic/stations/index.shtml (accessed June 12, 2003).

Mount Erebus Volcano Observatory. http://www.ees.nmt.edu/Geop/mevo/mevo.html (accessed June 12, 2003).

"Warnings from the Ice," *Nova*. http://www.pbs.org/wgbh/nova/warnings/almanac.html (accessed June 12, 2003).

Antigua and Barbuda

- **Official name:** Antigua and Barbuda

- **Area:** 440 square kilometers (170 square miles) total area; Antigua, 280 square kilometers (108 square miles); Barbuda, 161 square kilometers (62 square miles); Redonda, 1.3 square kilometers (5 square miles)

- **Highest point on mainland:** Boggy Peak (402 meters/1,319 feet)

- **Lowest point on land:** Sea level

- **Hemispheres:** Northern and Western

- **Time zone:** 8 A.M. = noon GMT

- **Longest distances:** 14.4 kilometers (9 miles) from east to west; 22.4 kilometers (14 miles) from north to south

- **Land boundaries:** No international boundaries

- **Coastline:** 153 kilometers (95 miles)

- **Territorial sea limits:** 22 kilometers (12 nautical miles); exclusive economic zone: 370 kilometers (200 nautical miles)

1 ⊕ LOCATION AND SIZE

Antigua and Barbuda, a dependency of the United Kingdom, is part of the Leeward Islands, in the eastern part of the Caribbean Sea. Its total area, which is nearly two-and-one-half times that of Washington, D.C., includes the islands of Antigua (280 square kilometers/108 square miles) and Barbuda (161 square kilometers/62 square miles), and the uninhabited island of Redondo (1.3 square kilometers/5 square miles). The country is divided into six parishes.

2 ⊕ TERRITORIES AND DEPENDENCIES

Antigua and Barbuda has no territories or dependencies.

3 ⊕ CLIMATE

Temperatures average 29°C (84°F) in July and 24°C (75°F) in January, a result of the cooling trade winds from the east and northeast. Rainfall averages 117 centimeters (46 inches) per year, with September through November being the wettest months. The islands are subject to both the occasional summer drought and autumn hurricanes, although the low humidity gives them one of the most temperate climates in the world.

Season	Months	Average Temperature: °C (°F)
Summer	April to October	24–30°C (75–86°F)
Winter	November to March	22–27°C (72–81°F)

4 ⊕ TOPOGRAPHIC REGIONS

Antigua, the largest of the British Leeward Islands, is partly volcanic and partly coral in makeup. Many islets line its northeastern coast, and its central area is a fertile plain. Barbuda is a coral island. Redonda is a rocky, low-lying islet.

5 ⊕ OCEANS AND SEAS

Antigua and Barbuda is located in the eastern Caribbean Sea. The open Atlantic Ocean lies to the north and east. The island of Guadeloupe lies to the south, on the far side of the Guadeloupe Passage from Antigua.

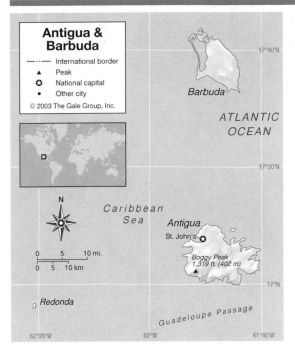

Antigua & Barbuda

--- International border
▲ Peak
✪ National capital
• Other city
© 2003 The Gale Group, Inc.

Barbuda

ATLANTIC OCEAN

17°40'N

17°20'N

N

Caribbean Sea

0   5   10 mi.
0   5   10 km

Antigua

St. John's ✪

Boggy Peak
1,319 ft. (402 m) ▲

17°N

Redonda

Guadeloupe Passage

62°20'W   62°W   61°40'W

Coastal Features

Antigua and Barbuda is famous for its beaches, particularly those on Antigua itself. When advertising to attract vacationers, the country claims it has 365 beaches.

Antigua has deeply indented shores lined by shoals and reefs, with many natural harbors. Barbuda has large stretches of both white and pink sand beaches. Codrington Lagoon, enclosed by a narrow finger of land that stretches northward, lies in northwest Barbuda.

6 ⊕ INLAND LAKES

Antigua and Barbuda lacks any lakes of significant size.

7 ⊕ RIVERS AND WATERFALLS

Antigua and Barbuda lacks any large rivers.

8 ⊕ DESERTS

There are no deserts on Antigua and Barbuda.

9 ⊕ FLAT AND ROLLING TERRAIN

Antigua has a central plain that is relatively fertile due to the volcanic ash in the soil. Like other parts of the island with the same soil composition, it supports some agriculture, as well as tropical vegetation.

10 ⊕ MOUNTAINS AND VOLCANOES

Antigua is a partly volcanic island, but there have been no eruptions in recent history. Its highest elevations are in the southwestern part of the island. This is where Boggy Peak (402 meters/1,319 feet), the tallest mountain on the island, is located. There are no significant elevations on either Barbuda or Redonda.

11 ⊕ CANYONS AND CAVES

There are a number of large caves, both above and under ground, on Barbuda, including an underground cave that extends for 1.6 kilometers (1 mile) at Two Foot Bay.

Seacoast and Undersea Features

There are many coral reefs near Antigua and Barbuda. Antigua is surrounded by an almost continuous band of coral. Devil's Bridge, an unusual formation on Antigua's northeastern shore, is a natural arch created by the erosion of limestone over time.

Sea Inlets and Straits

The coastline of Antigua features many small bays.

Islands and Archipelagos

Redonda, a rocky outcropping less than two square kilometers (less than one square mile) in area, lies 40 kilometers (25 miles) southwest of Antigua. Redonda is uninhabited. Guiana Island, a tiny island off the northeast coast of Antigua, provides a forest habitat for a number of nesting bird species.

ANTIGUA AND BARBUDA

EPD Photos

The beach at Galley Bay is one of the hundreds of beaches lining the islands of Antigua and Barbuda.

12 ⊕ PLATEAUS AND MONOLITHS

There are no plateaus or monoliths on Antigua and Barbuda.

13 ⊕ MAN-MADE FEATURES

There are no significant man-made features affecting the geography of Antigua and Barbuda.

14 ⊕ FURTHER READING

Books

Corum, Robert. *Caribbean Time Bomb; the United States' Complicity in the Corruption of Antigua.* New York: Morrow, 1993.

Dyde, Brian. *Antigua and Barbuda; the Heart of the Caribbean.* Macmillan Caribbean Guides. London: Macmillan, 1993.

U.S. Department of State, Bureau of Western Hemisphere Affairs. *Background Notes. Antigua and Barbuda.* Washington, DC: U.S. Department of State, 2001.

Vaitilingham, Adam. *Antigua: The Mini Rough Guide.* New York: Penguin Books, 1998.

Web Sites

Welcome to Antigua and Barbuda. http://www.Antigua-barbuda.org/ (accessed June 5, 2003).

Official Travel Guide. http://www.geographia.com/Antigua-barbuda/ (accessed June 5, 2003).

DID YOU KN⊕W?

The Frigate Bird Sanctuary, in Barbuda's Codrington Lagoon, is home to more than 170 bird species, including its namesake, the frigate bird (*fregata magnificens*).

Argentina

- **Official name:** Argentine Republic
- **Area:** 2,766,890 square kilometers (1,068,302 square miles)
- **Highest point on mainland:** Cerro Aconcagua (6,960 meters/22,835 feet)
- **Lowest point on land:** Salinas Chicas (40 meters/131 feet below sea level)
- **Hemispheres:** Southern and Western
- **Time zone:** 9 A.M. = noon GMT
- **Longest distances:** 3,650 kilometers (2,268 miles) from north to south; 1,430 kilometers (889 miles) from east to west

- **Land boundaries:** Total boundary length 9,665 kilometers (6,006 miles); Bolivia, 832 kilometers (517 miles); Brazil, 1,224 kilometers (761 miles); Chile, 5,150 kilometers (3,200 miles); Paraguay, 1,880 kilometers (1,168 miles); Uruguay, 579 kilometers (360 miles)
- **Coastline:** 4,989 kilometers (3,100 miles)
- **Territorial sea limits:** 22 kilometers (12 nautical miles)

1 ⊕ LOCATION AND SIZE

Argentina is the second-largest country in South America, covering most of the southern peninsula of the continent. It is bordered by Bolivia and Paraguay to the north; Brazil, Uruguay, and the South Atlantic Ocean to the east; and Chile to the west and south. With an area of 2,766,890 square kilometers (1,068,302 square miles), the nation is a little less than one-third the size of the United States. Argentina is divided into twenty-three provinces and one autonomous city.

2 ⊕ TERRITORIES AND DEPENDENCIES

Argentina has a territorial claim in Antarctica. As of 2002, it was involved in a long-standing dispute with the United Kingdom over which nation controls the Falkland Islands, South Georgia, and the South Sandwich Islands. All of these territories lie off the coast of Argentina but are governed by the United Kingdom.

3 ⊕ CLIMATE

Argentina's climate ranges from subtropical in the north, to humid in the central regions, to subantarctic in the south. Winter is the driest period of the year. The coldest months are June and July; the warmest month is January. Climate variations are due to the country's range of altitude as well as of latitude.

Average rainfall declines from east to west. Buenos Aires receives an average of 94 centimeters (37 inches) of rain annually and experiences light snow during the winter months. Areas north of Río Negro experience little precipitation during winter. The Pampas receives enough rainfall to support its crops, but it is also subject to flooding. The northeastern region bordering Brazil and Uruguay also receives sufficient rainfall. The Gran Chaco region north of the Pampas receives an average of 76 centimeters (30 inches) of rainfall per year. The Andes region is subject to intense changes in weather, including flash floods during the summer months.

Some areas of Argentina are prone to natural geological disturbances such as earthquakes, violent windstorms known as pamperos, and volcanic activity.

Season	Months	Average Temperature Range (Celsius/Farenheit)
Summer	January to March	16° to 35°C (60° to 95°F)
Winter	May to August	8° to 18°C (47° to 65°F)

4 ⊕ TOPOGRAPHIC REGIONS

The terrain of Argentina varies dramatically across the country's different regions, since both elevation and latitude play a major role in Argentina's geography. The country's four major geographic regions are the Andes Mountains, the lowland north, the central Pampas, and the Patagonia region in the south. Patagonia includes Tierra del Fuego, the southernmost point of the South American continent, which is shared by Argentina and Chile.

5 ⊕ OCEANS AND SEAS

Seacoast and Undersea Features

Argentina has an eastern coast on the Atlantic Ocean.

Sea Inlets and Straits

The Atlantic coast of Argentina, curving from northeast to southwest, features a number of gulfs, bays, and inlets. Starting in the north, the bay on which Buenos Aires sits is Samborombón Bay. At the city of Bahía Blanca the coast abruptly turns southward, forming Blanca Bay. To the south are the San Matías Gulf and the San Jorge Gulf. The Strait of Magellan separates the mainland from Tierra del Fuego, the southernmost tip of the country.

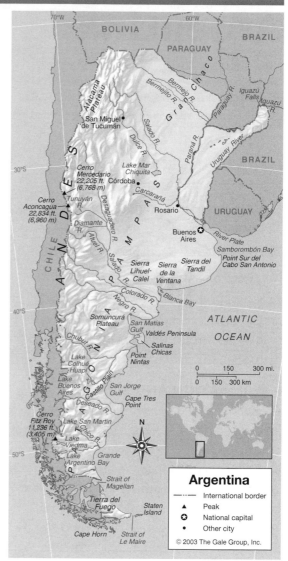

Islands and Archipelagos

Argentina shares the offshore island territory of Tierra del Fuego with Chile. Eons ago, Tierra del Fuego existed under the sea. The land slowly rose and mountains formed as the South American and Scotia Tectonic Plates pushed together. By the Ice Age, most of what is now the Patagonian continental shelf had become land. About 9,000 years ago, the waters of the Strait of Magellan broke through the tip of the continent.

EPD/Cynthia Bassett

The landscape of southern Argentina is dotted with many lakes.

Argentina also owns the Isla de los Estados, which is separated from the southern point of Tierra del Fuego by the Strait of Le Maire. Both Argentina and the United Kingdom claim the Falkland Islands (Islas Malvinas) as their own.

Coastal Features

The Valdés Peninsula (Península Valdés), with its miles of beaches and tall cliffs, forms the southern rim of the San Matías Gulf, at about the midpoint of the country's Atlantic coast. This area is home to large colonies of marine mammals, including penguins and the southern elephant seal, which mate in the protected lagoons of the peninsula. The area also hosts one of the world's largest concentrations of the Atlantic Right Whale (*Eubalaena glacialis*). In 1999, the United Nations Educational, Scientific, and Cultural Organization (UNESCO) designated the peninsula as a World Heritage Site. Salinas Chicas, Argentina's lowest elevation (40 meters/131 feet below sea level), also is found here. Just south of Valdés Peninsula is a tiny bay that is bordered to the south by Point Ninfas.

Cape Horn is the southernmost tip of the continent.

A popular destination for both tourists and Argentines is the Mar del Plata, a city on the Atlantic coast known for its sprawling beaches, which cover about 8 kilometers (5 miles). This area boasts more than 140 bird species, including flamingos.

6 ⊕ INLAND LAKES

The Lake District, straddling the border between Chile and Argentina in the Andes Mountains, contains many glacial lakes that were carved out of the mountains and later filled up with water from the melting glaciers, snow, and rain. The most significant of these is Lago Buenos Aires, also known as General Carrera Lake. It is located in southern Argentina and shared with Chile. It is the largest lake in the country, and the fifth largest in all of South America, with an average surface area of 2,240 square kilometers (860 square miles). South of Lago Buenos Aires are Lago San Martín, Lago Viedma, and finally Lago Argentino. Not far from Lago Buenos Aires, on the Castillo Plain near Comodoro Rivadavia, is Lake Colhué Huapí.

One of the world's largest salt lakes, and the second-largest lake in Argentina, is Lago Mar Chiquita (Little Sea), located in central Argentina. Its surface area varies from year to year and season to season, but during its wettest periods it has spanned 5,770 square kilometers (2,228 square miles).

7 🌐 RIVERS AND WATERFALLS

The Rio Paraná is the longest river in Argentina and the second-longest river in South America (after the Amazon). It flows approximately 4,900 kilometers (3,060 miles), separating Brazil from Paraguay and Paraguay from Argentina. The Rio Paraná is navigable only as far as Rosário. Its upper reaches feature many waterfalls. Once the Rio Paraná enters Argentina in the northeast, the Iguazú River (Río Iguaçu) joins it. This area is well known throughout the world for the spectacular Iguazú Falls (Cataratas Iguaçu, meaning "great water"). The falls are located on the border between Argentina and Brazil, with two-thirds of them in Argentina. They include approximately 275 smaller falls, with heights ranging between 60 and 80 meters (197 and 262 feet). These falls are higher and wider than Niagara Falls, on the border between Canada and the United States.

Other tributaries of the Rio Paraná that feed in from the west are the Rios Bermejo, Bermejito, Salado, and Carcarañá.

The Uruguay River (1,600 kilometers/1,000 miles) forms part of the borders between Argentina, Brazil, and Uruguay. It is navigable for about 300 kilometers (190 miles), from its mouth to Concordia. The Paraguay River, extending for 2,550 kilometers (1,594 miles), forms part of the border between Paraguay and Argentina, and it flows into the Rio Paraná north of Corrientes and Alto Paraná. These waterways all join to flow into the Río de la Plata, and eventually into the Atlantic Ocean in northern Argentina. Where these rivers meet, a wide estuary is formed, which can reach a maximum width of 222 kilometers (138 miles).

In north-central Argentina, several rivers flow into Lago Mar Chiquita. Rio Dulce originates near San Miguel de Tucumán and flows southwest into the lake. Rios Primero and Segundo also feed into Lago Mar Chiquita from the southwest.

In the northern Patagonia region, the major rivers are the Río Colorado and Río Negro, both of which rise in the Andes and flow to the Atlantic Ocean. The Colorado is fed by the Rio Salado, which flows from Pico Ojos del Salado in a southeasterly direction to the Colorado. Tributaries of the Rio Salado include the Rios Atuel, Diamante, Tunuyán, Desaguadero, and the San Juan, all of which originate in the northwest Andes. The Río Negro also has two main tributaries of its own, the Rio Neuquén and the Rio Limay. In the central Patagonia region, the Rio Chubut rises in the Andes and flows east to form a sizable lake before making its way to the ocean. The Lake District also contains its share of rivers, all originating in the mountains and flowing to the Atlantic.

EPD/Cynthia Bassett

The western Pampas leading up to the Andes mountains, is home to horse, cattle, and sheep ranches.

These include the Rios Deseado, Chico, Santa Cruz, and Gallegos.

8 ⊕ DESERTS

Narrow strips of desert area extend eastward from the mountains down into the Patagonian plains of Argentina. The land is dry, wind-eroded, and marked by sparse scrub vegetation and remnants of a petrified forest.

9 ⊕ FLAT AND ROLLING TERRAIN

The Pampas comprises fertile grasslands that cover much of central Argentina. This area is oval-shaped and extends more than 800 kilometers (500 miles) both north and south and east to west. The eastern half of the Pampas is humid, with fertile agricultural lands well suited to the cultivation of wheat. The western Pampas approaching the Andes mountain range is dry, open land, providing grazing for Argentina's famous horse, cattle, and sheep ranches. This region, along with the northeastern Gran Chaco region, is subject to violent windstorms known as pamperos (pahm-PARE-ohss).

Patagonia, the southern region of Argentina, is a combination of pastoral steppes (flat grasslands) and glacial regions. Near the Chilean border is Glacier National Park (Parc Nacional Los Glaciares), where some three hundred glaciers make up part of the Patagonian Ice Cap (21,760 square kilometers/8,400 square miles). The ice cap, flowing into the Pacific Ocean from the Andes, is the largest in the southern hemisphere outside of Antarctica. Thirteen of these glaciers feed lakes in the region. The Upsala Glacier, at 60 kilometers (37 miles) long and 10 kilometers (6 miles) wide, is the largest in South America. It can only be reached by boat, since it floats in Lago Argentino. The next largest glacier is Perito Moreno, 4.8 kilometers (3 miles) wide and stretching about 35 kilometers (22 miles) long to Lago Argentino, where it forms a natural dam.

The lowland north, including the Gran Chaco and Mesopotamia regions, consists of tropical and subtropical lowlands. The landscape ranges from dry savannas (flat grasslands) to swamps (lands partially submerged under standing water).

Iberá, in the northeast of Argentina, is a biologically rich region, with more than sixty ponds joined to marshes and swampland. The area is extremely humid, and is home to hundreds of bird species and thousands of insects, including a wide variety of butterflies. The area hosts a diverse array of flora and fauna, notably the royal water lily, silk-cotton tree, alligators, and capybara, the largest rodent species in the world.

10 ⊕ MOUNTAINS AND VOLCANOES

The Andean region makes up 30 percent of Argentina. Stretching more than 7,000 kilometers (4,500 miles), the Andes Mountains form the western border of Argentina, which is nearly parallel to the coast of the Pacific Ocean. First formed by tectonic movement approximately seventy million years ago, the mountain range is the highest in the western hemisphere. Its peaks reach nearly 7,015 meters (23,000 feet) and stretch to form a natural border with Chile for more than 3,219 kilometers (2,000 miles).

The Argentinean Andes contain some of the tallest mountains in South America, including Cerro Aconcagua, which at 6,960 meters (22,834 feet) is the tallest peak on the continent and in the entire Western Hemisphere, and Cerro Mercedario (6,768 meters/22,205 feet). Both of these peaks are located near the Chile border southwest of San Juan. The Andes region is also home to arid basins (low-lying areas that receive almost no rainfall); lush foothills covered with grape vineyards; glacial mountains; and half of the Lake District (the other half is in Chile).

Throughout the Andes there are more than 1,800 volcanoes, 28 of which are considered to be active. These include Tipas, Cerro el Condor, and Antofalla, all of which are over 6,000 meters (19,685 feet) high and are some of the highest volcanoes in the world.

Jagged mountain peaks formed from granite include Cerro Fitz Roy (3,405 meters/11,236 feet), Cerro Torre (3,102 meters/10,346 feet), and Cerro Pináculo (2,160 meters/7,128 feet).

Smaller mountain ranges also exist in central South America. These ranges cut across the center of the country and separate the

DID YOU KN⊕W?

Patagonia, in the southern region of Argentina, has a geography that ranges from a vast, windy, and treeless plateau to several glacial regions in the southern area of Tierra del Fuego. Patagonia extends more than 2,000 kilometers (1,200 miles) from Rio Colorado in the north to Cape Horn at the southernmost tip of the continent. The region of Patagonia takes its name from the Patagon, the native inhabitants believed by travelers in the 17th and 18th century to be the tallest people in the world.

DID YOU KN🌐W?

The Strait of Magellan was named for Ferdinand Magellan (1480–1521), the Portuguese navigator who traveled the strait in 1520 while trying to find a western route to the Spice Islands. He spent the winter of that year in the area of Patagonia. When he continued his trip, Magellan became the first European traveler to cross the Pacific Ocean, which he named because of the calm, peaceful weather he experienced on his journey. Unfortunately, he was killed in a skirmish between native people that he encountered when he reached the Philippines.

southern Patagonia region from the northeastern Pampas. From west to east, these ranges are the Sierra Lihuel-Calel, the Sierra de la Ventana, and the Sierra del Tandil.

11 🌐 CANYONS AND CAVES

The Cave of the Hands (Cueva de las Manos) is named for the stenciled, painted outlines of human hands that cover the walls of the cave. These outlines are surrounded by paintings of animals and stick-figured people, as well as by other geometric shapes.

Archaeologists believe that ancient inhabitants of the land painted the caves approximately 9,500 to 13,000 years ago. Cueva de las Manos has been designated a World Heritage Site by UNESCO (United Nations Educational, Scientific, and Cultural Organization).

12 🌐 PLATEAUS AND MONOLITHS

The Somuncurá Plateau is a basalt plateau with alternating hills and depressions. It stretches across the area from the Rio Chubut to the Rio Negro. The region undergoes severe climate changes between the winter and summer months. The area has lava (molten rock) formations and contains many fruit and alfalfa plantations. Cattle ranchers find this area to be ideal for raising their livestock. A smaller plateau, the Atacama Plateau, occupies the region just east of the Andes Mountains in northern Argentina and extends east to the city of San Miguel de Tucumán.

13 🌐 MAN-MADE FEATURES

The reservoir created by the Chocón dam, located on the Río Negro, is one of the country's largest man-made lakes. The Chapetón and Pati Dams, both on the Rio Paraná, are the second- and third-largest dams in the world.

14 🌐 FURTHER READING

Books

Argentina. London: APA Publications, 1997.

Bernhardson, Wayne. *Argentina, Uruguay, and Paraguay.* Oakland, CA: Lonely Planet, 1999.

Hintz, M. *Argentina.* Chicago: Children's Press, 1985.

Nickles, Greg. *Argentina: The Land.* New York: Crabtree, 2001.

Web Sites

Argentina Travel Net. http://www.argentinatraveln et.com/indexE.htm (accessed August 13, 2003).

Mayell, Hillary. "Patagonia Penguins Make a Comeback." *National Geographic,* Dec. 26, 2001. http://news.nationalgeographic.com/news/ 2001/12/1221_patapenguins.html (accessed May 2, 2003).

United Nations Educational, Scientific, and Cultural Organization (UNESCO). http://www.whc.unesco.org/heritage.htm (accessed June 17, 2003).

Armenia

- **Official name:** Republic of Armenia
- **Area:** 29,800 square kilometers (11,500 square miles)
- **Highest point on mainland:** Mt. Aragats (4,095 meters/13,425 feet)
- **Lowest point on land:** Debed River Valley (400 meters/1,320 feet)
- **Hemispheres:** Northern and Eastern
- **Time zone:** 4 P.M. = noon GMT
- **Longest distances:** 400 kilometers (240 miles) from northwest to southeast; 200 kilometers (120 miles) from west to east

- **Land boundaries:** 1,254 kilometers (778 miles) total boundary length; Azerbaijan, 789 kilometers (488 miles), 221 kilometers/137 miles of which is in the Naxçivan enclave; Georgia, 164 kilometers (102 miles); Iran, 35 kilometers (22 miles); Turkey, 268 kilometers (166 miles)
- **Coastline:** None
- **Territorial sea limits:** None

1 ⊕ LOCATION AND SIZE

Armenia is a small, landlocked nation located in the mountainous region southwest of Russia between the Black Sea and the Caspian Sea. With a total area of 29,800 square kilometers (11,500 square miles), it is somewhat larger than the state of Maryland. Armenia is divided into eleven provinces.

2 ⊕ TERRITORIES AND DEPENDENCIES

Armenia has no territories or dependencies.

3 ⊕ CLIMATE

Although Armenia lies not far from several seas, its high mountains block their effects and give it a continental highland climate. It has cold, dry winters and hot, dusty summers. Temperature and precipitation depend greatly on elevation, with colder and wetter seasons in the high north and northeast.

The widest variation in temperature between winter and summer occurs in the central Armenian Plateau, where in midwinter the mean temperature is 0°C (32°F); in midsummer the mean temperature is over 25°C (77°F). Overall, Armenia is a sunny country. Precipitation rates depend on altitude and location, but are heaviest during autumn. In the lower Aras River Valley, the average annual precipitation is 25 centimeters (10 inches). It can reach 80 centimeters (32 inches) in the mountains.

4 ⊕ TOPOGRAPHIC REGIONS

Armenia's terrain is composed largely of plateaus and rugged mountain ranges, with the exception of a few fertile river valleys and the area around Lake Sevan, in the east-central part of the country. The geological formation known as the Armenia Plateau occupies the western part of the country.

5 ⊕ OCEANS AND SEAS

Armenia is landlocked and has no coast.

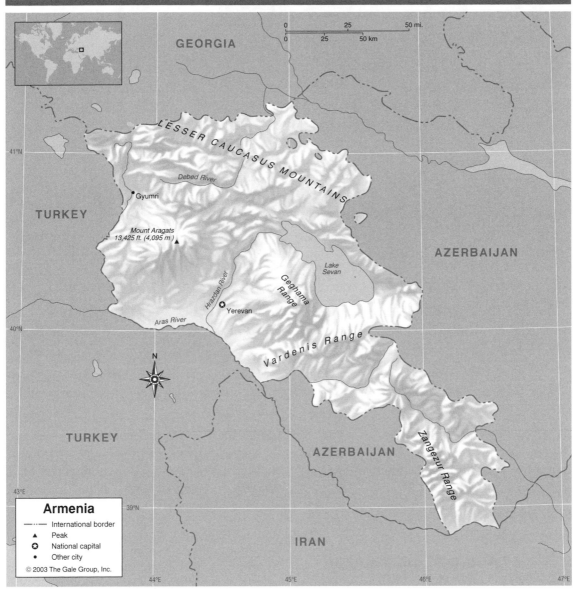

6 ⊕ INLAND LAKES

Lake Sevan lies 2,070 meters (6,200 feet) above sea level on the Armenian Plateau. With an area of 1,244 square kilometers (480 square miles), it is the country's largest lake—and one of the largest high-elevation lakes in the world. At its widest point, Lake Sevan measures 72.5 kilometers (58 miles) across; it is 376 kilome-

ters (301 miles) long. The lake's greatest depth is about 83 meters (272 feet). Many tributaries flow into the lake from the south and southeast, but the Hrazdan River is its only outlet.

7 ⊕ RIVERS AND WATERFALLS

The Aras River, which is 914 kilometers (568 miles) long, is Armenia's largest and longest river. Its chief tributary in Armenia is the

EPD Photos/©2003 Robert Kurkjian

Mount Aragats (Aragats Lerr) as seen from the village of Garni, which lies to the north.

Hrazdan. The Debed River in the north of the country flows northeast into Georgia. The Bargushat River drains the southeastern part of Armenia.

8 ⊕ DESERTS

Armenia has no deserts.

9 ⊕ FLAT AND ROLLING TERRAIN

The Aras River and the Debed River valleys in the far north are the lowest points in Armenia, with elevations of 380 meters (1,158 feet) and 400 meters (1,320 feet), respectively. The rich soils of the arable river valleys contain vineyards and orchards.

10 ⊕ MOUNTAINS AND VOLCANOES

The Lesser Caucasus Mountains enter into Armenia in the north and extend across the entire country along the border with Azerbaijan and into Iran. The Lesser Caucasus system in-

cludes the P'ambaki, Geghama, Vardenis, and Zangezur ranges. Composed largely of granite and crystalline rock, the mountains are high, rugged, and include some extinct volcanoes and many glaciers.

The terrain is particularly rugged in the extreme southeast. Some smaller mountain ranges and extinct volcanoes are located on the Armenia Plateau; included in one of these ranges is Mount Aragats (Aragats Lerr), which at 4,095 meters (13,425 feet) is the highest point in Armenia.

11 ⊕ CANYONS AND CAVES

There are many caves throughout Armenia, and several steep canyons. The longest cave is the Arjeri Cave in the Vayots Dzor region to the south. The Debed Canyon drops to the lowest elevation in the country (400 meters/ 1,320 feet).

EPD Photos/©2003 Robert Kurkjian

Wheat is grown in the southwestern region of Armenia.

12 ⊕ PLATEAUS AND MONOLITHS

Half of Armenia is above 2,000 meters (6,090 feet) in elevation. The Armenian Plateau, which occupies the western part of the country, was formed in a geological upheaval of the earth's crust twenty-five million years ago. It slopes down from the Lesser Caucasus Mountains toward the Aras River Valley.

13 ⊕ MAN-MADE FEATURES

The 1.8-kilometer-long (1-mile-long) tunnel through the Pushkin Pass in northern Armenia, built in 1970 and reopened after reconstruction in 2000, is a major route linking Armenia and Georgia.

14 ⊕ FURTHER READING

Books

Lang, David Marshall. *Armenia: Cradle of Civilization*. London: Allen and Unwin, 1980.

Lynch, H. F. B. *Armenia: Travels and Studies* (2 vols.). Beirut, Lebanon: Khayats, 1965.

Suny, Ronald G. *Armenia in the Twentieth Century*. Chico, CA: Scholars Press, 1983.

Suny, Ronald G. *Looking Toward Ararat: Armenia in Modern History*. Bloomington: Indiana University Press, 1993.

Periodicals

Walker, Christopher J. "Armenia: A Nation in Asia." *Asian Affairs* 19 (February 1988): 20-35.

Web Sites

Armenia Resource Page. http://www.eurasianet.org/resource/Armenia/index.shtrr (accessed June 5, 2003).

Tour Armenia. http://www.tacentral.com (accessed June 5, 2003).

Australia

- **Official name**: Commonwealth of Australia
- **Area:** 7,686,300 square kilometers (2,966,200 square miles)
- **Highest point on mainland:** Mount Kosciusko (2,229 meters/7,314 feet)
- **Highest point in Australian territory:** Mawson Peak (2,745 meters/9,000 feet), an active volcano on Heard Island near Antarctica
- **Lowest point on land:** Lake Eyre (16 meters/52 feet below sea level)
- **Hemispheres:** Southern and Eastern
- **Time zone:** 10:00 P.M. in New South Wales, Australian Capital Territory, Victoria, Tasmania and Queensland = noon GMT; 9:00 P.M. in South Australia and Northern Territory = noon GMT; 8:00 P.M. in Western Australia = noon GMT
- **Longest distances:** 4,000 kilometers (2,485 miles) from east to west; 3,837 kilometers (2,374 miles) from north to south
- **Land boundaries:** None
- **Coastline:** 36,735 kilometers (22,831 miles)
- **Territorial sea limits:** 4.8 kilometers (3 miles)

1 ⊕ LOCATION AND SIZE

The nation of Australia, which also happens to be the world's smallest continent, is situated in the Southern Hemisphere southeast of Asia, between the Pacific and Indian Oceans. Australia covers an area of 7,686,300 square kilometers (2,966,200 square miles). It is slightly smaller than the contiguous United States (not including Alaska and Hawaii). Australia is divided into six states and two territories.

Many Australian place-names reflect the country's history as a British colony, as well as the influence of Dutch and French explorers who visited the region during the seventeenth, eighteenth, and nineteenth centuries. In the late twentieth century, some Aboriginal place-names replaced the British colonial names.

The following table lists the area of each of the six Australian states in both metric and English units:

STATE	AREA IN SQUARE KILOMETERS	AREA IN SQUARE MILES
New South Wales	801,600	309,500
Queensland	1,727,200	666,900
South Australia	985,000	379,900
Tasmania (Island)	67,800	26,200
Victoria	227,600	87,900
Western Australia	2,525,500	975,100

2 ⊕ TERRITORIES AND DEPENDENCIES

Mainland Australia has two territories: Northern Territory and Australian Capital Territory. The following table lists the area of each region in metric and English units:

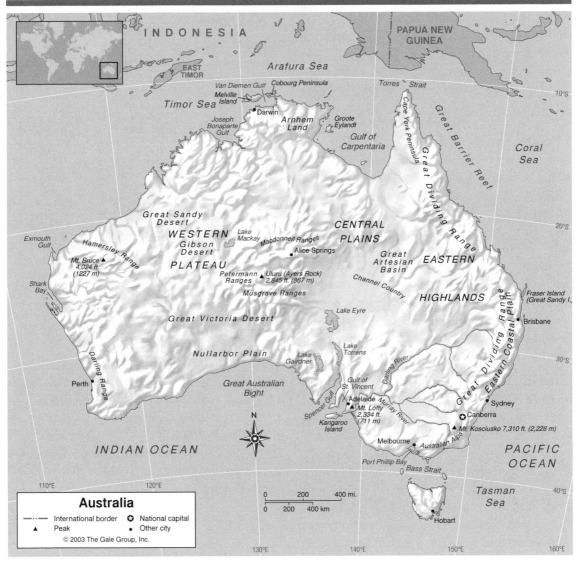

Map labels:

INDONESIA

PAPUA NEW GUINEA

EAST TIMOR

Arafura Sea

Van Diemen Gulf • Cobourg Peninsula

Torres Strait

Timor Sea

Melville Island

Darwin

Arnhem Land

Joseph Bonaparte Gulf

Groote Eylandt

Gulf of Carpentaria

Cape York Peninsula

Great Barrier Reef

Coral Sea

10°S

Exmouth Gulf

Hamersley Range

Great Sandy Desert

WESTERN

Lake Mackay

Macdonnell Ranges

CENTRAL PLAINS

Great Dividing Range

20°S

Gibson Desert

Alice Springs

Great Artesian Basin

EASTERN

Mt. Bruce ▲ 4,024 ft. (1227 m)

PLATEAU

Petermann Ranges

Uluru (Ayers Rock) ▲ 2,845 ft. (867 m)

Channel Country

HIGHLANDS

Fraser Island (Great Sandy I.)

Shark Bay

Musgrave Ranges

Lake Eyre

Eastern Coastal Plain

Brisbane

Great Victoria Desert

Lake Torrens

Darling River

30°S

Perth

Darling Range

Nullarbor Plain

Lake Gairdner

Gulf of St. Vincent

Great Dividing Range

Sydney

Great Australian Bight

Spencer Gulf

Adelaide ▲ Mt. Lofty 2,334 ft. (711 m)

Murray River

Canberra ✪

▲ Mt. Kosciusko 7,310 ft. (2,228 m)

Kangaroo Island

Melbourne

Australian Alps

INDIAN OCEAN

N

Port Phillip Bay

Bass Strait

PACIFIC OCEAN

110°E   120°E

Tasman Sea

40°S

Australia

- - - - International border ✪ National capital
▲ Peak • Other city
© 2003 The Gale Group, Inc.

0   200   400 mi.
0   200   400 km

Hobart

130°E   140°E   150°E   160°E

Territory	Area in Square Kilometers	Area in Square Miles
Northern Territory	1,346,200	519,800
Australian Capital Territory	2,400	900

Since 1936, Australia has claimed an additional 6.1 million square kilometers (2.4 million square miles) on the continent of Antarctica as Australian Antarctic Territory—about 40 percent of the total land area. Three

scientific bases are in operation there: Mawson (established in February of 1954), Davis (established in January of 1957), and Casey (established in February of 1969).

Furthermore, Australia claims authority over several nearby inhabited islands including Christmas Island, which is located in the Indian Ocean 2,623 kilometers (1,630 miles) northwest of Perth. Christmas Island covers an area of about 135 square kilometers (52 square miles), and in 1996 it had an estimated population of 813; 61 percent of the island's residents were Chinese and 25 percent were Malay. Not far from Christmas Island, the Cocos (Keeling) Islands consist of twenty-seven islets with a total land area of 14 square kilometers (5 square miles), two of which are inhabited. In 1996, the estimated population of these two islands was 609. Another possession, Norfolk Island, is northeast of Sydney and covers an area of 36 square kilometers (14 square miles). British explorer James Cook discovered Norfolk Island in 1774; the British government later sent prisoners here during the late eighteenth and early nineteenth centuries. In 1856, descendants of the British sailors who had carried out a mutiny on the ship, *HMS Bounty*, in 1789, joined the prisoners and settled on Norfolk Island. As of 1996, the estimated permanent population was 2,209.

Australia also claims authority over a number of uninhabited islands. The Coral Sea Islands were declared a territory of Australia in 1969; they have no permanent inhabitants, but researchers temporarily take up residence at a meteorology station on one of the islands. The mountainous Heard Island, which is about 4,000 kilometers (2,500 miles) southwest of Perth, covers an area of 910 square kilometers (350 square miles) and has a dormant volcano known as Big Ben (at an elevation of 2,740 meters/8,990 feet). Shag Island is just north of Heard Island; only 42 kilometers (26 miles) to the west are the small McDonald Islands. About 1,600 kilometers (1,000 miles) southeast of Tasmania, the rocky Macquarie Island measures 34 kilometers (21 miles) in length and about 3 to 5 kilometers (2 to 3 miles) in width. Macquarie Island is uninhabited except for a base maintained at its northern end since February 1948; at its southern end, it houses the biggest penguin rookery (a breeding ground) in the world.

3 ⊕ CLIMATE

The climate of Australia is warm and dry. The following table summarizes seasonal temperatures and precipitation levels in the capital city of Sydney:

SEASON	MONTHS	AVERAGE TEMPERATURE: °CELSIUS (°FAHRENHEIT)	RAINFALL IN SYDNEY MILLIMETERS (INCHES)
Summer	December to February	22°C (71°F)	89 mm (3.5 in.)
Fall	March to May	18°C (65°F)	1345 mm (5.3 in.)
Winter	June to August	12°C (54°F)	76 mm (3.0 in.)
Spring	September to November	19°C (67°F)	74 mm (2.9 in.)

4 ⊕ TOPOGRAPHIC REGIONS

Australia has one of the flattest terrains of any country in the world. Erosion over thousands of years has rounded and flattened the mountains of Australia, so that only 6 percent of the land is over 610 meters (2,000 feet) above sea level. The country may be divided into regions according to topography (description of the surface of the land).

The Eastern Highlands (also called the Eastern Uplands) encompass the eastern portion of the country, stretching from the Cape York Peninsula in northern Queensland south through New South Wales and Victoria. Average elevation in this region is about 152 meters (500 feet). The country's highest peak, Mount Kosciusko—at 2,229 meters (7,314 feet)—is found in the southeast corner of the mainland between Melbourne and Canberra.

The Western Plateau is a large desert region, covering approximately the western two-thirds of the country. The Western Plateau rests on an ancient rock shield or foundation, and the average elevation throughout is 305 meters

(1,000 feet) above sea level. The Western Plateau has one mountain range (Hamersley) at its western edge, and three mountain ranges (Macdonnell, Musgrave, and Petermann) that stretch to its eastern edge. From these ranges southward, the Western Plateau is generally a flat tableland, with dramatic outcroppings of granite or sandstone. Four deserts are situated on the Western Plateau. The dry central part of the Western Plateau is popularly referred to as the "Outback." The Darling Range, also known as the Darling Scarp, is found along the plateau's southwest coast.

5 ⊕ OCEANS AND SEAS

Several bodies of water surround Australia. Along the northern coast lie the Timor Sea (northwest of Darwin) and the Arafura Sea (directly north of Darwin between Australia and the neighboring nations of Indonesia and Papua New Guinea). The Coral Sea lies east of the Cape York Peninsula along the northeast coast. Stretching directly east is the Pacific Ocean. The Tasman Sea lies along the southeast shore of mainland Australia northeast of Tasmania Island. (Tasmania and the Tasman Sea are both named for the Dutch explorer Abel Tasman, who arrived in Tasmania in 1642.) Finally, the Indian Ocean surrounds the southern and western coasts of mainland Australia.

Seacoast and Undersea Features

The Great Barrier Reef, the world's longest coral reef, extends for 2,010 kilometers (1,250 miles) just off the northeast coast of Queensland. It encompasses 207,000 square kilometers (79,902 square miles), and it supports a marine ecosystem that includes islands as well as coral reefs. Lake Alexandrina, a coastal inlet that is sometimes referred to as a coastal lake, is situated near Meningie to the southeast of Adelaide and to the east of the Great Australian Bight.

Sea Inlets and Straits

The coastline of Australia features a number of gulfs where the land curves around the sea. The Gulf of Carpentaria forms a deep U-shape on the northeast coast between Arnhem Land and Cape York Peninsula. In 1623 Djan Carstensz, a Dutch explorer, named the gulf in honor of Pieter de Carpentier, who was then the governor-general of the Dutch East Indies (present-day Indonesia). Another Dutch East Indies governor-general, Anthony van Diemen, gave his name in 1644 to Van Diemen Gulf, which lies just west of the Gulf of Carpentaria between Darwin and Melville Island. To the south of Van Diemen Gulf is Joseph Bonaparte Gulf, named in honor of eighteenth-century French emperor Napoleon Bonaparte's older brother by a French explorer in 1803.

To the south, the Great Australian Bight is formed by a large semicircular curve in the southern coast. ("Bight" describes a bend in a coastline or the bay that is formed by a curving coastline.) Along its eastern edge near Port Lincoln is Spencer Gulf, a finger-shaped gulf which points northward about 320 kilometers (198 miles) into South Australia. Bass Strait lies between Tasmania and the mainland. In 1798, explorers George Bass and Matthew Flinders sailed through the strait, demonstrating for the first time that Tasmania was an island.

Islands and Archipelagos

The state of Tasmania (sometimes called Tasmania Island) is a large island located 241 kilometers (150 miles) off the southeastern coast of the mainland. Tasmania has the same geology as the Eastern Highlands, with rugged terrain and a large central plateau. Elevations reach 1,524 meters (5,000 feet) on Tasmania. Between Tasmania and the mainland in the Bass Strait lie King Island and Flinders Island.

This rugged terrain lies on the east coast of Tasmania.

Two of Australia's largest islands lie off the northern coast of Northern Territory. To the west of Darwin is the largest, Melville Island, measuring 5,786 square kilometers (2,333 square miles). To the east in the Gulf of Carpentaria is Groote Eylandt (Dutch for "Great Island"), which covers 2,285 square kilometers (882 square miles), and Mornington Island. North of Broome in Western Australia lie the three uninhabited Ashmore Islands, as well as Cartier Island, which was annexed as part of the Northern Territory in 1938. Kangaroo Island, off the southern coast near Adelaide in South Australia, measures 4,416 square kilometers (1,718 square miles). Fraser Island, a part of Queensland that covers 1,643 square kilometers (634 square miles), is the largest all-sand island in the world.

To the northwest, the Bonaparte Archipelago features numerous small, rocky islands and a deeply indented coastline.

Coastal Features

Many peninsulas extend along the coast. In the northeast, the Cape York Peninsula points north toward Papua New Guinea. Across the Gulf of Carpentaria, Arnhem Land represents the edge of the Western Plateau and features rugged highlands and broad valleys. To the northwest, the Eighty Mile Beach, a stretch of sandy beachfront, marks the coastal edge of the Great Sandy Desert. Just off the high cliffs that mark the shore southwest of Melbourne, limestone pillars known as the Twelve Apostles emerge from the sea.

A river system is made up of a principal river and its tributaries (the rivers that flow into it). A river system begins with the drainage of rainfall and ends in a large body of water, usually an ocean. After a rainstorm, rainwater—called runoff—drains downhill until it eventually accumulates at a low point and begins to flow. As the water flows from higher to lower elevations, two or more small rivers join together to form a larger river. This larger river—usually the one that gives its name to the river system—continues to flow. Sometimes several other smaller rivers, called tributaries, join with the main river as it flows toward a larger body of water such as a lake or ocean.

The point at which a river flows into the ocean is called its mouth. A river system begins at a place called the source or headwaters. The source is the point farthest away from the mouth where water begins to flow. Ports—cities that support shipping activity—often develop at a river's mouth. Ports have docks and roads to allow goods to be transported by ships and other vehicles into and out of the country.

6 ⊕ INLAND LAKES

There are no notable lakes in Australia.

7 ⊕ RIVERS AND WATERFALLS

The most important and longest continuous river system in Australia, referred to as the Murray-Darling River System, flows through parts of four states: Queensland, New South Wales, Victoria, and South Australia. This river system provides the water for 80 percent of the irrigated land in the country. With an annual runoff volume of 22.7 billion cubic meters (801.6 billion cubic feet) of water, the Murray-Darling River System is Australia's largest. Compared to the world's largest river system, the Amazon River in South America, however, the Murray-Darling River system carries less than one percent of the water volume that is transported by the Amazon

The Murray-Darling River System drains an area of 1.1 million square kilometers (410,318 square miles), or about 14 percent of the total land area of the country. Measured from its source in Queensland to its mouth at Lake Alexandrina south of Adelaide, Murray-Darling measures 3,370 kilometers (2,022 miles), or about one-half the length of the world's longest river, the Nile in Egypt. The Murray River, the Darling River, and their tributaries are among the few river systems in Australia that have year-round water flow.

The Murray River measures 2,520 kilometers (1,512 miles), flowing west and southwest, eventually emptying into Lake Alexandrina, a coastal lake south of Adelaide that opens into the Indian Ocean. The Murrumbidgee River, one of the Murray's tributaries, measures 1,575 kilometers (950 miles). Other tributaries include the Lacklan and Goulburn Rivers.

The Darling River, flowing from the junction of the Culgoa and Barwon Rivers in New South Wales, measures 1,390 kilometers (834 miles).

*The interior of Australia is made up of rocky desert. It is often called
"the red center" because of its red sandstone rocks.*

The headwaters of the Darling River originate in the MacIntyre River, which forms part of the border between Queensland and New South Wales. The MacIntyre River eventually flows into the Barwon River, generally agreed to be the main source of the Darling River. The Barwon-MacIntyre section, sometimes called the Upper Darling River, measures 1,140 kilometers (700 miles).

8 ⊕ DESERTS

About 35 percent of the land area of Australia is categorized as desert because it receives so little rainfall. The Great Victoria Desert (Western Australia and South Australia) is the largest individual desert, covering about 4.5 percent of Australia's total land area at approximately 348,750 square kilometers (134,618 square miles).

Other deserts, in descending order from largest to smallest, are: the Great Sandy Desert (Western Australia), representing 3.5 percent of Australia's total land area, covering 267,250 square kilometers (130,160 square miles); the Tanami (or Tanamy) Desert (Western Australia and Northern Territory), representing 2.4 percent of Australia's total land area, covering 184,500 square kilometers (71,220 square miles) just north of the MacDonnell Ranges; the Simpson Desert (Northern Territory, Queensland, and South Australia), representing 2.3 percent of Australia's total land area, covering 176,500 square kilometers (68,130 square miles); the Gibson Desert (Western Australia), representing about 2 percent of Australia's total land area, covering approximately 156,000 square kilometers (60,200

State/Territory	Dam Name	Reservoir Name	Capacity (in millions of cubic meters)	Capacity (in millions of cubic feet)
Tasmania	Gordon	Lake Gordon	12,450	439,485
Western Australia	Ord River	Lake Argyle	5,797	204,634
New South Wales	Eucumbene	Lake Eucumbene	4,798	169,369
Victoria	Dartmouth	not named	4,000	141,200
Queensland	Burdekin Falls	Lake Dalrymple	1,860	65,658
Northern Territory	Darwin River	not named	259	9,140
Australian Capital Territory	Corin	not named	75.5	2,665
South Australia	Mount Bold	Mount Bold	45.9	1,620

square miles) in the center of the state along its western border; the Little Sandy Desert (Western Australia), representing about 1.5 percent of Australia's total land area, covering 111,500 square kilometers (43,040 square miles); the Strzelecki Desert (South Australia, Queensland, New South Wales), representing 1 percent of Australia's total land area, covering 80,250 square kilometers (30,980 square miles); the Sturt Stony Desert (South Australia, Queensland, New South Wales), representing less than 1 percent of Australia's total land area, covering 29,750 square kilometers (11,484 square miles); the Tirari Desert (South Australia), representing less than 1 percent of Australia's total land area, covering 15,250 square kilometers (5,888 square miles); and the Pedirka Desert (South Australia), representing less than 1 percent of Australia's total land area, covering 1,250 square kilometers (482 square miles).

9 ⊕ FLAT AND ROLLING TERRAIN

Rimming the southern edge of the Western Plateau is the Nullarbor Plain, a flat lowland region of limestone along the Great Australian Bight. (Nullarbor comes from the Latin, meaning "no trees.")

The Central Plains, also called the Central Eastern Lowlands or the Interior Lowlands, rest on large horizontal deposits of sedimentary rock, and run from the Gulf of Carpentaria in the north to western Victoria. Lake Eyre, the nation's lowest point, lies in this region.

There are rolling hills on the west coast near Perth. Other hilly areas lie near Adelaide in South Australia, and in the Eastern Highlands.

10 ⊕ MOUNTAINS AND VOLCANOES

Australia is one of the flattest continents on Earth. The summit (highest point) of the highest mountain, Mount Kosciusko (2,229 meters/7,314 feet) in the southeast, can be reached by car. Mount Kosciusko, along with its surrounding plateaus and extinct volcanoes, is in the larger range known generally as the Australian Alps; the specific system that includes Mount Kosciusko is known as the Snowy Mountains.

Geographers use the term Great Divide to describe the mountains that run the length of the country in the east. These mountains are also referred to as the Great Dividing Range. The coastline in this area features deep gorges and high, sheer rock cliffs. Moving north, the highlands gradually decrease in altitude. Along the northeastern coast, the Great Divide also includes the Eastern Highlands, where the elevation is just over 900 meters (3,000 feet).

Uluru, located in Australia's Western Plateau, is the world's largest monolith.

The Western Plateau features several mountain ranges. At the far western edge lies the highest of these, the Hamersley Range, which includes a peak that exceeds 1,219 meters (4,000 feet). Extending to the eastern edge of the Western Plateau are the Macdonnell Range, the Musgrave Range, and the Petermann Range.

All three ranges run from east to west and are characterized by deep gorges. The Macdonnell and Musgrave Ranges have peaks that rise to almost 1,500 meters (4,900 feet). The Darling Range, named for Sir Ralph Darling, a former governor of New South Wales, lies in the extreme southwest corner of the country. Its highest peak is Mount Cooke (582 meters/ 1,920 feet).

11 ⊕ CANYONS AND CAVES

A network of caves punctuate the Nullarbor Plain. Among the best known are the Abrakurrie Cave and the Koonalda Caves, huge caves which are situated about 76 meters (250 feet) below ground.

Some of the most spectacular caverns are underwater along the coast. These attract scuba divers from around the world.

12 ⊕ PLATEAUS AND MONOLITHS

Forming the northern edge of the large Western Plateau, on the northwestern border of the state of Western Australia, lies the Kimberley Plateau, with elevations reaching over 900 meters (3,000 feet).

The western portion of the Western Plateau is generally a flat tableland, with dramatic

DID YOU KN⊕W?

The Outback is a popular term that refers to the interior of the country, especially the dry center of the Western Plateau and the northern plains. Australians use the term "the bush" to refer to rural areas, especially wilderness.

Life in the Outback may be compared loosely to the rough cowboy lifestyle of the historic American West. "Outback" was first used to describe remote areas far away from civilization. Now, however, "Outback" refers to a broader picture—a place where men and women struggle to live and work in a challenging environment; "the bush" simply describes the geographical places located far from cities and towns.

outcroppings of granite or sandstone. The most well known of these is Uluru, the Aboriginal name for the location formerly known as Ayers Rock. Uluru is the world's largest monolith—a large cylindrical stone outcropping—and is over 335 meters (1,100 feet) high.

In the southwest near the Darling Range, limestone pillars about the size of a person protrude from the surface of a flat, barren plain.

13 ⊕ MAN-MADE FEATURES

Dams have been built to create water storage reservoirs in every state and territory.

14 ⊕ FURTHER READING

Books

Australia. Des Plaines, IL: Heinemann Library, 1999.

Berendes, Mary. *Australia.* Chanhassen, MN: Child's World, 1999.

Darian-Smith, Kate. *Exploration into Australia.* Parsippany, NJ: New Discovery Books, 1996.

Dolce, Laura. *Australia.* Philadelphia: Chelsea House Publishers, 1999.

Israel, Fred L. *Australia: The Unique Continent.* Philadelphia: Chelsea House Publishers, 2000.

Lowe, David. *Australia.* Austin, TX: Raintree Steck-Vaughn, 1997.

McCollum, Sean. *Australia.* Minneapolis, MN: Carolrhoda Books, 1999.

North, Peter. *Welcome to Australia.* Milwaukee, WI: Gareth Stevens, 1999.

Williams, Brian, and Brenda Williams. *World Book Looks at Australia.* Chicago: World Book, 1998.

Periodicals

"Australia's Southern Seas." *National Geographic,* March 1987, p. 286–319.

Brian, Sarah Jane. "What's Up Down Under." *Contact Kids,* September 2000, p. 20.

Bryson, Bill. "Australian Outback." *National Geographic Traveler,* October 1999, p. 86ff.

Gore, Rick. "People Like Us." *National Geographic,* July 2000, p. 90.

Web Sites

Australia's National Mapping Agency. http://www.auslig.gov.au (accessed March 12, 2003).

Australia Speleological Federation. http://www.caves.org.au/ (accessed March 12, 2003).

Bureau of Meteorology. "Climate Facts." http://www.bom.gov.au/ (accessed March 12, 2003).

Austria

- **Official name:** Republic of Austria
- **Area:** 83,858 square kilometers (32,378 square miles)
- **Highest point on mainland:** Grossglockner (3,798 meters/12,461 feet)
- **Lowest point on land:** Neusiedler See (115 meters/377 feet)
- **Hemispheres:** Eastern and Northern
- **Time zone:** 1 P.M. = noon GMT; has Daylight Savings Time
- **Longest distances:** 573 kilometers (356 miles) from east to west; 294 kilometers (183 miles) from north to south
- **Land boundaries:** 2,562 kilometers (1,592 miles) total boundary length; Czech Republic, 362 kilometers (225 miles); Germany, 784 kilometers (487 miles); Hungary, 366 kilometers (227 miles); Italy, 430 kilometers (267 miles); Liechtenstein, 35 kilometers (22 miles); Slovakia, 91 kilometers (57 miles); Slovenia, 330 kilometers (205 miles); Switzerland, 164 kilometers (102 miles)
- **Coastline:** None
- **Territorial sea limits:** None

1 ⊕ LOCATION AND SIZE

Centrally situated at the heart of central Europe and bordering eight different countries, Austria historically has been a political, economic, and cultural crossroads. For hundreds of years, the small, landlocked country (does not have access to the sea) was at the center of a great empire—the Hapsburg regime that ruled much of Europe until World War I (1914-18). Austria has an area of 83,858 square kilometers (32,378 square miles), or slightly less than the state of Maine.

2 ⊕ TERRITORIES AND DEPENDENCIES

Austria has no territories or dependencies.

3 ⊕ CLIMATE

Austria has a transitional climate, with Atlantic maritime (ocean) influences in the north, a continental climate in the east, and an Alpine climate in the south and southwest. The coldest temperatures in Vienna are experienced in January and the warmest are in July. In the fall and spring, a warm, dry southern wind called the föhn moderates temperatures in the Alpine regions. It can also bring fog, and contributes to avalanches by causing snow to melt suddenly and fall from high elevations. Precipitation is heaviest in the mountains (as high as 102 centimeters or 40 inches annually) and lighter in the eastern plains (under 76 centimeters or 30 inches), especially east of the Neusiedler See. Average annual rainfall is 86 centimeters (34 inches) at Innsbruck in the mountainous Tyrol region, and 66 centimeters (26 inches) in Vienna.

SEASON	MONTHS	AVERAGE TEMPERATURE: °CELSIUS (°FAHRENHEIT)
Summer	June to August	15°C to 25°C (59°F to 77°F)
Winter	November to March	4°C to 1°C (25°F to 34°F)

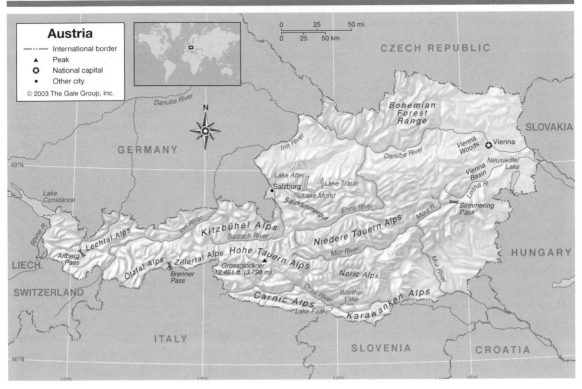

Austria

- –·–·– International border
- ▲ Peak
- ✪ National capital
- • Other city

© 2003 The Gale Group, Inc.

4 ⊕ TOPOGRAPHIC REGIONS

Austria's topography is dominated by the Alpine mountains (called the Alps) that extend eastward from Switzerland, covering the western two-thirds of the country. Austria's two other major regions are the Bohemian Highlands bordering the Czech Republic to the north, and the eastern lowlands, which include the Vienna Basin (lowland region), named for the capital city.

5 ⊕ OCEANS AND SEAS

Austria is a landlocked nation.

6 ⊕ INLAND LAKES

The many lakes in Austria's mountain valleys contribute to the country's scenic beauty. The largest lake that Austria does not share with another country is the Neusiedler See. It is over 32 kilometers (20 miles) long and about 8 kilometers (5 miles) wide. At the opposite end

of Austria, at its furthest northwestern tip, is a small part of Lake Constance (also known as the Bodensee), which lies along the course of the Rhine River, where Austria, Switzerland, and Germany meet. It is one of the largest lakes in Western Europe. There are well-known lake regions in the provinces of Salzburg, Upper Austria, and Styria. The Salzkammergut region near Salzburg includes a district that has about seventy lakes, of which the largest include the Attersee, the Mondsee, and the Traunsee. The southern province of Carinthia, which alone boasts a total of over twelve hundred lakes, is home to five of the most famous, known as the Five Sister Lakes (Funf Schwesterseen). The Drava (Drau) River Valley, where Carinthia is located, is known for other picturesque lakes, including the Faakersee.

7 ⊕ RIVERS AND WATERFALLS

Austria's principal river is the Danube (Donau), the second-longest river in Europe,

The landscape of Austria is mountainous.

which originates in Germany and flows southeastward to the Black Sea. The Danube flows eastward for 350 kilometers (217 miles) within Austria's borders, through the northern part of the country; Vienna, the Austrian capital, is situated on its banks. Three of Austria's other major rivers—the Inn, Salzach, and Enns—are tributaries of the Danube that flow eastward through the central part of the country. The major rivers in the southeast are the Mur and Mürz, in the industrial province of Styria. The Leitha flows northeast, draining the area from the Semmering Pass to the Hungarian border.

8 ⊕ DESERTS

Austria has no desert regions.

9 ⊕ FLAT AND ROLLING TERRAIN

East of the Alpine mountains is a region of low hills and level plains that forms part of the Hungarian Plain and constitutes Austria's lowland region. Even here, however, the land is often hilly, with elevations averaging 150 to 400 meters (500 to 1,300 feet). The Vienna Basin in the north contains the most productive agricultural land in the country.

The Northern Alpine Forelands is a region of foothills and valleys that lies between Austria's northern Alpine ranges and the Danube River valley. There are also foothills at the southeastern edge of the Alpine system, leading to the plains region bordering Hungary. Other hilly regions include the Waldviertel (wooded quarter) and Mühlviertel (mill district), rugged forested areas near the borders with Germany and the Czech Republic.

10 ⊕ MOUNTAINS AND VOLCANOES

More than three-fourths of Austria is mountainous. The Alps spread across the western and southern parts of the country, dividing into three major groups as they fan out across the land. The northern Alps section extends across the northern portion of the provinces of Vorarlberg and Tyrol in the west. This range continues through central and southern Salzburg and Upper Austria provinces, reaching as far as the Vienna Woods in the east. Many of its peaks rise above 2,400 meters (8,000 feet). The central group of mountains is the largest and has the highest elevations. Many of its peaks—including the Grossglockner, the highest point in Austria—exceed 3,000 meters (10,000 feet), The major ranges of the central Alps include the Hohe Tauern and Niedere Tauern, and the Otztaler, Zillertaler, Lechtaler, and Kitzbühel Alps. Austria's southern Alps belong to a group of ranges that lies mostly in northern Italy. Within Austria, they occupy a relatively narrow strip in the southeast, along Austria's borders with Italy and Slovenia, within the province of Carinthia. They include the Karawanken mountain range.

11 ⊕ CANYONS AND CAVES

Austria has several deep caves, including a cave near Salzburg that is 1,600 meters (5,100 feet) deep. The caves are not open to tourists.

12 ⊕ PLATEAUS AND MONOLITHS

North of the Danube River and northwest of Vienna lie the granite and gneiss (granite-like) highlands of the Bohemian Massif, a plateau region that extends northward into the Czech Republic at elevations of up to 1,200 meters (4,000 feet). These highlands account for roughly one-tenth of Austria's total area.

DID YOU KN⊕W?

Although the composer Johann Strauss Jr. immortalized the Danube River in his famous waltz entitled "On the Beautiful Blue Danube," the Danube River is not blue—its waters appear either greenish or brown.

13 ⊕ MAN-MADE FEATURES

A bridge in Austria has the highest columns (184 meters / 607 feet) of any bridge in the world. The roads through the mountainous terrain of Austria travel through numerous long tunnels, some as long as 8 kilometers (5 miles).

14 ⊕ FURTHER READING

Books

Austria. Oakland, CA: Lonely Planet, 1996.

Frommer's Austria. New York: Macmillan, 1997.

Rice, Christopher, and Melanie Rice. *Essential Austria*. Lincolnwood, IL: Passport Books, 2000.

Web Sites

Austrian Press and Information Service. http://www.Austria.org/ (accessed February 17, 2003).

Lonely Planet World Guide: Destination Austria. http://www. lonelyplanet.com/destinations/europe/austria/ (accessed June 22, 2003).

Azerbaijan

- **Official name**: Republic of Azerbaijan
- **Area:** 86,600 square kilometers (33,400 square miles)
- **Highest point on mainland:** Mount Bazardyuze (Bazarduzu Dagi) (4,485 meters /14,800 feet)
- **Lowest point on land:** The shore of the Caspian Sea (28 meters/92 feet below sea level)
- **Hemispheres:** Northern and Eastern
- **Time zone:** 4 P.M. = noon GMT
- **Longest distances:** Approximately 510 kilometers (320 miles) from east to west; 380 kilometers (240 miles) from north to south

- **Land boundaries:** 2,013 kilometers (1,251 miles) total boundary length; Armenia (with Azerbaijan proper) 566 kilometers (353 miles); Armenia (with Azerbaijan-Naxcivan exclave), 221 kilometers (137 miles); Georgia, 322 kilometers (200 miles); Iran (with Azerbaijan proper), 432 kilometers (268 miles); Iran (with Azerbaijan-Naxcivan exclave), 179 kilometers (111 miles); Russia, 284 kilometers (176 miles); Turkey (with Azerbaijan-Naxcivan exclave), 9 kilometers (6 miles)
- **Coastline:** 800 kilometers (500 miles) along the Caspian Sea
- **Territorial sea limits:** None

1 ⊕ LOCATION AND SIZE

Azerbaijan is located in southwestern Asia between Iran to the south and Russia to the north, with its eastern border along the Caspian Sea. With a total land area of 86,600 square kilometers (33,400 square miles), Azerbaijan is slightly smaller than the state of Maine. It is divided into fifty-nine rayons, eleven cities (administrative districts), and one autonomous republic.

2 ⊕ TERRITORIES AND DEPENDENCIES

Both Armenia and Azerbaijan claim the land in the Azerbaijan-Naxcivan exclave (territory not connected to the main land area of a country), surrounded by Iran on the southwest and Armenia on the northeast. Most of the exclave's residents are exclave Armenian, but the area is generally considered to be part of Azerbaijan. The country also claims several small islands that lie in the Caspian Sea. As of 2002, the countries surrounding the Caspian Sea—Azerbaijan, Iran, Kazakhstan, Russia, and Turkmenistan—had not agreed on territorial limits and boundaries.

3 ⊕ CLIMATE

In the central and eastern regions, the climate is generally dry and semiarid (little annual rainfall). In the southeast, it is humid and subtropical. Along the shores of the Caspian Sea it is temperate (moderate), while the higher mountain elevations are generally cold.

Season	Months	Average temperature in the capital, Baku
Summer	June to August	25° C (77° F)
Winter	November to March	4° C (39° F)

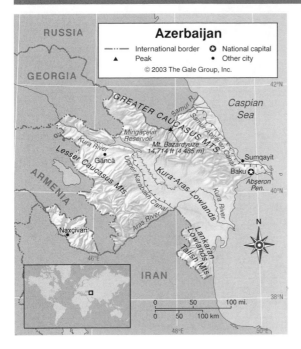

Azerbaijan

--- --- International border   ✪ National capital
▲ Peak   • Other city

© 2003 The Gale Group, Inc.

RUSSIA

GEORGIA

GREATER CAUCASUS MTS.

Caspian Sea

Samur R.

Samur-Abseron Canal

Mingäçevir Reservoir

Mt. Bazardyuze 14,714 ft (4,485 m)

Kura River

Gäncä

Lesser Caucasus Mts.

Upper Karabakh Canal

Kura-Aras Lowlands

ARMENIA

Sumqayit

Baku ✪

Abseron Pen.

Kura River

Naxçivan

Aras River

Lankaran Lowlands

Talish Mts.

IRAN

N

0   50   100 mi.
0   50   100 km

42°N
40°N
38°N
46°E
48°E
50°E

Most of Azerbaijan receives little rainfall—only 15 to 25 centimeters (6 to 10 inches) annually. The greatest precipitation falls in the highest elevations of the Caucasus Mountains, but significant rainfall also occurs in the Lankaran Lowlands of the extreme southeast. The yearly average in these areas can exceed 100 centimeters (39 inches). Drought (lack of rainfall) is a natural and frequent hazard, as is flooding in some lowland areas by rising levels of the Caspian Sea.

4 ⊕ TOPOGRAPHIC REGIONS

Azerbaijan is the easternmost country of Transcaucasia (the southern portion of the Caucasus region between the Black and Caspian Seas). It lies within the southern part of the isthmus between the Black and Caspian Seas. About half of Azerbaijan is covered by mountain ranges, primarily the Great Caucasus Mountains. These mountains surround the central Kura-Aras Lowlands on three sides. The shoreline along the Caspian Sea is essentially flat. The rise in elevation, from lowlands to highlands, occurs over a relatively small area. The Karabakh Uplands are in the west.

5 ⊕ OCEANS AND SEAS

Seacoast and Undersea Features

Azerbaijan has an 800-kilometer-long (500-mile-long) shoreline along the Caspian Sea. The Caspian Sea is a saltwater lake and the largest inland body of water in the world. The sea extends approximately 1,210 kilometers (750 miles) from north to south and between 210 and 436 kilometers (130 and 271 miles) from east to west. Its total area is 371,000 square kilometers (143,000 square miles). Its mean (average) depth is about 170 meters (550 feet).

Although connected to the Baltic Sea, the White Sea, and the Black Sea by extensive inland waterways (primarily the Volga River), the Caspian Sea has no natural outlet. Pollution from agricultural chemicals (especially pesticides), industry, and oil drilling has had a serious adverse impact on the Caspian Sea shoreline environment.

Sea Inlets and Straits

The Bay of Baku is a natural harbor located in the wide curve on the southern side of the Apsheron Peninsula. The port city of Baku is the nation's capital.

Islands and Archipelagos

The islands of the Baku archipelago are located just off of the southern shore of the Apsheron Peninsula and form the partial boundary of Baku Bay. The islands include Nargin, Zhiloy, Bulla, Svinoy, and Glinyany, all of which were formed by underwater mud volcanoes.

Coastal Features

The Apsheron Peninsula juts out into the Caspian Sea. The northern shore of the peninsula boasts beautiful orchards and vineyards, with

ARAMCO/Brynn Bruijn

The natural harbor of the Port of Baku is part of Azerbaijan's capital city.

land particularly suited for agriculture and cattle breeding. The oil and gas fields of this peninsula region are the most important natural resources of Azerbaijan.

6 ⊕ INLAND LAKES

There are more than 250 lakes in Azerbaijan; however, most of them are very small. Many of them were formed as a result of runoff water used in industry or agriculture. This is particularly true of those located along the Apsheron Peninsula. The Mingechevir Reservoir is the largest inland body of water totally within the borders of Azerbaijan. It is a man-made lake, formed by a dam built on the Kura River, and covers an area of 605 square kilometers (234 square miles). The largest natural lake is Lake Gadzhikabul, which only covers 16 square kilometers (6 square miles). Lake Goygol is another natural lake located on the northeastern slope of the Murovdag Range in the Caucasus Mountains.

7 ⊕ RIVERS AND WATERFALLS

There are more than 8,350 rivers in Azerbaijan's river system, but most of them are very small. Most of the country's rivers flow down from the Caucasus ranges into the central Kura-Aras Lowlands. The Kura River (1,500 kilometers / 940 miles) flows through Turkey, Georgia, and Azerbaijan and enters the Caspian Sea south of Baku. It is the longest river of the Transcaucasia Region. The Aras River, which is 914 kilometers (568 miles) long, flows from the east through Armenia and Azerbaijan until it joins the Kura River. Several canals connect the Kura to the Aras River.

8 ⊕ DESERTS

There are no desert regions in Azerbaijan.

9 ⊕ FLAT AND ROLLING TERRAIN

The country's only flatlands can be found along the shore.

The Kura-Aras Valley (lowlands) lies in the center of the country, between the mountain ranges and the Caspian Sea. It is primarily an area of wetlands that includes alluvial flatlands (flatlands containing deposits of clay, silt, sand, or gravel deposited by running water, such as a stream or river) and low seacoast deltas. Since the area is naturally arid, water is often supplied through irrigation. Mineral springs in the valleys are particularly high in iodine.

10 ⊕ MOUNTAINS AND VOLCANOES

Azerbaijan is nearly surrounded by mountains. The Greater Caucasus range, with the country's highest elevations, lies to the northeast along the border with Russia. The country's highest peak, Mount Bazardyuze (Bazarduzu Dagi), rises 4,485 meters (14,800 feet) above sea level. The Greater Caucasus mountains extend into northeastern Azerbaijan and run southeast to the Apsheron Peninsula on the Caspian Sea. The Lesser Caucasus range, with elevations up to 3,500 meters (11,500 feet), lies to the west along the border with Armenia. The Talysh Mountains form part of the border with Iran at the southeast tip of the country. There are several hot and cold mineral springs located in these mountains. Kobustan Mountain, located near Baku, contains deep ravines, from which bubble mineral springs and very active mud volcanoes.

11 ⊕ CANYONS AND CAVES

There are many small caves in the mountainous regions of the Caucasus. The most notable one in Azerbaijan is Azykh, located in the southern part of the Karabakh region, where archeologists have found a number of stone tools left by the ancient cave dwellers. Ancient artifacts also have been found in the Taglar, Damjyly, and the Dashsalakhly Caves of the western Kazakh region. The Gobustan Cave, located near Baku, and other caves located on the Apsheron Peninsula contain numerous petrographs (rock drawings) that have helped scientists learn about the customs and culture of the area's earliest inhabitants.

12 ⊕ PLATEAUS AND MONOLITHS

A number of plateaus exist in Azerbaijan near the country's mountain regions. The major ones include the Baku and Guzdek. Several lava plateaus also form part of the Karabakh Uplands.

13 ⊕ MAN-MADE FEATURES

A dam built in 1953 on the Kura River created the Mingechevir Reservoir. The Upper Karabakh Canal channels water from this reservoir to the Kura and Aras Lowlands to irrigate farmlands during the dry summer months. More than fifty additional water reservoirs in Azerbaijan have been designed for irrigation.

14 ⊕ FURTHER READING

Books

Edwards-Jones, Imogen. *The Taming of Eagles: Exploring the New Russia*. London: Weidenfeld & Nicolson, 1993.

Richards, Susan. *Epics of Everyday Life: Encounters in a Changing Russia*. New York: Viking, 1991.

Streissguth, Thomas. *The Transcaucasus*. San Diego, CA: Lucent Books, 2001.

Web Sites

The United Nations Environment Programs, Azerbaijan. http://www.grida.no (accessed June 17, 2003).

The U.S. Embassy, Baku, Azerbaijan. http://www.usembassybaku.org (accessed June 17, 2003).

The Bahamas

- **Official name:** Commonwealth of the Bahamas

- **Area:** 13,940 square kilometers (5,382 square miles)

- **Highest point on mainland:** Mount Alvernia, Cat Island (63 meters/206 feet)

- **Lowest point on land:** Sea level

- **Hemispheres:** Northern and Western

- **Time zone:** 7 A.M. = noon GMT

- **Longest distances:** 950 kilometers (590 miles) from southeast to northwest; 298 kilometers (185 miles) from northeast to southwest

- **Land boundaries:** Bahamas is made up of islands.

- **Coastline:** 3,542 kilometers (2,201 miles)

- **Territorial sea limits:** 22 kilometers (12 nautical miles)

---

1 ⊕ LOCATION AND SIZE

The Commonwealth of the Bahamas occupies an archipelago that straddles the Tropic of Cancer at the northwestern end of the West Indies (islands lying between southeastern North America and northern South America), about 80 kilometers (50 miles) off the southeast coast of Florida. The Bahamas have a land area of 13,940 square kilometers (5,382 square miles), spread out over approximately 233,000 square kilometers (90,000 square miles) of water in the southwestern portion of the North Atlantic Ocean.

2 ⊕ TERRITORIES AND DEPENDENCIES

The Bahamas claims no territories or dependencies.

3 ⊕ CLIMATE

The Bahamas have a subtropical marine climate moderated by warm breezes from the Gulf Stream (a warm current flowing north from the Gulf of Mexico along eastern North America) and the Atlantic Ocean. Rainfall averages 127 centimeters (50 inches) annually, with some variation among the different islands. Occasional hurricanes occur between mid-July and mid-November. Hurricanes can cause major damage from winds and flooding.

Season	Months	Average temperature: °Celsius (°Fahrenheit)
Summer	May–November	27°C (81°F)
Winter	December–April	23°C (73°F)

4 ⊕ TOPOGRAPHIC REGIONS

The Bahamas encompass roughly seven hundred islands, as well as some two thousand rock formations, islets, and cays (pronounced keys, or low-lying islands). Nassau, the capital of the Bahamas, is located on New Providence Island, which occupies a central position in the archipelago (island chain) and is the most densely populated. Collectively, the rest of the inhabited Bahamas islands are known as the Family Islands. Most of these land masses are long, narrow, and fringed by coral reefs.

5 ⊕ OCEANS AND SEAS

The Bahamas are spread over approximately 233,000 square kilometers (90,000 square

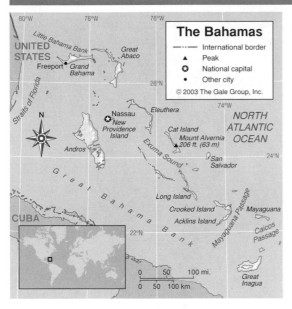

The Bahamas

- – – – – International border
- ▲ Peak
- ✪ National capital
- ⊙ Other city

© 2003 The Gale Group, Inc.

miles) of water in the southwestern portion of the North Atlantic Ocean, between the Atlantic and the Caribbean Sea.

Seacoast and Undersea Features

The numerous coral reefs on the shorelines of the Bahamas combine with iron compounds to produce rare and beautiful colors in the shallow seas surrounding the islands. The Pelican Cay National Park, an underwater nature preserve, is found on Abaco Island.

Sea Inlets and Straits

Numerous inlets and straits separate the islands of the Bahamas from each other and from neighboring islands and archipelagos. Sea passages that lie between islands of the Bahamas include the Northeast and Northwest Providence Channels, Exuma Sound (which lies roughly at the center of the Bahamas), Crooked Island Passage, and Mayaguana Passage. The Caicos Passage separates the Bahamas from the Turks and Caicos islands to the southeast, and the Old Bahama Channel separates Great Bahamas Bank from Cuba to

the south. To the west, the Straits of Florida lie between the Bahamas and Florida.

Islands and Archipelagos

The most important island is New Providence, home to the capital city of Nassau. It has an area of 13,939 square kilometers (5,382 square miles). Andros, at 10,688 square kilometers (4,160 square miles) is the largest island; other inhabited islands include Great Abaco, Eleuthera, Grand Bahama, Cat Island, San Salvador, Long Island, Great Exuma, Crooked Island, Acklin Island, Mayaguana, Bimini (just 77 kilometers/48 miles from Florida), and Great Inagua. On Great Inagua, reptiles, wild boar, and other wildlife roam freely.

Coastal Features

The eastern shore is generally the lowest point on the islands. Some of the islands (especially the long narrow ones in the middle section of the archipelago) have smooth coastlines, while others have numerous indentations, including peninsulas and lagoons. Coastal wetlands and mangrove swamps are common throughout the archipelago.

6 ⊕ INLAND LAKES

There are a few small lakes and ponds on the islands of the Bahamas.

7 ⊕ RIVERS AND WATERFALLS

None of the islands of the Bahamas is large enough to support significant rivers or lakes, although there are many small streams.

8 ⊕ DESERTS

The Bahamas has no desert areas.

9 ⊕ FLAT AND ROLLING TERRAIN

The terrain of the Bahamas is mostly flat and low, rising only a few feet above sea level in most places.

EPD/Cory Langley

The waters surrounding The Bahamas are generally calm and clear.

10 ⊕ MOUNTAINS AND VOLCANOES

There are no true mountains in the archipelago, and only a few hills. The tallest point is the limestone-cliff-sided Mount Alvernia on Cat Island (63 meters /206 feet), which once hosted a monastery on its summit.

11 ⊕ CANYONS AND CAVES

There are a number of caves on the islands, some of which were used as refuges for earlier settlers. On Eleuthera, there is a cave that extends for more than 1.6 kilometers (1 mile) and contains impressive stalagmites and stalactites.

12 ⊕ PLATEAUS AND MONOLITHS

The Bahamas has no plateaus.

13 ⊕ MAN-MADE FEATURES

There are a number of bridges connecting the islands of the Bahamas. Paradise Island Bridge connects New Providence Island (Nassau) to Paradise Island. A bridge joins the Eleuthera mainland to Windemere Island. The Dam Bridge connects Alexander, Exuma, Brigantine Cay, and Barreterra.

14 ⊕ FURTHER READING

Books

Dulles, Wink, and Marael Johnson. *Fielding's Bahamas*. Redondo Beach, CA: Fielding Worldwide, 1997.

Lloyd, Harvey. *Isles of Eden: Life in the Southern Family Islands of the Bahamas*. Akron, OH: Benjamin Publishing, 1991.

Permenter, Paris, and John Bigley. *The Bahamas: A Taste of the Islands*. Edison, NJ: Hunter, 2000.

Web Sites

Geographia Tourist Guide to the Bahamas. http://www. geographia.com/bahamas/ (accessed February 7, 2003).

Bahrain

- **Official name:** State of Bahrain
- **Area:** 620 square kilometers (239 square miles)
- **Highest point on mainland:** Ad-Dukhān Hill (134 meters /440 feet)
- **Lowest point on land:** Sea level
- **Hemispheres:** Northern and Eastern
- **Time zone:** 3 P.M. = noon GMT

- **Longest distances:** Archipelago extends 19 kilometers (12 miles) from east to west; 48 kilometers (30 miles) from north to south.
- **Land boundaries:** No international boundaries
- **Coastline:** 126 kilometers (78 miles)
- **Territorial sea limits:** 22 kilometers (12 nautical miles)

1 ⊕ LOCATION AND SIZE

Bahrain is a Middle Eastern (southwestern Asia and northern Africa) country consisting of thirty-three islands, six of which are inhabited. The country's position in an inlet of the Persian Gulf has given it a regional importance as a trade and transportation center. With an area of 620 square kilometers (239 square miles), Bahrain is more than three times as large as Washington, D.C.

2 ⊕ TERRITORIES AND DEPENDENCIES

Bahrain claims no territories or dependencies.

3 ⊕ CLIMATE

Summers are very hot and humid with southwest winds raising dust storms and drought conditions. Winters are mild, cool, and pleasant. Prevailing southwest winds contribute to dust storms and occasional drought. Rainfall averages less than 10 centimeters (4 inches) annually and occurs primarily from December to March.

Season	Months	Average temperature: °Celsius (°Fahrenheit)
Summer	May to September	29 to 37°C (84 to 99° F)
Winter	December to March	14 to 20°C (57 to 68°F)

4 ⊕ TOPOGRAPHIC REGIONS

Low rolling hills, rocky cliffs, and wadis (dry river or stream beds) comprise the majority of this barren land, although a narrow strip of land along the north coast of the island of Bahrain is irrigated by natural springs and artesian wells (water that flows to the surface without pumping). As of 2002, increasing demands on the natural water resources had begun to deplete them, and some of the lush date palms and other vegetation had begun to decline.

Most of the lesser islands are flat and sandy, although date groves cover the island of Nabih Salih. Bahrain also encompasses the Hawār Islands, off the coast of Qatar.

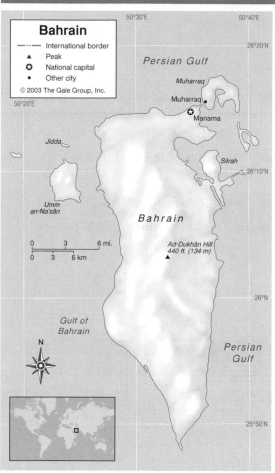

Bahrain

- ·—·—· International border
- ▲ Peak
- ✪ National capital
- ● Other city

© 2003 The Gale Group, Inc.

Umm an-Na'sān; Nabih Salih; and Jidda. At low tide, extensive mud flats along the east coast of Al Muhurraq attract wading birds.

In 2001, the International Court of Justice awarded the Hawār Islands, long disputed with Qatar, to Bahrain. The remaining islands are little more than exposed rock and sandbar.

Coastal Features

Damage to coral reefs and sea vegetation from oil spills and other petroleum-related discharges has adversely affected Bahrain's coastline and beaches.

6 ⊕ INLAND LAKES

Bahrain has no notable lakes.

7 ⊕ RIVERS AND WATERFALLS

Comprised of mostly barren land, Bahrain has little fresh water, and no rivers. There are 10 square kilometers (about 6.2 square miles) of land on the main island of Bahrain that are irrigated by natural springs and artesian wells.

8 ⊕ DESERTS

Bahrain is primarily desert. Only desert vegetation can survive on the sand-covered limestone rock that makes up most of the country's terrain.

9 ⊕ FLAT AND ROLLING TERRAIN

On the main island of Bahrain, the land gradually rises from the shoreline to the center, where rocky cliffs surround a basin. Near the center of this basin is the country's highest elevation, Ad-Dukhān Hill, which rises only 134 meters (440 feet) above sea level.

10 ⊕ MOUNTAINS AND VOLCANOES

Bahrain has no mountains or volcanoes.

5 ⊕ OCEANS AND SEAS

Bahrain is located in the Persian Gulf, which is connected to the Arabian Sea by the Strait of Hormuz and the Gulf of Oman.

Seacoast and Undersea Features

Oil spills and other environmental hazards have damaged Bahrain's coastline and beaches.

Sea Inlets and Straits

Within the Persian Gulf, Bahrain occupies an inlet called the Gulf of Bahrain.

Islands and Archipelagos

The six major islands in the archipelago are Bahrain (the largest); Al Muharraq; Sitrah;

ARAMCO/Burnett H. Moody

The scimitar-horned oryx once faced extinction, but now thrives in the protected environment of Bahrain's Al Areen wildlife park.

11 ⊕ CANYONS AND CAVES

Bahrain has no canyons or caves.

12 ⊕ PLATEAUS AND MONOLITHS

Bahrain has no plateaus.

13 ⊕ MAN-MADE FEATURES

Several bridges connect the island of Bahrain to the other major islands in the archipelago; the King Fahd Causeway links the island to Saudi Arabia. In 2002, plans were underway to construct a 45-kilometer (28-mile) bridge connecting Qatar to Bahrain.

14 ⊕ FURTHER READING

Books

Crawford, Harriet E. W. *Dilmun and Its Gulf Neighbors.* New York: Cambridge University Press, 1998.

Jenner, Michael. *Bahrain, Gulf Heritage in Transition.* New York: Longman, 1984.

Vine, Peter. *Pearls in Arabian Waters: The Heritage of Bahrain.* London: Immel Publications, 1986.

Web Sites

Bahrain government home page. http://www.bahrain.gov.bh/english/index.asp (accessed July 19, 2003).

Bahrain Tourism website. http://www.bahraintourism.com/subpage1.htm (accessed July 19, 2003).

Bangladesh

- **Official name**: People's Republic of Bangladesh

- **Area:** 143,998 square kilometers (55,598 square miles)

- **Highest point on mainland:** Reng Mountain (Keokradong) (1230 meters / 4,034 feet)

- **Lowest point on land:** Sea level

- **Hemispheres:** Northern and Eastern

- **Time zone:** 6 P.M. = noon GMT

- **Longest distances:** 767 kilometers (477 miles) from south-southeast to north-northwest; 429 kilometers (267 miles) from east-northeast to west-southwest

- **Land boundaries:** 4,246 kilometers (2,638 miles) total boundary length; India, 4,053 kilometers (2,518 miles); Myanmar, 193 kilometers (120 miles)

- **Coastline:** 574 kilometers (357 miles) on the Bay of Bengal of the Indian Ocean

- **Territorial sea limits:** 22 kilometers (12 nautical miles)

1 ⊕ LOCATION AND SIZE

Bangladesh is located in southern Asia between Myanmar and India, along the Bay of Bengal. With a total area of 143,998 square kilometers (55,598 square miles), the country is slightly smaller than the state of Wisconsin.

2 ⊕ TERRITORIES AND DEPENDENCIES

Bangladesh has no territories or dependencies.

3 ⊕ CLIMATE

The climate of Bangladesh is generally tropical with three seasons. The humidity ranges from 90 percent to almost 100 percent during the monsoon season. Bangladesh receives a heavy average annual rainfall of approximately 119 to 145 centimeters (47 to 57 inches). About 80 percent of Bangladesh's rain falls during the monsoon season. Parts of Bangladesh are also subject to severe seasonal flooding, cyclones, tidal bores, tornadoes, hailstorms, and moderate earthquakes.

Season	Months	Average temperature: °Celsius (°Fahrenheit)
Summer	March to May	29 to 37°C (84 to 99° F)
Monsoon	June to October	31°C (88°F)
Winter	October to March	5°C to 22°C (41°F to 72°F)

4 ⊕ TOPOGRAPHIC REGIONS

Most of Bangladesh is situated on river deltas. The Chittagong coastal region to the southeast has a narrow attachment to the bulk of the country. Small hill regions in the northeast and southeast are the only variations of the land's flat alluvial plains (flatlands containing deposits of clay, silt, sand, or gravel deposited by running water, such as a stream or river). Since 90 percent of Bangladesh is only about 10 meters (33 feet) above sea level, there is concern that permanent flooding will occur if the Indian Ocean rises as predicted due to global warming.

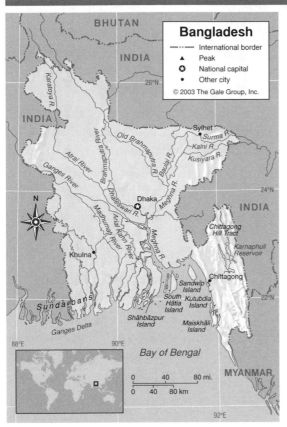

Bangladesh
- — - — - International border
- ▲ Peak
- ✪ National capital
- ● Other city
© 2003 The Gale Group, Inc.

A tidal bore is a unique wave that sweeps up a shallow river or estuary (place where a river joins a larger body of water) on the incoming tide but against the river's current. Conditions are right for tidal bores to occur only in a few places in the world — and one of these is Bangladesh.

5 ⊕ OCEANS AND SEAS

Seacoast and Undersea Features

The Bangladesh coastline lies at the apex (top) of the Bay of Bengal, an inlet of the Indian Ocean. Sri Lanka and India border the bay on the west, Bangladesh forms its north shore, and Myanmar and Thailand surround it on the east. The bay covers an area that is about 2,090 kilometers (1,300 miles) long and 1,610 kilometers (1,000 miles) wide. The ocean often threatens catastrophe for Bangladesh in the form of cyclones and tidal bores.

Islands and Archipelagos

Several flat islands lie just offshore in the Bay of Bengal; many are inhabited by fishing communities. The largest of the permanent islands are Shāhbāzpur, North Hātia, South Hātia, and Sandwīp. Along the Chittagong coast in the

south lie Kutubdia and Maiskhāl islands. In the Padma-Meghna estuary triangle there are a number of permanent islands, including many that surface only at low tide. There are also temporary "chars," land forms built up by silting that may either become permanent or erode.

Coastal Features

Rivers and streams fragment Bangladesh's coastline in the delta region (an area, usually triangular in shape, where rivers deposit soil). In contrast, in the southeast Chittagong region, the coastline includes an uninterrupted stretch of sand at Cox's Bāzār that is about 120 kilometers (75 miles) long.

The section of the Kulna delta that covers the coastline area from the western border to the Padma-Meghna estuary is called the Sundarbans. This is a forested, tidal-flushed, salt marsh region; so much of it is shifting, low, and swampy that humans cannot live there.

6 ⊕ INLAND LAKES

The largest lake, Kaptai Lake, is artificial. (Kaptai Lake is also known as the Karnaphuli Reservoir.) It covers an area of 253 square miles (655 square kilometers) in the Chittagong Hill Tracts. Much smaller lakes, called "mils" or "haors," are formed within the network of rivers that wind across Bangladesh's plains. The

DID YOU KN◉W?

Most people travel from place to place in Bangladesh by river boat. Ferries are available for tourists and others who wish to travel longer distances. One of the best-known ferries is a paddlewheel steamboat, called the "Rocket," that runs between the capital, Dhaka, and Kulna in the west.

large number of these lakes in the Meghna and Surma river plains causes frequent flooding in this area.

7 ⊕ RIVERS AND WATERFALLS

The longest river in Bangladesh is the Brahmaputra River, also commonly known as the Jamuna River once it enters Bangladesh. It starts in the Himalaya Mountains and flows through Tibet in China and India before reaching the northern border of Bangladesh. It has a total length of 2,900 kilometers (1,700 miles). The section that runs through Bangladesh, however, is only 337 kilometers (209 miles) long. The Ganges River, called the Padma River in Bangladesh, enters from the northwest border with India. Branches of the Barak River—the Surma and the Kusiyara—enter the country from the northeast border. They meet to form the Kalni River, which soon widens into the Meghna River. The Brahmaputra-Jamuna, the Ganges-Padma, and the Meghna all intersect with one another before heading toward the Bay of Bengal.

The rivers deposit rich soil through the country and provide fish and transportation for the people of Bangladesh. The rivers also cause hardship due to seasonal flooding and erosion.

The rivers often silt up (become filled with soil) to form marshlands (soft, wet areas). Two-thirds of the Kulna Division in the west is marsh and mangrove forest (a tidal wetland with low-growing trees and a salt bog).

The Rajshahi Division, a triangle of land between the Padma and Jamuna Rivers, is a wetland region, also called the "paradelta" by geographers. It is cut by many old river courses as well as by newer, active rivers. Similar to the rest of the country, this area is subject to disastrous flooding.

8 ⊕ DESERTS

There are no deserts in Bangladesh.

9 ⊕ FLAT AND ROLLING TERRAIN

Only 5 percent of the land in Bangladesh is considered to be permanent pasture. Seventy-three percent of the land is arable (land that is naturally suitable for cultivation by plowing and is used for growing crops).

Clearing land for agricultural uses, logging, and firewood has caused large-scale deforestation. Less than 8 percent of Bangladesh is forested. Small pockets of rainforest still exist in the eastern regions, however.

Bangladesh's significant hill regions are the Chittagong and Bandarban Hill Tracts, which are a series of ridges along the Myanmar frontier. The countryside north and east of the town of Sylhet features sedimentary hills, some of which exceed 90 meters (300 feet) in elevation. Also in the Sylhet District are six hill ranges connecting to the Tripura Hills of India. In these ranges, the maximum elevation is about 335 meters (1,100 feet).

10 ⊕ MOUNTAINS AND VOLCANOES

The country's highest peak is Reng Mountain, also known as Keokradong. It has an elevation of 1,230 meters (4,034 feet) and is located near the intersection of Myanmar, India, and Bangladesh.

ARAMCO/Kevin Bubriski

Rivers in Bangladesh often become marshy as their waters carry large quantities of soil.

11 ⊕ CANYONS AND CAVES

There are no significant canyons or caves in Bangladesh.

12 ⊕ PLATEAUS AND MONOLITHS

There are no significant plateaus or monoliths in Bangladesh.

13 ⊕ MAN-MADE FEATURES

The Karnaphuli Reservoir, also known as Kapti Lake, is located in the Chittagong Hill Tracts. A dam built along the Karnaphuli River in 1963 to generate hydroelectric power formed this man-made lake.

14 ⊕ FURTHER READING

Books

Heitzman, James, ed. *Bangladesh: A Country Study.* Washington, DC: Library of Congress, 1988.

Lauré, J. *Bangladesh.* Chicago: Children's Press, 1992.

Novak, James. *Bangladesh: Reflections on the Water.* Bloomington: Indiana University Press, 1993.

Periodicals

Cobb, Charles E. Jr. "Bangladesh: When the Water Comes." *National Geographic*, June 1993, 118-34.

Web Sites

USAID Bangladesh. USAID Bangladesh, Making a Difference. http://www.usaid.gov/bd (accessed February 22, 2003).

Virtual Bangladesh. Welcome to Bangladesh. http://www.virtualbangladesh.com (accessed February 22, 2003).

Barbados

- **Official name:** Barbados
- **Area:** 430 square kilometers (166 square miles)
- **Highest point on mainland**: Mount Hillaby (336 meters / 1,102 feet)
- **Lowest point on land:** Sea level
- **Hemispheres**: Northern and Western
- **Time zone:** 8 A.M. = noon GMT

- **Longest distances:** 23 kilometers (14 miles) from east to west; 34 kilometers (21 miles) from north to south
- **Land boundaries:** None
- **Coastline:** 97 kilometers (60 miles)
- **Territorial sea limits:** 22 kilometers (12 nautical miles)

1 ⊕ LOCATION AND SIZE

The second-smallest independent country in the Western Hemisphere and the easternmost Caribbean island, Barbados lies between the Caribbean Sea and the North Atlantic Ocean. It is located roughly 320 kilometers (200 miles) north-northeast of Trinidad and Tobago. It has an area of 430 square kilometers (166 square miles), or nearly two-and-one-half times the size of Washington, D.C.

2 ⊕ TERRITORIES AND DEPENDENCIES

Barbados claims no territories or dependencies.

3 ⊕ CLIMATE

The northeasterly trade winds that blow across Barbados's Atlantic coast moderate the island's tropical maritime climate. The weather is cool and dry in winter, and hotter and humid during the rainy season. Rainfall is heaviest between June and December but occurs throughout the year. Average annual precipitation varies from about 100 centimeters (40 inches) in coastal areas to 230 centimeters (90 inches) at higher elevations.

Season	Months	Average Temperature: °Celsius (°Fahrenheit)
Rainy	June to December	23 to 30°C (73 to 86°F)
Winter	December to May	21 to 28°C (70 to 82°F)

4 ⊕ TOPOGRAPHIC REGIONS

A series of terraces rises from the western coast to a central ridge, culminating in Mount Hillaby in the north-central part of the island. Hackleton's Cliff, at the eastern edge of the island's central plateau, extends over several miles. South and east of this elevated area is the smaller Christ Church Ridge. The St. George Valley separates Hackleton's Cliff from Christ Church Ridge.

5 ⊕ OCEANS AND SEAS

The western coast of Barbados borders the Caribbean Sea, and its eastern coast borders the North Atlantic Ocean.

Seacoast and Undersea Features

The low-lying island is almost totally ringed with undersea coral reefs.

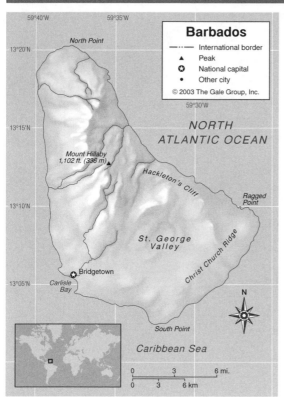

Barbados

- — ·— · — International border
- ▲ Peak
- ✪ National capital
- • Other city

© 2003 The Gale Group, Inc.

Sea Inlets and Straits

Barbados has no notable sea inlets or straits.

Islands and Archipelagos

Barbados consists of one island.

Coastal Features

Flat land and wide strips of sandy beach ring the coast. At the eastern end of the island, flat rocks at Ragged Point form a low, jagged rim to the ocean. The port city of Bridgetown is located on Barbados's only natural harbor, Carlisle Bay, at the southwestern end of the island. The southern and northern ends of the island are known as South Point and North Point, respectively.

6 ⊕ INLAND LAKES

Barbados has no inland lakes.

7 ⊕ RIVERS AND WATERFALLS

Barbados has no rivers and little surface water of any kind. A few springs are fed by underground water stored in limestone beds, and some ravines may become temporarily filled by heavy rains. The best known of Barbados's underground water channels is Cole's Cave in the middle of the island. Two dry streams known as Indian River and Joes River are of no use for either fishing or navigation.

8 ⊕ DESERTS

Barbados has no deserts.

9 ⊕ FLAT AND ROLLING TERRAIN

Other than the terraces that rise from the western coast to the center of the island, Barbados is mostly flat.

10 ⊕ MOUNTAINS AND VOLCANOES

The highest point, Mount Hillaby (336 meters /1,102 feet), rises in the north-central part of the island. At 305 meters (1,000 feet), Hackleton's Cliff is the next-highest point. Numerous inland cliffs were created by past seismic activity.

11 ⊕ CANYONS AND CAVES

Harrison's Cave, near the center of the island, is a large underground cave with stalactites and stalagmites. Streams flow through the cave, spilling over rock formations to form

DID YOU KN⊕W?

Barbados was once two separate islands. A shallow sea, at the site of the present-day St. George Valley, divided the large ridge of Mount Hillaby from the smaller Christ Church Ridge to the south.

EPD/©Stephen Mendes

Along the northeast coast of Barbados, the sea has carved the sandstone into interesting formations.

waterfalls which feed into deep pools of emerald-green water.

12 ⊕ PLATEAUS AND MONOLITHS

There are no notable plateaus on Barbados.

13 ⊕ MAN-MADE FEATURES

As of 2002, the port of Bridgetown was being dredged to allow large cruise ships to dock. As part of this process, the Barbados Marine Trust was transplanting coral from the harbor to other coastline areas. Another aspect of their coral reef preservation activity was the installation of concrete balls, called reef balls, to support and sustain the growth of the coral.

14 ⊕ FURTHER READING

Books

Beckles, Hilary. *A History of Barbados*. Cambridge: Cambridge University Press, 1990.

Spark, Debra. *The Ghost of Bridgetown*. Saint Paul, MN: Graywolf Press, 2001.

Stow, Lee Karen. *Essential Barbados*. Lincolnwood, IL: Passport Books, 2001.

Web Sites

Barbados Daily Nation. http://www. nationnews.com (accessed February 18, 2003).

Barbados Marine Trust. http://www.barbados marinetrust.com/index.htm (accessed June 17, 2003).

Belarus

- **Official name:** Republic of Belarus

- **Area:** 207,600 square kilometers (80,154 square miles)

- **Highest point on mainland:** Dzerzhinskaya Mountain (346 meters / 1,135 feet)

- **Lowest point on land:** Neman River (90 meters / 295 feet)

- **Hemispheres:** Northern and Eastern

- **Time zone:** 2 P.M. = noon GMT

- **Longest distances:** 640 kilometers (400 miles) from southwest to northeast; 490 kilometers (310 miles) from north to south

- **Land boundaries:** 3,098 kilometers (1,925 miles) total boundary length; Latvia, 141 kilometers (88 miles); Lithuania, 502 kilometers (312 miles); Poland, 605 kilometers (376 miles); Russia, 959 kilometers (596 miles); Ukraine, 891 kilometers (554 miles)

- **Coastline:** None

- **Territorial sea limits:** None

1 ⊕ LOCATION AND SIZE

The Republic of Belarus is a landlocked country (does not have access to the sea) in east-central Europe, about 260 kilometers (161 miles) southeast of the Baltic Sea coastline. With a total area of 207,600 square kilometers (80,154 square miles), it is slightly smaller than the state of Texas.

2 ⊕ TERRITORIES AND DEPENDENCIES

Belarus claims no territories or dependencies.

3 ⊕ CLIMATE

The Belarusian climate is considered transitional between continental and maritime. Cool temperatures and high humidity predominate, with a moderating influence from the nearby Baltic Sea. Winter temperatures at times have dropped below -40°C (-40°F) in the north. Summer lasts up to 150 days, while winter ranges from 105 to 145 days. Precipitation ranges between 57 and 61 centimeters (22.5 and 26.5 inches) in an average year; the central region generally receives the highest amount. The popular claim in Belarus that it either rains or snows every two days is fairly accurate.

SEASON	MONTHS	AVERAGE TEMPERATURE: °CELSIUS (°FAHRENHEIT)
Summer	May to August	19°C (67°F)
Winter	December to March	-5°C (23°F)

4 ⊕ TOPOGRAPHIC REGIONS

Although its topography is chiefly flat to hilly, Belarus does have five distinct geographic regions. In the north is the Polotsk Lowland, an area of lakes, hills, and forests. The Neman Lowland in the northwest is similar. The Belorussian Ridge and smaller uplands separate these lowlands from each other and from the rest of the country. Plains and grasslands lie in the east and central part of the country.

Belarus

- – – – – International border
- ▲ Peak
- ✪ National capital
- ✦ Other city

© 2003 The Gale Group, Inc.

0   50   100 mi.

0   50   100 km

The Polesye Marshes dominate the south region, a vast swampy area that extends into Ukraine. Belarus has no natural geographic borders.

5 ⊕ OCEANS AND SEAS

Belarus is landlocked and has no coast.

6 ⊕ INLAND LAKES

Belarus has over four thousand lakes. Lakes Drisvyaty and Osveyskoye are near the northern border. The largest is Lake Naroch (Narach), covering 80 square kilometers (50 square miles) in the northwest.

7 ⊕ RIVERS AND WATERFALLS

At 2,290 kilometers (1,420 miles), the Dnieper is the longest river in Belarus. It is the third-longest river in Europe; only the Volga and Danube Rivers are longer. Its main tributaries are the Berezina in the central region and the Pripyat in the south. The Pripyat and its tributaries are surrounded by the Polesye (or Pripyat) Marshes. The Bug River flows north along part of the border with Poland. The major rivers in the north of the country are the Western Dvina and the Neman Rivers.

8 ⊕ DESERTS

Belarus has no desert area.

9 ⊕ FLAT AND ROLLING TERRAIN

Aside from the highland of the Belorussian Ridge, most of the country is relatively flat (average elevation 162 meters/100 feet) and well watered. About 25 percent of Belarus is covered in peat bogs and marshes. The Polesye Marshes are poorly drained lowlands around the Pripyat River, with low hills that dominate the southern part of Belarus and northern Ukraine. Roughly 485 kilometers (300 miles) across from east to west and 225 kilometers (140 miles) from north to south, they represent the largest wetland in Europe.

Near the border with Poland, the Belavezhskaja Pushcha Nature Reserve protects the largest area of ancient forest in Europe, home to a free-ranging herd of European bison. There are large stands of birch trees across the country.

10 ⊕ MOUNTAINS AND VOLCANOES

Although its terrain is generally level, the Belorussian Ridge, a region of highlands,

DID YOU KN⊕W?

Roughly 23 percent of Belarus's territory was contaminated by radioactivity when a reactor at the Chernobyl nuclear power station in neighboring Ukraine exploded on April 26, 1986. The area affected was home to more than two million people.

EPD/Saxifraga/Jan van der Straaten

The Pripyat River in Belarus is bordered by marshland.

runs across the center of the country from the southwest to the northeast. The highest elevation is Dzerzhinskaya Mountain (Dzyarzhynskaya Hara; 346 meters/1,135 feet).

11 ⊕ CANYONS AND CAVES

Belarus has no notable canyons or caves.

12 ⊕ PLATEAUS AND MONOLITHS

There are no notable plateaus on Belarus.

13 ⊕ MAN-MADE FEATURES

The Dnieper-Bug Canal connects the Bug River to the Pripyat-Dnieper system. Canals also link both the Western Dvina and the Neman with the Dnieper, helping to make it one of the main waterways linking the Black and the Baltic Seas.

14 ⊕ FURTHER READING

Books

Zaprudnik, Jan. *Belarus: At a Crossroads in History.* Boulder, CO: Westview Press, 1993.

Periodicals

Glover, Jeffrey. "Outlook for Belarus." *Review and Outlook for the Former Soviet Union.* Washington: PlanEcon, August 1995, pp. 89-104.

"In the Slav Shadowlands." *Economist*, 335, no. 7915, May 20, 1995, pp. 47-49.

Web Sites

Interesting WWW Sites in and around Belarus. http://www.ac.by/country/ (accessed May 2, 2003).

Virtual Guide to Belarus. http://www.belarusguide.com/main/index.html (accessed May 2, 2003).

Belgium

- **Official name:** Kingdom of Belgium
- **Area:** 30,510 square kilometers (11,780 square miles)
- **Highest point on mainland:** Mount Botrange (694 meters/2,277 feet)
- **Lowest point on land:** Sea level
- **Hemispheres:** Northern and Eastern
- **Time zone:** 1 P.M. = noon GMT
- **Longest distances:** 280 kilometers (174 miles) from southeast to northwest; 222 kilometers (137 miles) from northeast to southwest
- **Land boundaries:** 1,451 kilometers (902 miles) total boundary length; France, 620 kilometers (385 miles); Germany, 167 kilometers (104 miles); Luxembourg, 148 kilometers (92 miles); Netherlands, 450 kilometers (280 miles)
- **Coastline:** 66 kilometers (41 miles)
- **Territorial sea limits:** 22 kilometers (12 nautical miles)

1 ⊕ LOCATION AND SIZE

Belgium is one of Europe's smallest and most densely populated countries. It is located in a part of northwestern Europe that was once called the Low Countries and today is known as the Benelux region (primarily due to Belgium's economic partnership with its neighbors Luxembourg and the Netherlands). Centrally located in Western Europe with few natural frontiers, Belgium has been called the crossroads of Europe. For much of its history, it was a battleground for the major European powers of France, Britain, and Germany. Today, its capital, Brussels, is the seat of both NATO and the European Union.

2 ⊕ TERRITORIES AND DEPENDENCIES

Belgium has no territories or dependencies.

3 ⊕ CLIMATE

Belgium has a temperate maritime climate with moderate temperatures in both summer and winter.

The mean temperature in Brussels ranges from 2.2°C (36°F) in January to 18°C (64°F) in July.

Rainfall averages between 70 and 100 centimeters (28 and 40 inches) per year and is evenly spread out over the twelve months. The elevated Ardennes region can receive as much as 140 centimeters (55 inches) of rain annually.

Season	Months	Average Temperature: °Celsius (°Fahrenheit)
Summer	June to August	18°C (64°F)
Winter	December to March	3°C (37°F)

4 ⊕ TOPOGRAPHIC REGIONS

Belgium can be divided into three major geographic regions: the coastal plains to the northwest, a low central plateau region, and the Ardennes highlands to the southeast. The country also has a distinctive ethnic and linguistic division, influenced by its proximity to its Dutch and French neighbors. The Flemish,

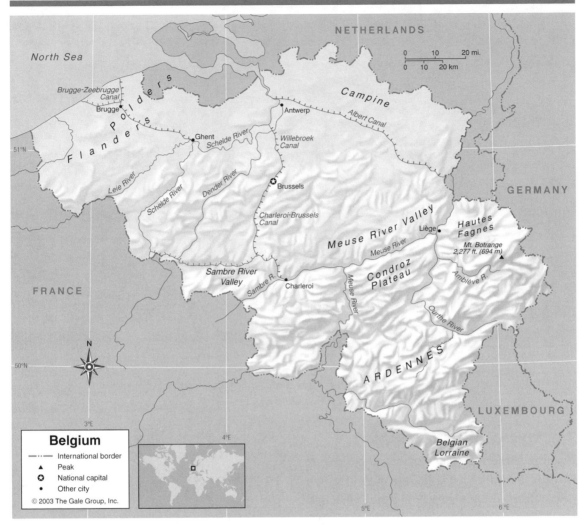

who speak a form of Dutch, live in the northern part of the country, while the French-speaking Walloons live in the southern part. A small German-speaking minority also lives in the east, near the German border.

5 ⊕ OCEANS AND SEAS

Belgium is situated at the southern tip of the North Sea.

Seacoast and Undersea Features

The coast of Flanders, a flat fringe of land reaching 8 to 16 kilometers (5 to 10 miles) in-

land from the sea, is protected from floods and tides by sand dunes and a network of dikes.

Coastal Features

Belgium's coastline is nearly straight, with white-sand beaches. Behind the beaches lie dunes, and behind them are polders (wetlands reclaimed for agricultural use during the Middle Ages).

6 ⊕ INLAND LAKES

Belgium has relatively few natural lakes. The largest complex of lakes is located in the southeast in the Ardennes region.

EPD/Saxifraga/Jan van der Straaten

The Gueule is typical of the many lowland brooks found in Belgium. These brooks feed the Schelde and the Meuse Rivers.

7 ⊕ RIVERS AND WATERFALLS

Belgium has two major rivers, the Schelde (Escaut) and the Meuse (Maas), both of which originate in France and flow east across Belgium. They gather numerous tributaries before continuing through the Netherlands and draining into the North Sea. Among the largest tributaries of the Schelde River are the Leie and Dender. In the south, the Sambre, Semois, Ourthe, and Amblève flow into the Meuse.

8 ⊕ DESERTS

Belgium has no desert regions.

9 ⊕ FLAT AND ROLLING TERRAIN

Belgium's northern lowlands belong to the Great European Plain. The western part of these lowlands is occupied by Flanders. The region northeast of Antwerp, which belongs to the delta of the Meuse and Rhine Rivers, is known as Kempenland, or the Campine.

10 ⊕ MOUNTAINS AND VOLCANOES

The heavily forested Ardennes highlands extend south of the Meuse River valley, continuing into France. They range in elevation from 400 meters (1,300 feet) to between 580 to 700 meters (1,900 and 2,300 feet). The Hautes Fagnes near the German border, which are part of the Ardennes, include Belgium's highest peak, Mount Botrange (Signal de Botrange), at 694 meters (2,277 feet) above sea level.

11 ⊕ CANYONS AND CAVES

A number of interesting caves may be found in the southeastern corner of the country, especially in the provinces of Namur, Liege, and Luxembourg, between Luxembourg and France.

12 ⊕ PLATEAUS AND MONOLITHS

Between the northern lowlands and the Ardennes highlands to the south lies Belgium's central plateau region. It extends across the middle of the country, from the Borinage area in the west to the Brabant region near the southeastern Dutch border. Elevations range from 20 meters (65 feet) to 200 meters (650 feet). The capital city of Brussels is located in this region.

13 ⊕ MAN-MADE FEATURES

The coastal area of Flanders includes polders (reclaimed land) that were formerly marshland. The salt marshes of the region were transformed into rich farmland behind a barrier of dikes.

An extensive network of canals extends throughout the coastal plains and central plateau region, connecting Belgium's major cities and rivers to the sea. The major arteries are the Brugge-Zeebrugge, Charleroi-Brussels, Willebroek, and Albert Canals.

14 ⊕ FURTHER READING

Books

Blyth, Derek. *Belgium.* 9th ed. New York: W.W. Norton, 2000.

Fielding's Belgium: The Most In-Depth and Entertaining Guide to the Charms and Pleasures of Belgium. Redondo Beach, CA: Fielding Worldwide, 1994.

Fox, Renie C. *In the Belgian Château: The Spirit and Culture of a European Society in an Age of Change.* Chicago: I.R. Dee, 1994.

Web Sites

Belgian Federal Govt Online. http://www.belgium.fgov.be/en_index.htm (accessed February 8, 2003).

Belgium: Overview. http://pespmc1.vub.ac.be/BELGCUL.html (accessed July 17, 2003).

Belize

- **Official name:** Belize
- **Area:** 22,806 square kilometers (8,803 square miles)
- **Highest point on mainland:** Victoria Peak (1,122 meters / 3,680 feet)
- **Lowest point on land:** Sea level
- **Hemispheres:** Northern and Western
- **Time zone:** 6 A.M. = noon GMT
- **Longest distances:** 109 kilometers (68 miles) from east to west; 280 kilometers (174 miles) from north to south.

- **Land boundaries:** 995 kilometers (618 miles) total boundary length; Guatemala, 269 kilometers (167 miles); Mexico, 251 kilometers (156 miles)
- **Coastline:** 475 kilometers (295 miles)
- **Territorial sea limits:** 22 kilometers (12 nautical miles)

1 ⊕ LOCATION AND SIZE

Belize is in Central America. Belize is located on the coast of the Caribbean Sea at the southeastern edge of Mexico's Yucatan Peninsula. Known as British Honduras until 1973, Belize has a land area of 22,806 square kilometers (8,803 square miles), which makes it slightly larger than the state of Massachusetts.

2 ⊕ TERRITORIES AND DEPENDENCIES

Belize has no outside territories or dependencies.

3 ⊕ CLIMATE

Belize's climate is subtropical and humid, but it is modified by the northeast trade winds that consistently blow toward the equator. Temperatures range between 16°C and 32°C (61°F and 90°F) along the coast and are slightly higher inland. Changes in humidity, rather than temperature fluctuations, mark the changes in seasons. The mean annual humidity is 83 percent, but many days the humidity is masked by cooling sea breezes. November to January are traditionally the coolest months, and

there are dry seasons from February to May and again in August. Some days and nights in the mountains can be very cold, but the mean annual temperature there is a comfortable 22°C (72°F). Annual rainfall averages from 127 centimeters (50 inches) in the northern portion of the country to more than 380 centimeters (150 inches) in the south. The number of rainy days varies considerably from place to place. The hurricane season lasts from July to October. Hurricanes can cause serious damage and flooding along the coast. Belize City, once the capital, has suffered severe damage from hurricanes since the 1930s. After hurricanes destroyed over half the buildings in Belize City in 1931 and again in 1961, the capital was relocated further inland, to Belmopan.

4 ⊕ TOPOGRAPHIC REGIONS

The country is divided into two main topographic regions. The Maya and Cockscomb Mountains and their associated basins and plateaus dominate the southern half of the country. The northern lowlands, drained by

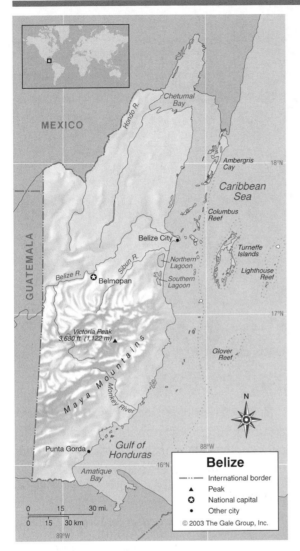

Belize

- --·--- International border
- ▲ Peak
- ✪ National capital
- ● Other city

© 2003 The Gale Group, Inc.

umal Bay, while the southern coast borders the Gulf of Honduras and Amatique Bay.

Seacoast and Undersea Features

The coastline of Belize, on the eastern coast of Central America, is full of indented areas, providing for many beaches as well as swamplands and lagoons. Belize's shore is sheltered by the second-longest barrier reef in the world, dotted with a large number of smaller coral reefs and cays. A barrier reef is an underwater formation of coral that lies parallel to the coast. The Lighthouse Reef contains an underwater cavern, known as Blue Hole Cave. Explored by Jacques Cousteau, the famous oceanographer, Blue Hole Cave measures 300 meters (1,000 feet) in diameter and 120 meters (400 feet) in depth.

Sea Inlets and Straits

Chetumal Bay lies between the northernmost points of Belize and its neighbor to the west, Mexico.

Islands and Archipelagos

To the north of the barrier reef, numerous islands and cays—including Ambergris Cay, the Turneffe Islands, Columbus Reef, and Glover's Reef—lie off the coast of Belize. More than one thousand small islands dot the coastline of Belize.

Coastal Features

The Belize coastline is flat and swampy and marked by many swamps and lagoons.

6 ⊕ INLAND LAKES

There are several small lakes in the northern half of the country. Two of the major inland bodies of water are the Northern and Southern Lagoons, which lie south of Belize City and near the coast.

numerous rivers and streams, make up the second region. Belize is located on the Caribbean Tectonic Plate.

In the far south lies the Cockscomb Basin Wildlife Sanctuary, where jaguars, pumas, ocelots, margays, agoutis, anteaters, armadillos, boa constrictors, and dozens of bird species thrive.

5 ⊕ OCEANS AND SEAS

Belize's eastern border lies on the Caribbean Sea. The central coast is on the open sea, but the northern shoreline forms one side of Chet-

EPD/Saxifraga/Wiel Pohlmans

Belize's Maya Mountains extend from the northeast to the southwest.

7 ⊕ RIVERS AND WATERFALLS

Seventeen rivers, among them the Belize River, crisscross the countryside. The Belize River runs across the center of the country, draining into the Caribbean Sea near Belize City. About 30 kilometers (19 miles) west of Belize City, an area along the Belize River features a nature preserve to provide a protected habitat for the black howler monkey. Dozens of other native bird and animal species thrive there as well.

Just south of the Belize River, the shorter Sibun River flows northeastward from the highlands in the center of the country to empty into the Caribbean Sea south of Belize City. Monkey River is located in the south of the country, emptying into the Caribbean near the Gulf of Honduras. In the north, the Hondo River marks the border with Mexico.

Hidden Valley Falls, aptly known as the Thousand Foot Falls for their 323-meter (1,000-foot) drop, are located near the Mountain Pine Ridge Forest Preserve in the mountains south of Belmopan. These scenic falls are the highest in Central America.

8 ⊕ DESERTS

There are no notable desert regions in Belize.

9 ⊕ FLAT AND ROLLING TERRAIN

The country north of Belize City is mostly level, interrupted only by the Manatee Hills.

10 ⊕ MOUNTAINS AND VOLCANOES

The Maya and Cockscomb mountain ranges form the backbone of the country. The Maya Mountains rise to a height of 1,100 meters (3,400 feet), extending northeast to southwest across the central and southern parts of the country. The country's highest elevation, Victoria Peak, is located in the Cockscomb Mountains.

11 ⊕ CANYONS AND CAVES

Because most caves in Belize contain artifacts from the ancient Mayans, the government requires all explorers to obtain a permit to explore them. There are numerous caverns in the limestone foothills of the Maya range. A region near the Southern Lagoon features limestone cones that rise above the citrus trees that grow in the area. Blue Creek Cave lies just north of Punta Gorda.

In western Belize, southwest of Belmopan, lie Chechem Ha and Barton Creek Caves, where archaeologists have unearthed ceremonial pots and human skulls and bones from the ancient Mayans.

12 ⊕ PLATEAUS AND MONOLITHS

There are no notable plateaus or monoliths in Belize.

13 ⊕ MAN-MADE FEATURES

Belize's Mayan ruins include the residential compounds and ritual sites found at El Pilar on the border with Guatemala.

14 ⊕ FURTHER READING

Books

Crandell, Rachel. *Hands of the Maya: Villagers at Work and Play.* New York: Henry Holt, 2002.

Hoffman, Eric. *Adventuring in Belize: The Sierra Club Travel Guide to the Islands, Waters, and Inland Parks of Central America's Tropical Paradise.* San Francisco: Sierra Club Books, 1994.

Jermyn, Leslie. *Belize.* New York: Marshall Cavendish, 2001.

Norton, Natasha. *Belize.* Old Saybrook, CT: Globe Pequot Press, 1997.

Wright, Peggy, and Brian E. Coutts, eds. *Belize.* Oxford: Clio Press, 1993.

Web Sites

Belize Audubon Society. http://www.belizeaudubon.org/html/parks.html (accessed July 20, 2003).

Belize Country Overview. http://www.belizenet.com/ (accessed July 20, 2002).

Belize Online. http://www.belize.com/ (accessed July 20, 2003).

Benin

- **Official name:** Republic of Benin
- **Area:** 112,620 square kilometers (43,483 square miles)
- **Highest point on mainland:** Mount Sokbaro (658 meters/2,159 feet)
- **Lowest point on land:** Sea level
- **Hemispheres:** Northern and Eastern
- **Time zone:** 1 P.M. = noon GMT
- **Longest distances:** 333 kilometers (207 miles) from east to west; 665 kilometers (413 miles) from north to south

- **Land boundaries:** 1,236 kilometers (1,989 miles) total boundary length; Burkina Faso, 306 kilometers (190 miles); Niger, 266 kilometers (165 miles); Nigeria, 773 kilometers (480 miles); Togo, 644 kilometers (400 miles)
- **Coastline:** 121 kilometers (75 miles)
- **Territorial sea limits:** 22 kilometers (12 nautical miles)

1 ⊕ LOCATION AND SIZE

Formerly a French colony known as Dahomey, Benin is a small country on the coast of West Africa, between Togo and Nigeria. It is bounded on the north by the Niger River and on the south by the Bight of Benin, which forms part of the Gulf of Guinea. Benin has an area of 112,620 square kilometers (43,483 square miles), or slightly less land than the state of Pennsylvania.

2 ⊕ TERRITORIES AND DEPENDENCIES

Benin has no outside territories or dependencies.

3 ⊕ CLIMATE

Southern Benin, which lies near the equator, has a hot, humid, tropical climate, with average temperatures around 27°C (80°F). The north has a semiarid climate with greater variability, ranging from 13°C (56°F) in June to 40°C (104°F) in January. Southern Benin has two rainy seasons: one from March to July, and another between September and November.

The hot, dry harmattan wind blows during the dry season. Average annual rainfall is highest (135 centimeters/53 inches) in the central part of the country and lower in the north (97 centimeters/38 inches). The driest part of Benin is the southwest, which averages just 82 centimeters (32 inches) of rain per year.

4 ⊕ TOPOGRAPHIC REGIONS

From south to north, Benin's major regions consist of a coastal belt that includes sandbanks and lagoons; a savannah-covered clay plateau; and, in the northern two-thirds of the country, a higher plateau region that includes the Atakora Mountains and the Niger Plains. A large swampy depression called the Lama Marsh extends across the plateau region.

5 ⊕ OCEANS AND SEAS

The North Atlantic Ocean lies to the south of Benin.

BENIN

Benin map showing Niger, Burkina Faso, Ghana, Togo, Nigeria, Atakora Mts., Mékrou, Alibori River, Sota River, Kandi, Ouémé River, Koufo River, Mono R., Lake Ahémé, Porto Novo, Cotonou, Bight of Benin, Gulf of Guinea.

Benin
- International border
- ▲ Peak
- National capital
- • Other city

© 2003 The Gale Group, Inc.

Seacoast and Undersea Features

Benin's coastal belt includes four lagoons (Grand Popo, Ouidah, Cotonou, and Porto Novo).

The sandbanks that form part of the country's shoreline impede access to the ocean, however.

Sea Inlets and Straits

The coast of Benin lies on a wide bay in the Gulf of Guinea called the Bight of Benin.

Islands and Archipelagos

Benin has no islands.

Coastal Features

Benin has no natural harbors.

6 ⊕ INLAND LAKES

Benin's principal lake is Lake Ahémé, in the southern part of the country.

7 ⊕ RIVERS AND WATERFALLS

Most of Benin's rivers flow in a north-south direction. Benin's longest river is the Niger River, which forms part of its border with Niger in the northeast and is navigable for 89 kilometers (55 miles) in Benin. The longest river located entirely within Benin's borders is the Ouémé, which is 459 kilometers (285 miles) long. It flows southward through about two-thirds of Benin. The rivers in the north, including the Alibori, the Mékrou, and the Sota, drain into the Niger. To the southwest, the Mono River forms part of the border with Togo.

8 ⊕ DESERTS

Benin has no significant desert regions.

9 ⊕ FLAT AND ROLLING TERRAIN

The low-lying coastal plain is flat and sandy.

10 ⊕ MOUNTAINS AND VOLCANOES

The Atakora Mountains extend northeast to southwest across the plateau of Upper Benin in the northwestern part of the country. They rise to elevations of 300 to 600 meters (1,000 to 2,000 feet). Heavily forested, they belong to the same system as the Togo Mountains to the south.

DID YOU KN⊕W?

The area of low precipitation in southwest Benin—a dramatic exception to the high rainfall elsewhere in this tropical region—is called the "Benin window." It is thought to have resulted from the destruction of the native rainforest.

UNESCO/Georges Malempré

Men in fishing boats near Cotonou on the coast of Benin.

11 ⊕ CANYONS AND CAVES

There are no notable caves or canyons in Benin.

12 ⊕ PLATEAUS AND MONOLITHS

North of the coastal region, 90 to 230 meters (300 to 750 feet) above sea level, lies a belt of the fertile, savannah-covered clay plateau called *terre de barre,* composed of lateritic clay (clay made from decayed rock) and bisected by the swampy Lama Marsh. The granite and gneiss tablelands of Upper Benin are farther north; these are traversed northeast to southwest by the Atakora Mountains.

13 ⊕ MAN-MADE FEATURES

The Nangbeto Dam is located on the Mono River, a waterway that comprises part of the border between Benin and Togo. The dam restricts the flow of the Mono River, and it also retains sediment that would be carried to the mouth of the river. Erosion along the coast may be traced to the existence of this dam.

14 ⊕ FURTHER READING

Books

Chatwin, Bruce. *The Viceroy of Ouidah.* New York: Summit Books, 1980.

Eades, J. S., and Chris Allen. *Benin.* Santa Barbara, CA: CLIO Press, 1996.

Manning, Patrick. *Slavery, Colonialism, and Economic Growth in Dahomey,*

1640-1960. Cambridge: Cambridge University Press, 1982.

Web Sites

Mbendi Profile. http://www.mbendi.co.za/land/af/ be/p0005.htm (accessed June 22, 2003).

World Desk Reference Web site. http://www. travel.dk.com/wdr/BJ/mBJ_Intr.htm# (accessed February 21, 2003).

Bhutan

- **Official name:** Kingdom of Bhutan
- **Area:** 47,000 square kilometers (18,147 square miles)
- **Highest point on mainland**: Kula Kangri (7,553 meters/24,781 feet)
- **Lowest point on land:** Drangme Chhu (River) (97 meters/318 feet)
- **Hemispheres**: Northern and Eastern
- **Time zone:** 5:30 P.M. = noon GMT
- **Longest distances:** 306 kilometers (190 miles) from east to west; 145 kilometers (90 miles) from north to south
- **Land boundaries**: 1,075 kilometers (668 miles) total boundary length; China, 470 kilometers (292 miles); India, 605 kilometers (376 miles)
- **Coastline:** None
- **Territorial sea limits:** None

1 ⊕ LOCATION AND SIZE

Bhutan is a small, landlocked country in the Himalaya Mountains, between China and India in Southern Asia. To the north and northwest, it borders the Chinese autonomous region of Tibet (Xizang Zizhiqu); to the south and southwest, the Indian states of West Bengal and Assam; and to the east, the Indian state of Arunachal Pradesh (formerly the North-East Frontier Agency). Bhutan has an area of 47,000 square kilometers (18,147 square miles), making it slightly more than half as large as the state of Indiana.

2 ⊕ TERRITORIES AND DEPENDENCIES

Bhutan has no territories or dependencies.

3 ⊕ CLIMATE

Bhutan has three distinct climates, corresponding to its three topographical regions. The Duārs Plain areas in the south have a hot, humid, subtropical climate, with heavy rainfall. Temperatures generally average between 15°C (59°F) and 30°C (86°F) year-round. Temperatures in the valleys of the southern foothills of the Himalayas may rise as high as 101°F (40°C) in the summer. The central Inner Himalayan region has a temperate climate, with hot summers, cool winters, and moderate rainfall. Temperatures in the capital city of Thimphu, located in the western part of this region, generally range from about 15°C (59°F) to 26°C (79°F) between June and September (the monsoon season), falling to between -4°C (25°F) and 16°C (61°F) in January. The high mountains of the Greater Himalayas in the north have more severe weather than the regions to the south. At their highest elevations, they are snow-covered year-round, with an arctic climate.

Like other aspects of Bhutan's climate, rainfall varies by region. The northern Himalayas are relatively dry, and most precipitation falls as snow. The Inner Himalayan slopes and valleys have moderate rainfall, averaging between 100 and 150 centimeters (39 and 59 inches) annually. Rainfall in the subtropical southern regions averages between about 500 centimeters and 750 centimeters (197 and 295 inches) per year. The greatest amount of rain falls dur-

BHUTAN

Bhutan
- - - International border
▲ Peak
✪ National capital
• Other city
© 2003 The Gale Group, Inc.

CHINA

Kula Kangri
24,781 ft. (7,553 m)

Chomo Lhari
23,997 ft. (7,314 m)

GREAT HIMALAYAS

Sankosh R.
Paro R.
Black Mountain Range
Himalayas
Lesser
✪ Thimphu
Amo River
Wong R.
Tongsa R.
Bumtang R.
Drangme R.
Black Mountain
16,154 ft. (4924 m)
Duars Plain
Manas R.

28°N
90°E
26°N
92°E

INDIA

ing the summer monsoon season, from late June through the end of September.

4 ⊕ TOPOGRAPHIC REGIONS

All of Bhutan is mountainous except for narrow fringes of land at the southern border where the Duārs Plain, the lowland of the Brahmaputra River, protrudes northward from India. The rest of Bhutan can be divided into two mountain regions: the Lesser Himalayas, or Inner Himalayas, which extend from the Duārs Plain through the central part of the country; and the snow-capped peaks of the Great Himalayas in the far north.

5 ⊕ OCEANS AND SEAS

Bhutan is landlocked.

6 ⊕ INLAND LAKES

There are no notable inland lakes in Bhutan.

7 ⊕ RIVERS AND WATERFALLS

All of Bhutan's numerous rivers flow south through gorges and narrow valleys, eventually draining into the Brahmaputra River in India. The headwaters of most streams are in the regions of permanent snow along the Tibetan border. None of the rivers in Bhutan is navi-

gable, but many of them are potential sources of hydroelectric power.

Bhutan contains four main river systems. The Tongsa River and its tributaries, the Bumtang and Drangme Rivers (river names in Bhutan are often followed by Chu or Chhu, which means river), drains the area east of the Black Mountain watershed. West of the Black Mountains, the drainage pattern changes to a series of parallel streams, beginning with the Sankosh (or Puna Tsang) River and its tributaries, the Mo Chhu and Pho Chhu. These two waterways flow southward to Punakha; there they join the main river, continuing their southward course into the Indian state of West Bengal. Farther west is the third major system, the Wong Chhu and its tributaries. These flow through west-central Bhutan, joining to form the Raigye Chhu before flowing into West Bengal. Still farther west is the smallest system, the Torsa Chhu (called the Amo Chhu farther north), which flows through the Chumbi Valley before entering India.

8 ⊕ DESERTS

There are no notable desert regions in Bhutan.

9 ⊕ FLAT AND ROLLING TERRAIN

The Duārs Plain, which lies mostly in India, extends northward across Bhutan's border in strips 10 to 15 kilometers (6 to 9 miles) wide. The northern edges of these plains, which border the Himalayan foothills, have rugged terrain and porous soil. Fertile flatlands are found farther south. At the southern edge of the Inner Himalayas, sloping down to the Duārs Plain, are low, densely forested foothills called the Siwalik (or Southern) Hills.

10 ⊕ MOUNTAINS AND VOLCANOES

The mountains of Bhutan are known for their dramatic differences in elevation. Elevations vary from approximately 305 meters (1,000 feet) in the south to almost 7,620 meters

EPD/Cynthia Bassett

Bhutan's landscape features many narrow valleys.

(25,000 feet) in the north—in some places as close together as 100 kilometers (60 miles). The snowcapped Great Himalayas rise along the Tibetan border, stretching across Bhutan in a belt about 16 kilometers (10 miles) wide. Four peaks in this range have elevations above 6,096 meters (20,000 feet). The highest is Kula Kangri, north of Gasa Dzong, at 7,553 meters (24,781 feet). Next in height is the country's most famous peak, picturesque Chomo Lhari, which towers over the Chumbi Valley at an elevation of 7,314 meters (23,997 feet).

Spurs extending southward from the Great Himalayas make up the north-south ranges of Bhutan's Inner, or Lesser, Himalayas. The fertile valleys between its peaks form the watersheds of Bhutan's major rivers. The dominant range in this system is the Black Mountain Range, which divides the country almost exactly down the middle from north to south and forms the watershed between the Sankosh and Drangme Chhus (Rivers). Its peaks range from 1,500 to 2,700 meters (4,922 to 8,859 feet) above sea level.

Several strategically important passes follow the major river courses through the valleys of Bhutan's Himalaya Mountains. Formerly of great significance for trade, they now serve as escape routes for Tibetan refugees.

11 ⊕ CANYONS AND CAVES

There are no notable canyons or caves in Bhutan.

12 ⊕ PLATEAUS AND MONOLITHS

There are no notable plateaus or monoliths in Bhutan.

13 ⊕ MAN-MADE FEATURES

A 90-meter (295-foot) suspension bridge at Chazam, spanning the Dangmechu River, was opened on March 16, 2001. It is the most extensive single-span bridge of this type in the Himalayas.

14 ⊕ FURTHER READING

Books

Dompnier, Robert. *Bhutan, Kingdom of the Dragon.* Boston: Shambhala, 1999.

Hellum, A. K. *A Painter's Year in the Forests of Bhutan.* Edmonton: University of Alberta Press, 2001.

Zeppa, Jamie. *Beyond the Sky and the Earth: A Journey into Bhutan.* New York: Riverhead Books, 1999.

Web Sites

The Kingdom of Bhutan. http://www. kingdomofbhutan.com/ (accessed June 22, 2003).

Bolivia

- **Official name:** Republic of Bolivia

- **Area:** 1,098,580 square kilometers (424,164 square miles)

- **Highest point on mainland:** Mount Sajama (6,542 meters / 21,464 feet)

- **Lowest point on land:** Paraguá River (90 meters / 295 feet)

- **Hemispheres:** Southern and Western

- **Time zone:** 8 A.M. = noon GMT

- **Longest distances:** 1,450 kilometers (900 miles) from east to west; 1,530 kilometers (950 miles) from north to south

- **Land boundaries:** 6,743 kilometers (4,190 miles) total boundary length; Argentina, 832 kilometers (517 miles); Brazil, 3,400 kilometers (2,113 miles); Chile, 861 kilometers (535 miles); Paraguay, 750 kilometers (466 miles); Peru, 900 kilometers (559 miles)

- **Coastline:** None

- **Territorial sea limits:** None

1 ⊕ LOCATION AND SIZE

Home to the world's highest capital city and highest commercially navigable lake, Bolivia has been called the "rooftop of the world." This landlocked country in south-central South America is the continent's fifth-largest nation. With an area of 1,098,580 square kilometers (424,164 square miles), it is almost three times the size of Montana.

2 ⊕ TERRITORIES AND DEPENDENCIES

Bolivia has no territories or dependencies.

3 ⊕ CLIMATE

Although Bolivia is a tropical country, its climate varies widely with differences in elevation and terrain. The high peaks of the Cordillera Occidental to the west have a cool climate, and cold winds blow in the Altiplano (the high plains separating Bolivia's two mountain ranges). In the northern Altiplano, however, the climate is moderated by Lake Titicaca. The valleys of the lower Cordillera Oriental have a semiarid Mediterranean-like climate; but the climate becomes semitropical in the Yungas region on the eastern slopes of these mountains, and tropical in the eastern lowlands. The mean annual temperature in the capital city of La Paz, at the edge of the Altiplano, is about 8°C (46°F), compared with mean temperatures of 16° to 19°C (60° to 68°F) in the Yungas region, and 26°C (79°F) in the city of Trinidad, in the eastern plains. A strong wind originating in the nearby Argentine pampas, called the *surazo*, can bring fierce storms and plunging temperatures in the winter months (June through August).

Like climate conditions in general, rainfall in Bolivia varies greatly by region, ranging from 13 centimeters (5 inches) or less in the southwest to over 152 centimeters (60 inches) in the Amazon basin to the northeast. Rainfall in the Yungas region on the eastern slopes of the Cordillera Oriental averages 76 centimeters (30 inches) to 127 centimeters (50 inches)

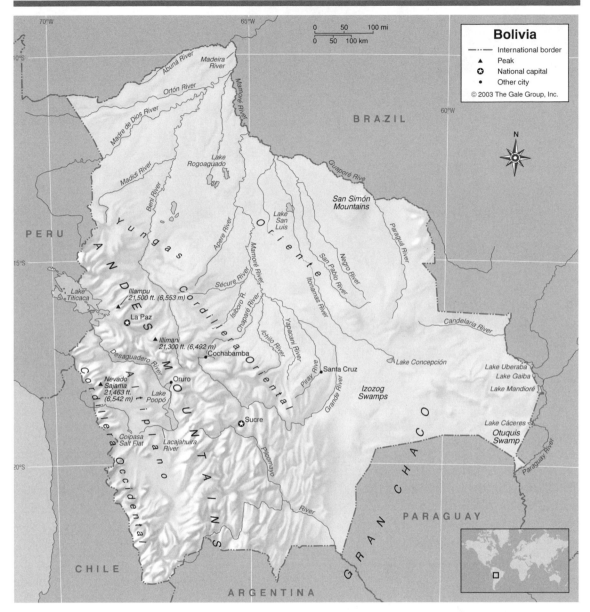

annually; it is heaviest between December and February but falls year-round.

The southern part of the country has a long summer dry season that can last from four to six months, while the dry season in the northern areas is shorter. Flooding often occurs in the northeast in March and April.

4 ⊕ TOPOGRAPHIC REGIONS

The Andean highlands of southwest Bolivia cover roughly one-third of the country. They include the mountain ranges of the Eastern and Western Cordilleras, separated by a high plateau called the Altiplano. The remaining two-thirds of Bolivia are part of the Oriente, the country's northern and eastern tropical

During the dry season, salt is harvested on the salt lake of Salar de Uyuni.

lowland region, which consists of forestland, savannahs, and marshes. At the far southeastern corner of the country lies the Bolivian portion of the Gran Chaco, a thinly populated plain that continues southward into Paraguay and northern Argentina.

5 ⊕ OCEANS AND SEAS

Bolivia is landlocked.

6 ⊕ INLAND LAKES

Lake Titicaca straddles the Peruvian border in the north. At 3,805 meters (12,484 feet) above sea level, it is both South America's largest inland lake and the world's highest navigable body of water. Lake Titicaca has a length of 222 kilometers (138 miles) and a width of 113 kilometers (70 miles), and contains depths of up to 213 meters (700 feet). There are twenty-five islands in the lake. Southeast of Lake Titicaca

and connected to it by the Desaguadero River, Lake Poopó is a shallow, salty body of brackish water with depths of 3 meters (10 feet) or less, and an area of around 386 square kilometers (1,000 square miles) when its waters are low. Bolivia also has several other large lakes, including Lake Rogoguado. Shallow lakes in the region of the Paraguá River in the east include Cáceres, Mandioré, Gaiba, and Uberaba. The water of Colorado Lake (Laguna Colorado) has a deep reddish color, caused by bacteria which thrive in its warm, volcanic waters.

7 ⊕ RIVERS AND WATERFALLS

Bolivia is drained by three different river systems. Flowing down from the Yungas area of the Cordillera Real, the Beni and Mamoré Rivers and the Mamoré's tributaries, including the Chaparé, Ichilo, and Grande, form part of the

Amazon River system. These Amazon headwaters flow north to join the Madeira River beyond the border with Brazil. At Bolivia's western border, the Desaguadero River, the only major waterway on the surface of the Altiplano, flows southward from Lake Titicaca into Lake Poopó. Lake Poopó, in turn, drains into the Lacajahuira River. Farther south, the Pilcomayo River rises in the heart of the Yungas and flows southward to the border with

DID YOU KN🌐W?

The Salar de Uyuni in southwest Bolivia is one of the world's largest (12,000 square kilometers/ 4,600 square miles in area) salt "lakes." During the dry season, vehicles can drive on its surface, which is firmer than sand. During the rainy season, the lake can still be traversed by four-wheel drive vehicles, since the water reaches depths of just 15 to 38 centimeters (6 to 15 inches). In the center of the salt plain lies a hotel, built of salt blocks with a thatched roof.

The layers of salt deposits are up to six meters (20 feet) thick. Villagers from Colchani harvest almost 90,000 kilograms (20,000 tons) of salt by chopping it up and shoveling it into piles. The salt is trucked into the village, where it is sifted and prepared for shipment by train to refiners, where it will be prepared for international sale.

Argentina and Paraguay to join the Paraguay River in Paraguay.

8 🌐 DESERTS

The region known as Gran Chaco that lies along the Paraguayan and Argentine borders is hot and dry.

9 🌐 FLAT AND ROLLING TERRAIN

Savannah grasslands cover much of the lowland Oriente region, which encompasses the eastern and northern two-thirds of Bolivia, or all the land east of the Eastern and Western Cordilleras. The region slopes from elevations of 610 to 762 meters (2,000 to 2,500 feet) at the foot of the Andes in the west to just 91 meters (300 feet) along parts of the Brazilian border.

10 🌐 MOUNTAINS AND VOLCANOES

The Andes Mountains reach both their greatest average elevations and their greatest width in Bolivia. The Bolivian Andes Mountains contain two mountain ranges separated by the high plateau called the Altiplano, which is the country's heartland.

On the west, the Cordillera Occidental (Western Cordillera), which forms the border with Chile, rises above 5,800 meters (19,000 feet), and includes Mount Sajama, Bolivia's highest peak. The chain also contains a number of both active and inactive volcanoes.

The eastern arm of the Bolivian Andes is called either the Cordillera Oriental or Cordillera Real. The name *Cordillera Real* is often used to describe only that section of the range that extends northward from the environs of Cochabamba and Oruro. This part of the Andes, where the capital city of La Paz is located, includes the country's most dramatic peaks, with average heights of over 5,486 meters (18,000 feet) for more than 322 kilometers (200 miles). The best known of these summits are Illampu (6,553 meters/21,500 feet) and the triple crown of Illimani, which rises to 6,492 meters (21,300 feet) behind the city of La Paz. The eastern slopes of the northern Cordillera Oriental, called the Yungas, are rugged, steep, and densely forested; they descend swiftly to the eastern plains. South of the Yungas is an area of valleys and mountain basins called the Valles.

11 ⊕ CANYONS AND CAVES

There are no notable canyons or caves in Bolivia.

12 ⊕ PLATEAUS AND MONOLITHS

The barren and forbidding landscape of the Altiplano extends southward for a distance of 804 kilometers (500 miles), with an average width of 50 kilometers (80 miles), and altitudes varying from 3,657 meters to 4,267 meters (12,000 to 14,000 feet). The Altiplano tilts upward from the center toward both the Eastern and Western Cordillera, and it descends gradually from north to south. The plateau floor is made up of sedimentary debris washed down from the adjacent mountains.

13 ⊕ MAN-MADE FEATURES

The Incan and pre-Incan ruins near Lake Titicaca on Bolivia's Altiplano are among the oldest in South America.

14 ⊕ FURTHER READING

Books

Bradt, Hilary. *Peru and Bolivia: Backpacking and Trekking.* Old Saybrook, CT: Globe Pequot Press, 1999.

Murphy, Alan. *Bolivia Handbook.* Lincolnwood, IL: Passport Books, 1997.

Swaney, Deanna. *Bolivia: A Lonely Planet Travel Survival Kit.* 3rd ed. Oakland, CA: Lonely Planet Publications, 1996.

Web Sites

Bolivia Web. http://www. boliviaweb.com (accessed February 25, 2003).

LANIC (Academic research resources). http://lanic.utexas.edu/la/sa/bolivia/ (accessed June 23, 2003).

Bosnia and Herzegovina

- **Official name**: Republic of Bosnia and Herzegovina

- **Area**: 51,129 square kilometers (19,741 square miles)

- **Highest point on mainland**: Mount Maglic (2,386 meters / 7,828 feet)

- **Lowest point on land**: Sea level

- **Hemispheres**: Northern and Western

- **Time zone**: 1 P.M. = noon GMT

- **Longest distances**: 325 kilometers (202 miles) from north to south; 325 kilometers (202 miles) from east to west

- **Land boundaries**: 1,459 kilometers (907 miles) total boundary length; Croatia, 932 kilometers (579 miles); Serbia and Montenegro, 527 kilometers (327 miles)

- **Coastline**: 20 kilometers (12 miles)

- **Territorial sea limits**: None

1 ⊕ LOCATION AND SIZE

The nation of Bosnia and Herzegovina is located in southeastern Europe on the Balkan Peninsula, between the countries of Croatia, Serbia, and Montenegro. With a total area of 51,129 square kilometers (19,741 square miles), the country is slightly smaller than the state of West Virginia.

2 ⊕ TERRITORIES AND DEPENDENCIES

Bosnia and Herzegovina has no outside territories or dependencies.

3 ⊕ CLIMATE

Most of the country has hot summers and cold winters. Areas of higher elevation have shorter, cooler summers and longer, severe winters. The areas closer to the coast have mild, rainy winters. Annual rainfall is about 62.5 centimeters (24.6 inches).

Season	Months	Average Temperature in Sarajevo
Summer	June to August	18.1°C (64.6°F)
Winter	November to March	0°C (32°F)

4 ⊕ TOPOGRAPHIC REGIONS

The Republic of Bosnia and Herzegovina lies inland along the eastern side of the Adriatic Sea, at the intersection of central Europe and the Mediterranean Sea. High plains and plateaus are in northern Croatia, between Bodanska Gradiška and Bijeljina.

The central region, between Banja Luka and Sarajevo, has low mountains; the higher Dinaric Alps cover the southwestern edge of the country.

Tectonic fault lines run through the central part of the country, from Bodanska Gradiška to Sarajevo, and also exist in the northwest corner between the Sana and Unac Rivers. A thrust fault also runs through southern Bosnia and Herzegovina in the vicinity of Mostar. These structural seams in Earth's crust periodically shift, causing tremors and occasional destructive earthquakes.

Bosnia and Herzegovina

International border — National capital
▲ Peak — • Other city

© 2003 The Gale Group, Inc.

5 ⊕ OCEANS AND SEAS

Seacoast and Undersea Features

The Adriatic coast of Bosnia and Herzegovina is only 20 kilometers (12 miles) long. There is one main town, Neum, on the coast, but the area is not suitable for shipping.

The Adriatic Sea is an extension of the Mediterranean Sea. It separates Italy from Croatia, Serbia, Montenegro, and Albania. It is about 772 kilometers (480 miles) long with an average width of 160 kilometers (100 miles), covering an area of about 160,000 square kilometers (60,000 square miles).

6 ⊕ INLAND LAKES

The country's largest lake is Buško Blato, which has a surface area of 55.8 square kilometers (21.5 square miles). It lies 716.6 meters (2,351.2 feet) above sea level within the Dinaric Alps and has a maximum depth of

17.3 meters (56.8 feet). Jablaničko Jezero is a long, narrow lake that lies at the bend of the Neretva River, southwest of Sarajevo.

Smaller lakes include Bilecko, Matura, Vijaka, Sanicani, Busko, Plivsko, Deransko, Boracko, and Ramsko.

7 ⊕ RIVERS AND WATERFALLS

The Sava River, the longest river in the country, travels 947 kilometers (589 miles). The first 221 kilometers (137 miles) flows through Slovenia, and the remaining 727 kilometers (452 miles) forms the border between Croatia and Bosnia and Herzegovina (as well as a small section of Serbia and Montenegro), eventually joining the Danube River.

The Bosna River (245 kilometers/152 miles) begins near Sarajevo and flows northward to the Sava. The Drina River (346 kilometers/215 miles) forms much of the border with Serbia and Montenegro and crosses through a south-eastern segment of Bosnia and Herzegovina.

8 ⊕ DESERTS

There are no desert regions in Bosnia and Herzegovina.

9 ⊕ FLAT AND ROLLING TERRAIN

The Peri-Pannonian Plain, near the northern border with Croatia, contains the country's most fertile soils, used for farmland and grazing. The plain was once occupied by an ancient sea that was filled in with rich soil carried from the mountains by the rivers and deposited on the plains.

The region contains wide valley basins, alluvial plains (areas where soil has been carried and deposited by rivers), sandy dunes, and low, rolling hills covered with fertile loam (a light soil mixture). In general, the area is low and flat.

AP Photo/World Monuments Fund, J. Calame

Mostar, which dates back to the sixteenth century, is built above the Radobolja River. In 1999 Mostar was designated as one of the world's 100-most-endangered places by the World Monuments Fund.

10 ⊕ MOUNTAINS AND VOLCANOES

About two-thirds of Bosnia and Herzegovina is mountainous. There are sixty-four mountains, with some peaks exceeding 1,500 meters (4,922 feet) above sea level. Mount Maglic, at 2,386 meters (7,828 feet), is the highest peak in the country, lying in the southeast adjacent to the Serbia and Montenegro border. Nearby are the country's second and third highest mountains: Volujak—at 2,336 meters (7,664 feet) and Velika Ljubušnja—at 2,238 meters (7,343 feet).

The Dinaric Alps consist of ridges that run parallel to the coast. The limestone ranges of the Dinaric Alps, referred to as karst or karstland, are marked by underground drainage channels, formed by water seepage down through the soluble limestone. Over the years, this water seepage has formed many large depressions and left the surface dry.

Beech forests cover much of the mountainous areas; mixed forests of beech, fir, and spruce blanket the higher mountains. Mount Maglic lies within the Sutjeska National Park, the country's oldest national park, which also contains the old-growth Perucica forest.

11 ⊕ CANYONS AND CAVES

At 1,300 meters (4,265 feet) deep, Tara Canyon is Europe's deepest canyon. The canyon follows the Tara River along the southeastern border with Yugoslavia.

12 ⊕ PLATEAUS AND MONOLITHS

There are no plateau regions in Bosnia and Herzegovina.

13 ⊕ MAN-MADE FEATURES

The sixteenth-century Mostar Bridge, destroyed by Croatian forces in violent conflict during 1993, was being rebuilt as of 2002. The bridge, measuring 20 meters (66 feet) in height and 30 meters (100 feet) in length, was first built in 1566 by Mimar Hajrudin, an Ottoman Empire architect.

14 ⊕ FURTHER READING

Books

Brân, Zoë. *After Yugoslavia*. Oakland, CA: Lonely Planet, 2001.

Filipovic, Zlata. *Zlata's Diary: A Child's Life in Sarajevo*. New York: Viking, 1994.

Lovrenovic, Ivan. *Bosnia: A Cultural History*. New York: New York University Press, 2001.

Malcolm, Noel. *Bosnia: A Short History*. New York: New York University Press, 1996.

Web Sites

The Embassy of Bosnia and Herzegovina, Washington, D.C. http://www.bhembassy.org (accessed June 1, 2003).

Federation of Bosnia and Herzegovina Government. http://www.fbihvlada.gov.ba (accessed April 29, 2002).

Republic of Srpska Government. http://www.vladers.net (accessed April 29, 2003).

Botswana

- **Official name:** Republic of Botswana
- **Area:** 600,370 square kilometers (231,802 square miles)
- **Highest point on mainland**: Tsodilo Hills (1,489 meters/4,884 feet)
- **Lowest point on land:** Junction of the Limpopo and Shashe Rivers (513 meters/ 1,683 feet)
- **Hemispheres**: Southern and Eastern
- **Time zone:** 2:00 P.M. = noon GMT
- **Coastline:** None

- **Longest distances:** 1,110 kilometers (690 miles) from north-northeast to south-southwest; 960 kilometers (597 miles) from east-southeast to west-northwest
- **Land boundaries:** 4,013 kilometers (2,488 miles) total boundary length; Zimbabwe, 813 kilometers (504 miles); South Africa, 1,840 kilometers (1,141 miles); Namibia, 1,360 kilometers (843 miles)
- **Territorial sea limits:** None

1 ⊕ LOCATION AND SIZE

Botswana is a landlocked country (does not have access to the sea) located in southern Africa. It is bordered by Zimbabwe to the northeast, South Africa to the south and southeast, and Namibia to the north and west. Botswana covers an area of 600,370 square kilometers (231,802 square miles), or slightly less than the state of Texas.

2 ⊕ TERRITORIES AND DEPENDENCIES

Botswana claims no territories or dependencies.

3 ⊕ CLIMATE

Most of the country has a subtropical climate, while the higher altitudes have cooler temperatures. Winter days are warm with cool nights, although the desert is commonly covered in heavy frost. Temperatures range from 33°C (91°F) in January to 22°C (72°F) in July. The August seasonal winds that blow from the west carry sand and dust across the landscape, often contributing to droughts. Normal rainfall averages 45 centimeters (18 inches)

throughout most of the country except for the Kalahari Desert, in the south, which receives less than 25 centimeters (10 inches), and the wet northern plateau regions, which receive about 69 centimeters (27 inches) annually.

SEASON	MONTHS	AVERAGE TEMPERATURE: °CELSIUS (°FAHRENHEIT)
Summer	December to February	22 to 40°C (72 to 104 °F)
Winter	April to October	33°C (91°F)

4 ⊕ TOPOGRAPHIC REGION

Botswana is a vast tableland with a mean altitude of 1,000 meters (3,300 feet). A gently undulating plateau, running northward from the South African border near Lobatse to the Zimbabwe border, forms a watershed between the two main natural divisions of Botswana. The fertile land to the south and east of this plateau is hilly bush country and grassland, or veld. To the west of the plateau, stretching over

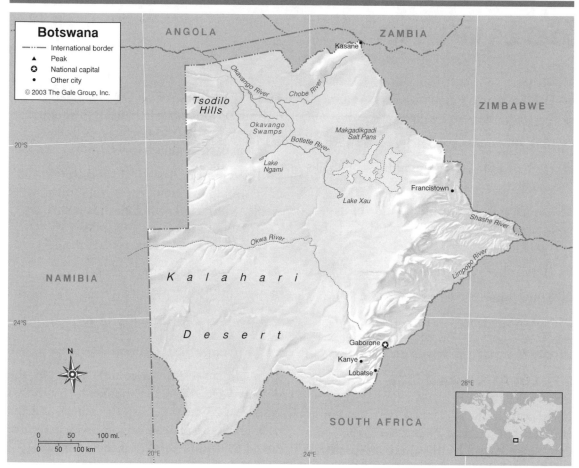

the border into Namibia, is the Kalahari Desert. In the north lies the area known as Ngamiland, which is dominated by the Okavango Delta and the Makgadikgadi Salt Pans.

5 ⊕ OCEANS AND SEAS

Botswana is a landlocked nation.

6 ⊕ INLAND LAKES

Temporary lakes form in the Okavango Swamps and the Makgadikgadi Salt Pans during seasons of heavy rainfall. Lakes Ngami and Xau are more permanent, but they also rely on the floodwaters that rush down the high plateaus.

7 ⊕ RIVERS AND WATERFALLS

There are few permanent rivers in Botswana, and its temporary rivers never reach the sea. One of the permanent waterways, the Chobe River in the north, is a major tributary of the Zambezi River. The Zambezi itself forms a short section of Botswana's border. The Limpopo River, a major waterway in the east, marks the border with South Africa. The Okavango River enters the country in the northwest and ends in the Okavango Swamps. The Boteti River flows south from these swamps into Lake Xau.

EPD/Cynthia Bassett

Hippopotamus in the Okavango River.

8 ⊕ DESERTS

The Kalahari Desert lies in the western portion of the country. It is a large, dry sandy basin that covers about 500,000 square kilometers (190,000 square miles). The Kalahari reaches from the Orange River in South Africa north to Angola, west to Namibia, and east to Zimbabwe.

9 ⊕ FLAT AND ROLLING TERRAIN

In the heart of the Kalahari Desert, the Okavango River spreads out into a seasonally flooded wetland covering some 16,835 square kilometers (6,500 square miles), or roughly the size of Massachusetts. It comprises swamps, channels, lagoons, and flood plains.

10 ⊕ MOUNTAINS AND VOLCANOES

There are no mountains in this elevated but relatively flat country. Botswana's highest elevations are found in the Tsodilo Hills, which are granite cliffs on the northwest fringe of the Kalahari Desert. The hills form a fortress-like ridge 20 kilometers (12 miles) in length and have long been considered sacred by the native people. At their highest point, the cliffs reach 1,489 meters (4,884 feet) above sea level.

11 ⊕ CANYONS AND CAVES

There are a number of caves in Botswana, some of which contain fossils as many as 3 million years old, notably in the area around Lake Ngami. In the southeast, south of Gaborone, lie the Lobatse Caves.

12 ⊕ PLATEAUS AND MONOLITHS

All of Botswana is located on a broad tableland with an average altitude of 1,000 meters (3,300 feet). A vast plateau, rising to about 1,219 meters (4,000 feet) above sea level, divides the country into two distinct topographical regions. This plateau extends from the southeastern part of the country to the border with Zimbabwe.

13 ⊕ MAN-MADE FEATURES

There are no notable man-made features affecting the geography of Botswana.

14 ⊕ FURTHER READING

Books

Alverson, Marianne. *Under African Sun*. Chicago: University of Chicago Press, 1987.

Augustinus, Paul. *Botswana: A Brush with the Wild*. Randburg, South Africa: Acorn Books, 1987.

Picard, Louis A., ed. *Politics and Rural Development in South Africa: The Evolution of Modern Botswana*. Lincoln: University of Nebraska Press, 1986.

DID YOU KN⊕W?

The Okavango Delta, one of the world's largest wetlands, provides a unique ecosystem and habitat for an astounding abundance of African wildlife, including mammals, birds, fish, amphibians, and reptiles.

Web Sites

The Government of Botswana Website. http://www.gov.bw/home.html (accessed July 3, 2003).

Mbendi Profile. http://www.mbendi.co.za/exch/5/p0005.htm (accessed July 3, 2003).

Brazil

- **Official name**: Federative Republic of Brazil
- **Area**: 8,511,965 square kilometers (3,286,488 square miles)
- **Highest point on mainland**: Neblina Peak (Pico da Neblina) (3,014 meters/9,888 feet)
- **Lowest point on land**: Sea level
- **Hemispheres**: Southern, Northern, and Western
- **Time zone**: There are four time zones. From east to west—noon GMT = 10 A.M. on the Fernando de Noronha islands; 9 A.M. in Rio de Janeiro; 8 A.M. in Manaus; 7 A.M. in Rio Branco (westernmost)
- **Longest distances**: 4,328 kilometers (2,689 miles) from north to south; 4,320 kilometers (2,684 miles) east to west

- **Land boundaries**: Total: 14,691 kilometers (9,108 miles); Argentina, 1,224 kilometers (759 miles); Bolivia, 3,400 kilometers (2,108 miles); Colombia, 1,643 kilometers (1,019 miles); French Guiana, 673 kilometers (417 miles); Guyana, 1,119 kilometers (694 miles); Paraguay, 1,290 kilometers (800 miles); Peru, 1,560 kilometers (967 miles); Suriname, 597 kilometers (307 miles); Uruguay, 985 kilometers (612 miles); Venezuela, 2,200 kilometers (1,364 miles)
- **Coastline**: 7,491 kilometers (4,655 miles)
- **Territorial sea limits**: 22 kilometers (12 nautical miles)

---

1 ⊕ LOCATION AND SIZE

Brazil is the largest country in South America and shares common boundaries with every South American country except Chile and Ecuador. Its eastern coastline borders the Atlantic Ocean. With an area of 8,511,965 square kilometers (3,286,488 square miles), it is slightly smaller than the United States. The country is divided into twenty-six states and one federal district. Brazil has land area in both the Northern and Southern Hemispheres, because the equator crosses through the northern part of the country.

2 ⊕ TERRITORIES AND DEPENDENCIES

Brazil designates the Fernando de Noronha Islands (Arquipelago de Fernando de Noronha), which lie off its northeast coast, as a territory.

The country also controls several small islands in the Atlantic Ocean.

3 ⊕ CLIMATE

Brazil's geographical diversity makes for a range of climatic conditions. Most of the country has a tropical climate. The southernmost regions lie outside the tropics and have a temperate climate. May through September are the coolest months, and the higher elevations in the south may receive snow during this time. In the north, the coastal areas experience tropical conditions, while the upland interior is relatively dry and moderate.

Rainfall varies widely across the country. In the southern and central part of the country, it generally ranges between 150 centimeters to 200 centimeters (58 inches to 78 inches)

annually, but it can be much higher in certain areas. Rainfall is heavier in the Amazon River basin, reaching as much as 300 centimeters (117 inches) annually. Parts of this region experience dry spells of three months or more each year. The northeast region is the driest and hottest part of the country, with lengthy droughts a regular occurrence.

Season	Months	Average Temperature, Rio de Janeiro °Celsius (°Fahrenheit)
Summer	November to March	29°C (84°F)
Winter	May to September	17°C (63°F)

4 ⊕ TOPOGRAPHIC REGIONS

The Amazon River basin and its many tributaries dominate the northern part of Brazil, occupying two-fifths of the country. The

Guiana Highlands, home to the country's highest point, Neblina Peak (Pico da Neblina) near the Venezuela border, are in the northernmost part of the Amazon River basin. To the south is a large plateau called the Brazilian Highlands. This plateau meets the Atlantic Ocean in a steep wall-like slope called the Great Escarpment. The highland block of the country is part of the South American Tectonic Plate.

5 ⊕ OCEANS AND SEAS

Seacoast and Undersea Features

Brazil's eastern seaboard borders the Atlantic Ocean, with a continental shelf that extends some 370 kilometers (200 nautical miles). The waters of the continental shelf are extremely shallow. Reefs and sandbars dot the shoreline.

Sea Inlets and Straits

Duck Lagoon (Lagoa dos Patos), on the southern coast of Brazil, is a long, shallow tidal lagoon separated from the Atlantic Ocean by a wide sandbar. It covers an area of 10,153 square kilometers (3,920 square miles) and is the largest lagoon in the world.

Harbors in Brazil include, from south to north: Pôrto Alegre, in Rio Grande do Sul; Santos, in the port of São Paulo; Rio de Janeiro; Vitória, just north of Rio de Janeiro in Espírito Santo; and Belem and Macapá, both at the mouth of the Amazon River.

Islands and Archipelagos

Many islands exist throughout the river system and delta area of the Amazon. One of the world's largest riverine islands, Marajó, is the largest island in the Amazon River Delta. (A riverine island is one situated in a river.) It lies in the center of the mouth of the Amazon River, separating the western arm from the eastern arm, known as the Pará River. Maracá Island lies north of the mouth of the Amazon, just to the south of Brazil's border with French Guiana.

The Fernando de Noronha Islands are a group of volcanic islands off the northeastern bulge of the country. The island state of Santa Catarina is located off the nation's southern coast, between São Paulo and Pôrto Alegre.

Coastal Features

Brazil's beaches are among the most famous in the world, including Copacabana and Ipanema, found near Rio de Janeiro. Near the Uruguay border, a large sandbar separates Duck Lagoon from the Atlantic Ocean.

6 ⊕ INLAND LAKES

Brazil has several small lakes throughout the Amazon River basin that formed naturally through flooding of the river systems. The largest of Brazil's natural lakes is the Duck Lagoon; the other large lakes are artificial, such as Sobradinho (3,970 square kilometers/ 1,533 square miles); Tucuruí (2,820 square kilometers/1,089 square miles); Balbina (2,360 square kilometers/911 square miles); and Serra da Mesa (1,784 square kilometers/689 square miles).

7 ⊕ RIVERS AND WATERFALLS

The Amazon River is Brazil's longest river and the second-longest river in the world. It covers 3,218 kilometers (2,000 miles) within the country of Brazil, but it has a total length of

---

DID YOU KN⊕W?

Tropical climate is typically hot and humid, with both abundant rainfall and intense sunshine; the main difference between seasons is the amount of rainfall. Temperate climate is generally mild, with greater differences in temperature from season to season.

The Pantanal is a wet lowland region known in the upper reaches of the Paraguay River.

about 6,570 kilometers (4,080 miles). It starts in Peru and flows through Colombia and Brazil before reaching the Atlantic Ocean. The Amazon has eighteen major tributaries, including ten that carry more water than the Mississippi River. The river is also known as having the world's largest flow of water, with about 303 million liters (80 million gallons) of water per second emptying into the Atlantic Ocean.

The Amazon River basin contains the world's largest tropical rain forest, which provides a natural replacement for 15 percent or more of the world's oxygen in the atmosphere. The number of species in this forest is unknown, but about one-fourth of the world's known plant species can be found in Brazil. Along much of the river in the Amazon basin, there are stretches of varzea (flat, swampy land) that is subject to frequent flooding and is underwater for part of every year.

The São Francisco River is the longest river contained entirely in Brazil. It starts near Belo Horizonte and flows northeastward along a line parallel to the coast before turning eastward toward the sea. At the border between the states of Sergipe and Alagoas, it drops 80 meters (265 feet) through a series of three spectacular waterfalls. The falls, known as Paulo Afonso Falls, lie about 305 kilometers (190 miles) from the mouth of the river on the Atlantic coast.

The Río de la Plata basin in the south includes three major rivers: Paraná, Uruguay, and Paraguay. The upper reaches of the Paraguay River contain a wet lowland system in western Mato Grosso called the Pantanal. Part of the region is protected as the Pantanal National Park, made up of swamp and marshland and supporting diverse wildlife. The Pantanal covers an area of about 140,000 square kilo-

EPD/Cynthia Bassett

The Serra do Mar runs along the coast of Brazil. Pedra Acu rises to the west of Rio de Janeiro.

meters (50,000 square miles) and is part of the world's largest freshwater wetland system.

The magnificent Iguazú Falls are located on the Iguazú River near the border with Argentina. The Iguazú River starts near the city of Curitaba and flows into the Paraná River. The Iguazú Falls include about 275 individual cataracts in a complex system that is 4.8 kilometers (3 miles) wide and 82 meters (270 feet) high.

8 ⊕ DESERTS

There are no desert regions in Brazil, although the northeast is arid, with dunes of white sand. Concern about desertification, the process where arid land becomes desert, is raised during periods of drought, but when the rains are normal, lagoons form between the dunes.

9 ⊕ FLAT AND ROLLING TERRAIN

Grasslands cover major portions of the south and west-central regions. The plains of Rio Grande do Sul, the southernmost state of Brazil, are called pampas and provide fields for cattle raising. The southern part of the west-central region is a rolling prairie with rivers draining southward. Its soils are particularly suited for agriculture.

The northern, western, and central areas of the Central Highlands (Brazilian Highlands) feature broad, rolling terrain with low, rounded hills. Names have been given to some systems of hills, but these hills do not reach altitudes high enough to be considered mountains.

10 ⊕ MOUNTAINS AND VOLCANOES

With an elevation of 3,014 meters (9,888 feet), the Neblina Peak (Pico da Neblina) in the Imeri range is Brazil's highest peak. It is located in the Guiana Highlands near the border with Venezuela.

The Serra do Mar runs along the coast for 1,609 kilometers (1,000 miles) from Santa Catarina to Rio de Janeiro and northward to join the Serra dos Orgaos. This extended range has an average height of about 1,524 meters (5,000 feet) topped by peaks above 2,133 meters (7,000 feet), including Pedra Acu, which rises to 2,318 meters (7,605 feet) just west of Rio de Janeiro. The Serra do Mar is so near the tidewater in many places that it rises almost directly from the shore.

The Serra da Mantiqueira is the highest and most rugged range of the Central Highlands. It includes the Bandeira Peak (Pico da Bandeira), which at 2,890 meters (9,482 feet) is the highest elevation in the Central Highlands.

The Serra do Espinhaço, or "Backbone Mountains," form a type of spine that determines the drainage divide between the São Francisco River to the west and short streams that tumble eastward to the Atlantic Ocean. It contains a great wealth of minerals. Sometimes the Serra do Espinhaço and the Serra da Mantiqueira are referred to collectively as the Serra Geral.

11 ⊕ CANYONS AND CAVES

There are no significant caves or canyons in Brazil.

12 ⊕ PLATEAUS AND MONOLITHS

The Central Highlands are often called the Brazilian Highlands or Brazilian Plateau. The region covers nearly all of Brazil south of the Amazon River basin.

The Guiana Highlands form part of an immense plateau that reaches higher altitudes than the Central Highlands. The Guiana Highlands extend into Venezuela, Guyana, Suriname, and French Guiana.

13 ⊕ MAN-MADE FEATURES

Most of Brazil's energy comes from the hydroelectric power created by dams. The Sete Quedas hydroelectric power project is located on the Paraná River. The Tucuruí Dam created Lake Tucuruí, near the mouth of the Amazon River. It was the first large dam ever built in a tropical rainforest and has created one of the largest man-made lakes to exist in such a region. The Sobradinho Dam created Lake Sobradinho along the São Francisco River. The Itaipú Hydroelectric Power Station created the Itaipu Reservoir, located near Iguazú Falls.

14 ⊕ FURTHER READING

Books

Burns, E. Bradford. *A History of Brazil*. 3rd ed. New York: Columbia University Press, 1993.

Haverstock, Nathan A. *Brazil in Pictures*. Minneapolis: Lerner, 1987.

Munro, David. *The Oxford Dictionary of the World*. New York: Oxford University Press, 1995.

Periodicals

Van Dyk, Jere. "The Amazon." *National Geographic*, February 1995, pp. 2-39.

Web Sites

CIA World Factbook. http://www.odci.gov/cia/publications/factbook/geos/cg.html (accessed July 22, 2003).

Fernando de Noronha Islands. http://www.noronha.com.br/indexe.htm (accessed July 22, 2003).

Brunei Darussalam

- **Official name:** Negara Brunei Darussalam
- **Area:** 5,770 square kilometers (2,228 square miles)
- **Highest point on mainland:** Mt. Pagon (1,850 meters/6,070 feet)
- **Lowest point on land:** Sea level
- **Hemispheres:** Northern and Eastern

- **Time zone:** 8 P.M. = noon GMT
- **Longest distances:** Not available
- **Land boundaries:** 381 kilometers (237 miles)
- **Coastline:** 160 kilometers (100 miles)
- **Territorial sea limits:** 22 kilometers (12 nautical miles)

1 ⊕ LOCATION AND SIZE

The small country of Brunei is an enclave (distinct cultural area or country surrounded by a larger country) on the northern coast of the island of Borneo. Brunei shares the island with two neighbors: the Malaysian state of Sarawak and Indonesia. Brunei has an area of 5,770 square kilometers (2,228 square miles), or slightly more than the state of Delaware.

2 ⊕ TERRITORIES AND DEPENDENCIES

Brunei believes it has rights to a fishing zone in an area of the Spratly Islands, land whose ownership is disputed among the Philippines, Malaysia, China, Taiwan, and Vietnam. Although Brunei has not made a formal claim on the territory, it does claim to have rights to fish in the waters around the islands.

3 ⊕ CLIMATE

The temperature of Brunei, a tropical country, averages from 23°C to 32°C (73°F to 89°F) year round. Humidity stays at around 80 percent. The northeast monsoon affects Brunei with heavy rains in November and December. On Brunei's coast the annual rainfall averages around 275 centimeters (110 inches), while inland rainfall amounts to 500 centimeters (200 inches) or more. Brunei is out of the path of most ocean storms such as typhoons, although it can be affected by tidal surges.

4 ⊕ TOPOGRAPHIC REGIONS

Brunei consists of distinct eastern and western segments, separated by Malaysia's Limbang River valley, but linked by the waters of Brunei Bay. The terrain in both the eastern segment (the Temburong District) and the more populated western segment is composed of a coastal plain rising gradually to hills and cut through by rivers running north to the sea.

5 ⊕ OCEANS AND SEAS

Brunei is strategically located on shipping lanes linking the trade routes of the Indian Ocean and Pacific Ocean through the South China Sea. The immensely valuable hydrocarbon deposits that have produced Brunei's petroleum export boom lie mainly under the South China Sea off Brunei's coast.

Seacoast and Undersea Features

The waters along the Brunei coast are filled with nutrients carried by the rivers, so there is an abundance of marine life, making the area productive for fishing. An estimated five hundred species of fish have been identified in the coastal waters.

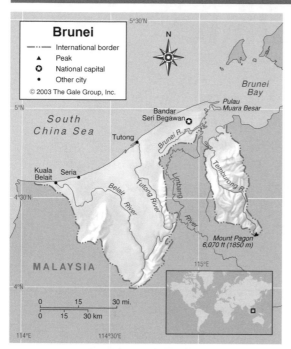

Brunei

- – – – International border
- ▲ Peak
- ✪ National capital
- • Other city

© 2003 The Gale Group, Inc.

South China Sea

Brunei Bay

Pulau Muara Besar

Bandar Seri Begawan

Tutong

Brunei R.

Kuala Belait

Seria

Belait River

Tutong River

Limbang River

Temburong R.

Mount Pagon
6,070 ft (1850 m)

MALAYSIA

0   15   30 mi.
0   15   30 km

Sea Inlets and Straits

In Temburong District, in the east, the steep muddy banks of Brunei Bay and its inlets form a major wildlife habitat.

Islands and Archipelagos

Brunei has thirty-three islands, comprising 1.4 percent of its land area. Two are in the South China Sea. The others are river islands or, like Pulau Muara Besar, are situated in Brunei Bay. The islands are important wildlife habitats and are mostly uninhabited by humans.

Coastal Features

The western section of Brunei has a coastline on the South China Sea, where sandbars lie between estuaries and the open ocean. The Belait, Tutong, and Brunei districts have three river estuaries and significant mangrove forests.

6 ⊕ INLAND LAKES

There are a few lakes in Brunei. In Tutong District, a 77-square-kilometer (30-square-mile) nature park surrounds the unusual, S-shaped Tasek Merimbun. The Wong Kadir and Teraja lakes are in Belait District.

7 ⊕ RIVERS AND WATERFALLS

Four indigenous river systems and one originating in the Malaysian state of Sarawak flow north through and between the regions of Brunei to the South China Sea. The Belait River, Brunei's longest waterway, flows through western Brunei, as does the Tutong River.

The Brunei River runs southwest from an inlet of Brunei Bay (where Bandar Seri Begawan is located). In the eastern segment of Brunei, the Temburong River provides drainage for the entire Temburong District. The Limbang River valley, which belongs to Sarawak, splits Brunei in two.

8 ⊕ DESERTS

Brunei has no deserts.

9 ⊕ FLAT AND ROLLING TERRAIN

In the west of Brunei, hills lower than 90 meters (295 feet) rise toward an escarpment and the higher hills approaching the Sarawak border. Brunei's highest peak, Mount Pagon (1,850 meters/6,070 feet), is located in this region. Brunei's eastern sector is also covered with low hills, which gain height close to the border with Sarawak. The mangrove forests of Brunei's estuaries are an ecological treasure, considered among the most intact in Southeast Asia. Mangrove forests cover an estimated 3.2 percent of Brunei's land.

DID YOU KN⊕W?

Brunei's ecologically intact peat swamps (rare in north Borneo) are found in western Brunei.

ARAMCO/Tor Eigeland

Brunei's Batu Apoi forest reserve.

10 ⊕ MOUNTAINS AND VOLCANOES

Brunei has no mountains.

11 ⊕ CANYONS AND CAVES

There are no notable caves.

12 ⊕ PLATEAUS AND MONOLITHS

There are no notable plateaus.

13 ⊕ MAN-MADE FEATURES

There are no man-made features affecting the geography of Brunei.

14 ⊕ FURTHER READING

Books

Edwards, David S. *A Tropical Rainforest: The Nature of Biodiversity in Borneo at Belalong, Brunei.* Torrance, CA: Heian International, 1995.

Pelton, Robert Young. *Fielding's Borneo.* Redondo Beach, CA: Fielding Worldwide, 1995.

Thia-Eng, Chua. *Brunei Darussalam: Coastal Environmental Profile of Brunei Darussalam.* Washington, DC: U.S. Agency for International Development, 1987.

Web Sites

Brunei Home Page. http://www.brunei.bn/ (accessed June 5, 2003).

Government of Brunei Darussalam website. http://www.brunei.gov.bn/index.htm (accessed June 5, 2003).

Bulgaria

- **Official name**: Republic of Bulgaria
- **Area:** 110,910 square kilometers (42,811 square miles)
- **Highest point on mainland:** Musala (2,925 meters/9,596 feet)
- **Lowest point on land:** Sea level
- **Hemispheres:** Northern and Eastern
- **Time zone:** 2 P.M. = noon GMT
- **Longest distances:** 330 kilometers (205 miles) from north to south; 520 kilometers (323 miles) from east to west

- **Land boundaries:** 1,808 kilometers (1,343 miles) total boundary length; The Former Yugoslav Republic of Macedonia (Macedonia), 148 kilometers (92 miles); Greece, 494 kilometers (307 miles); Romania, 608 kilometers (378 miles); Turkey, 240 kilometers (149 miles); Serbia and Montenegro (formerly part of Yugoslavia), 318 kilometers (197 miles)
- **Coastline:** 354 kilometers (214 miles)
- **Territorial sea limits:** 22 kilometers (12 nautical miles)

1 ⊕ LOCATION AND SIZE

Bulgaria is part of the Balkan Peninsula (peninsula surrounded by, from west to east, the Adriatic, Ionian, Aegean, and Black Seas) in southeastern Europe. It has an eastern coastline on the Black Sea and shares borders with Romania, Turkey, Greece, the former Yugoslav republic of Macedonia (Macedonia) and Serbia and Montenegro (formerly part of Yugoslavia). With an area of about 110,910 square kilometers (42,811 square miles), the country is slightly larger than the state of Tennessee. Bulgaria is divided into twenty-eight provinces.

2 ⊕ TERRITORIES AND DEPENDENCIES

Bulgaria claims no territories or dependencies.

3 ⊕ CLIMATE

Overall, Bulgaria's climate is temperate, with cold, damp winters and hot, dry summers. There is, however, a modified Mediterranean climate in the Thacian Plain, because of the protection offered by the Balkan Mountains.

Rainfall is generally light in the plateaus, averaging about 65 centimeters (25 inches) per year, and higher in the mountain ranges, where it can reach up to 152 centimeters (60 inches). Most rainfall occurs during the winter months.

Season	Months	Average Temperature °Celsius (°Fahrenheit)
Summer	May to September	22 to 24°C (72 to 75°F)
Winter	November to February	0 to 2°C (32 to 36°F)

4 ⊕ TOPOGRAPHIC REGIONS

Bulgaria occupies a relatively small area, but is nevertheless a land of unusual scenic beauty. It has picturesque mountains, wooded hills, sheltered valleys, grain-producing plains, and a seacoast along the Black Sea that has both rocky cliffs and long sandy beaches.

In the north of the country is the Danubian Plain. The central portion of the country houses

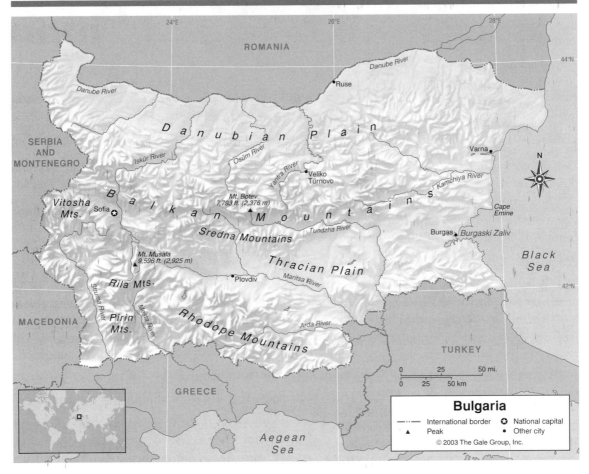

the Balkan Mountains and south of them is the Maritsa River. The Rhodope Mountains are found in the south and southwest areas of the country. Located on the Eurasian Tectonic Plate, Bulgaria is crossed by fault lines that cause frequent earthquakes.

5 ⊕ OCEANS AND SEAS

Seacoast and Undersea Features

Bulgaria has an eastern coastline on the Black Sea, an inland body of water between Europe and Asia. The waters of the Black Sea are calm and free of tides or dangerous marine life. Called the "Hospitable Sea" by the ancient Greeks, the Black Sea is half as salty as the Mediterranean Sea and has gentle sandy slopes, making it ideal for swimming.

Sea Inlets and Straits

Burgaski Zaliv is a bay that indents the coast deeply in the south. Cape Emine extends eastward in the north.

Coastal Features

Bulgaria's coast on the Black Sea is curved, providing for many beaches along its 354 kilometers (214 miles) of shoreline. Many of the country's beaches have received awards from the European Union for their environmental excellence. The coastline is varied, with coves, rugged shores, wooded hills, orchards, and fishing villages dotting the expansive area.

EPD/Saxifraga/Adriaan Dijksen

Ropotamo River near the Black Sea.

6 ⊕ INLAND LAKES

Most of the estimated 280 glacial lakes are situated in the Rila and Pirin Mountains, at altitudes of 2,200 to 2,400 meters (7,216 to 7,872 feet). The highest of these, Ledenika Lake in the Rila Mountains, lies at an altitude of 2,715 meters (8,905 feet). Located in the Pirin Mountains, Popovo Lake, also known as the "Pirin Sea," is the largest lake in the country. It covers an area of 12.4 hectares (30.7 acres) and is 480 meters (1,575 feet) long and 336 meters (1,102 feet) wide.

7 ⊕ RIVERS AND WATERFALLS

The Danube (Dunav) River, which forms the majority of Bulgaria's border with Romania, is by far the longest river in the country and is the second-longest waterway in Europe. With a total length of 2,850 kilometers (1,770 miles), it is deep and wide enough to be navigable by ocean vessels throughout Bulgaria. Most of the northern part of the country drains into the

Black Sea via the Danube and its tributaries. Many of these tributaries, including the Yantra and the Osum, rise in the Balkan Mountains. One notable exception is the Iskur, which rises in the Rila Mountains and flows northward, passing through Sofia's eastern suburbs before it cuts a valley through the Balkan Mountains.

South of the Balkan Mountains, most rivers flow south into the Aegean Sea. Most notable among these rivers are the Mesta, the Struma, and the Maritsa, and the Maritsa's tributaries, the Tundzha and Arda. Together, these waterways provide drainage for most of the Thracian Plain. The Kamchiya River in the northeast is the only large river to flow directly into the Black Sea. In the southeast, the Ropotamo River is the center of a large habitat for birds.

8 ⊕ DESERTS

There are no desert regions in Bulgaria.

9 ⊕ FLAT AND ROLLING TERRAIN

The Thracian Plain and Danubian Plain, both of which exist on large plateaus, have great varieties of vegetation. They are both densely populated and cultivated.

The north-flowing rivers have cut deep valleys through the Balkan Mountains and the Danubian Plain.

The famous Valley of Roses lies between the Balkan and Sredna Mountains. In this valley, hundreds of thousands of roses are in bloom during the months of May and June. At least 80 percent of the world's attar of roses (the fragrant oil used in perfumes) is produced here.

10 ⊕ MOUNTAINS AND VOLCANOES

The Balkan Mountains (Stara Planina) comprise the biggest and longest mountain chain. As an extension of the Carpathian Mountains, the Balkans cover 700 kilometers (435 miles) across the central portion of the entire country,

DID YOU KN⊕W?

The Balkan Peninsula, the southernmost peninsula of Europe, borders the Adriatic and Ionian Seas to the west, the Black and Aegean Seas to the east, and the Mediterranean Sea to the south. The countries within this region are collectively called the Balkan States. These nations include Albania, Bulgaria, continental Greece, southeast Romania, European Turkey, Serbia and Montenegro, Slovenia, Croatia, Bosnia and Herzegovina, and Macedonia.

declining in altitude towards the east. The range's highest peak is Botev at 2,376 meters (7,793 feet). Just to the south of the central part of this range are the Sredna Mountains (Sredna Gora), a 160-kilometer (100-mile) long ridge that runs almost directly from east to west at an average height of 1,600 meters (5,249 feet).

The other major mountain range is the Rhodope. These mountains mark the southern and southwestern borders of Bulgaria and include the Vitosha, Rila, and Pirin Mountains. These last two ranges are largely volcanic in origin and are the highest mountains on the Balkan Peninsula. Musala in the Rila Mountains is the tallest peak in the country at 2,925 meters (9,596 feet).

The densest forests in the country are in the mountainous regions. Broadleaf forests blanket the low areas of both the Balkan and Rhodope ranges, while conifers thrive at the higher elevations. In general, broadleaf forests are the predominant forest throughout the country.

11 ⊕ CANYONS AND CAVES

Tirgard Gorge is located in the West Rhodope Mountains, near the town of Devin. The gorge is about 500 meters (1,640 feet) long with cliffs above 300 meters (984 feet) high. The path to the gorge consists of an 80-meter (262 feet) rock tunnel.

Novi Iskur Gorge, surrounding the Iskara River, is located between the towns of Novi Iskur and Chomakovtsi. This gorge stretches for a length of about 156 kilometers (97 miles) and features a variety of rock formations.

More than two thousand caves are scattered amidst the limestone layers of the Pirin and the Balkan Mountains. The most notable of these caves are Bacho Kiro, Ledenika, Magura, Snezhanka, and Jamova Dupka.

12 ⊕ PLATEAUS AND MONOLITHS

The Danubian Plain extends from the Serbia and Montenegro border to the Black Sea. The plateau rises from cliffs along the Danube River and extends south to the Balkan Mountains at elevations as high as 457 meters (1,500 feet). On the southern side of the Balkan Mountains is another plateau, the Thracian Plain, which is drained by the Maritsa River. Both plateaus are fertile regions of hills and plains, gradually declining in elevation as they approach the Black Sea.

The Melnik Pyramids are natural rock formations found in the southwestern slopes of the Pirin Mountains. These amazing monolithic sculptures come in a variety of shapes, including some that look like Egyptian pyramids and Gothic temples.

13 ⊕ MAN-MADE FEATURES

The Ivanovo Rock Monasteries, located in the Roussenski Lom River valley in northeast Bulgaria, have been designated as a UNESCO (United Nations Educational, Scientific, and Cultural Organization) World Heritage Site. Hermit monks built the monastery during the twelfth century, carving the cells and chapels of the structure into the rocks. Two hundred years after the construction, the walls of most of the rooms were covered with exquisite fresco paintings.

14 ⊕ FURTHER READING

Books

Cary, William. *Bulgaria Today: The Land and the People, a Voyage of Discovery.* New York: ExpositionPress, 1965.

Detrez, Raymond. *Historical Dictionary of Bulgaria.* Lanham, MD: Scarecrow Press, 1997.

Hoddinott, Ralph F. *Bulgaria in Antiquity: An Archaeological Introduction.* New York: St. Martin's Press, 1975.

Pettifer, James. *Bulgaria.* New York: W.W. Norton, 1998.

Web Sites

Bulgarian Travel Guide: Explore Bulgaria. http://www.travel-bulgaria.com/content/explore_bulgaria.shtml (accessed May 2, 2003).

Burkina Faso

- **Official name:** Burkina Faso

- **Area:** 274,200 square kilometers (105,869 square miles)

- **Highest point on mainland:** Tena Kourou (747 meters/2,451 feet)

- **Lowest point on land:** Black Volta River (200 meters/656 feet)

- **Hemispheres:** Northern, Eastern, and Western

- **Time zone:** Noon = noon GMT

- **Longest distances:** 873 kilometers (542 miles) from east-northeast to west-southwest; 474 kilometers (295 miles) from south-southeast to north-northwest

- **Land boundaries:** 3,192 kilometers (1,983 miles) total boundary length; Benin, 306 kilometers (190 miles); Cote d'Ivoire, 584 kilometers (363 miles); Ghana, 548 kilometers (341 miles); Mali, 1,000 kilometers (621 miles); Niger, 628 kilometers (390 miles); Togo, 126 kilometers (78 miles)

- **Coastline:** None

- **Territorial sea limits:** None

1 ⊕ LOCATION AND SIZE

Burkina Faso (known as Upper Volta from 1960 until 1984) is a landlocked country (does not have access to the sea) in northwest Africa. It lies west of Niger; northwest of Benin; north of Mali, Togo, Ghana, and Côte d'Ivoire; and east and south of Mali. With an area of 274,200 square kilometers (105,869 square miles), the country is slightly larger than the state of Colorado. Burkina Faso is divided into thirty provinces.

2 ⊕ TERRITORIES AND DEPENDENCIES

Burkina Faso has no outside territories or dependencies.

3 ⊕ CLIMATE

High temperatures are typical in Burkina Faso, especially during the dry season. From March to May, the harmattan, a dry east wind, contributes to considerably hot temperatures that range from 40° to 48°C (104° to 119°F). From May to October, the weather is hot, but wet; and from November to March, it is dry and comfortable. January temperatures vary from 7° to 13°C (44° to 55°F).

The average annual rainfall varies from 115 centimeters (45 inches) in the southwest to a low of 25 centimeters (10 inches) in the extreme north and northeast portion of the country. The country suffers from recurring droughts.

4 ⊕ TOPOGRAPHIC REGIONS

Burkina Faso is situated on a single, vast plateau known as the Mossi Highlands. Three valleys are carved around the highlands by the Black, White, and Red Volta Rivers, and their main tributary, the Sourou. The rivers are either flooded or dry, making the terrain of this savannah arid and poor. This wild bush country has a mixture of grasslands and small

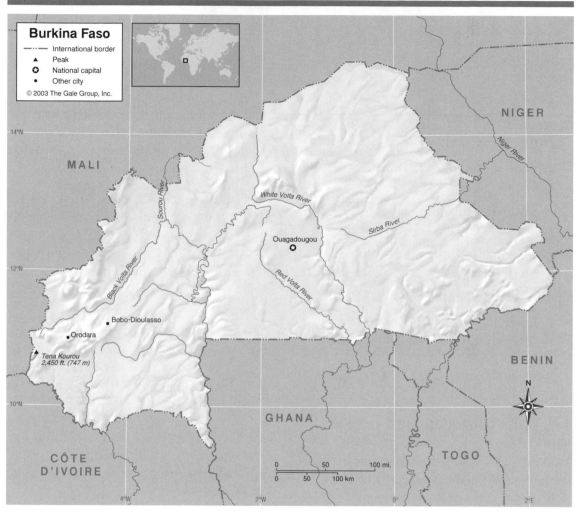

Burkina Faso

— — International border
▲ Peak
✪ National capital
• Other city

© 2003 The Gale Group, Inc.

trees. The northern provinces of Burkina Faso are part of the Sahel region, a long strip of savannah that marks the southern edge of the Sahara Desert. Though most of the country is flat, there is a hill region in the southwest.

5 ⊕ OCEANS AND SEAS

Burkina Faso is a landlocked country.

6 ⊕ INLAND LAKES

Burkina Faso has very few permanent natural lakes. One of them, Lake Tengréla, is located beyond the waterfalls of Karfiguéla near the city of Banfora. Lake Bam is found in the northern stretch of the White Volta River.

7 ⊕ RIVERS AND WATERFALLS

The longest river in Burkina Faso is the Black Volta (1,352 kilometers/840 miles), located in the southwestern bulge of the country. The two other principal rivers, the White Volta and Red Volta, run north to south in the central plateau region. All of the rivers flow southward and meet in Ghana to form the Volta River and Lake Volta. They are alternately dry or flooded and all are unnavigable.

The hill region of the southwest offers many waterfalls, particularly during the rainy

UNESCO/Dominique Roger

Burkinabe villagers have prepared bricks from the dry, clay-like earth.

season. The Karfiguéla waterfalls are located just outside of Banfora.

8 ⊕ DESERTS

Sahel is an Arabic word that means "shore." It refers to the 5,000-kilometer-long (3,125-mile-long) stretch of savannah that forms the edge of the Sahara Desert. The Sahel spreads east to west from Somalia to Mauritania and Senegal and covers most of the northern portion of Burkina Faso. Sparse rainfall means drought is common in this area, so even crops that need very little water often fail. Soil erosion is a great concern for this region, as the dry soil is blown away by the hot harmattans or washed into the rivers during the rains. To catch rainwater and reduce soil erosion on crop areas, farmers build diguettes around their fields. A diguette is a line of stones built up along the borders of a farmland that essentially creates a barrier to keep the rainwater on the crop field.

9 ⊕ FLAT AND ROLLING TERRAIN

The savannah region of Burkina Faso is primarily grassland during the rainy season.

The highest elevation is Tena Kourou at 747 meters (2,451 feet). It is located in a low hilly region near the Mali border, south of Orodara. The hills were formed by the incline of the central plateau.

10 ⊕ MOUNTAINS AND VOLCANOES

There are no significant mountain ranges in Burkina Faso.

11 ⊕ CANYONS AND CAVES

There are no significant caves or canyons in Burkina Faso.

12 ⊕ PLATEAUS AND MONOLITHS

For the most part, the country consists of a vast plateau in the West African savannah, approximately 198 to 305 meters (650 to 1,000 feet) above sea level. This plateau is slightly inclined toward the south, and it is notched by valleys formed by the three principal rivers, the Black, White and Red Volta Rivers.

13 ⊕ MAN-MADE FEATURES

Much of Burkina Faso relies on a system of dams and reservoirs to supply water for drinking and agriculture. Some of the largest dams include Douna and Moussodougou in the west; Sourou in the northwest; Bam, Loumbila, and Kanazoé in the central region; and Kompienga in the east. A number of smaller dams are used through the country to create temporary flooding for agriculture.

14 ⊕ FURTHER READING

Books

Baxter, Joan, and Keith Sommerville. *Burkina Faso*. New York: Pinter Publishers, 1989.

McFarland, Daniel Miles. *Historical Dictionary of Upper Volta*. Metuchen, NJ: Scarecrow Press, 1978.

Skinner, Elliott P. *African Urban Life: The Transformation of Ouagadougou*. Princeton, NJ: Princeton University Press, 1974.

Web Sites

Oxfam's Cool Planet - On The Line - Burkina Faso. http://www.oxfam.org.uk/coolplanet/ontheline (accessed June 13, 2003).

Burundi

- **Official name:** Republic of Burundi
- **Area:** 27,830 square kilometers (10,745 square miles)
- **Highest point on mainland:** Mount Heha (2,670 meters/8,760 feet)
- **Lowest point on land:** Lake Tanganyika (772 meters/2,533 feet)
- **Hemispheres:** Southern and Eastern
- **Time zone:** 2 P.M. = noon GMT
- **Longest distances:** 263 kilometers (163 miles) from north-northeast to south-southwest; 194 kilometers (121 miles) from east-southeast to west-northwest

- **Land boundaries:** 974 kilometers (605 miles) total boundary length; Rwanda, 290 kilometers (180 miles); Tanzania, 451 kilometers (280 miles); Democratic Republic of the Congo, 233 kilometers(145 miles)
- **Coastline:** None
- **Territorial sea limits:** None

1 ⊕ LOCATION AND SIZE

Burundi is a small, densely populated, land-locked country (does not have access to the sea) in east-central Africa, bounded by Rwanda, Tanzania, and Lake Tanganyika. It is slightly larger than the state of Maryland.

2 ⊕ TERRITORIES AND DEPENDENCIES

Burundi claims no territories or dependencies.

3 ⊕ CLIMATE

Although Burundi lies within fifty degrees of the equator, its high elevations keep temperatures at a comfortable level. Humidity, however, is high. The average annual temperature in the western plains (including the capital city of Bujumbura) is 23°C (73°F). Temperatures average 20°C (68°F) in the plateau region and 16°C (60°F) in the mountains.

Dry seasons occur from June to August and December to January, and rainy seasons from February to May and September to November.

SEASON	MONTHS
Long dry season (winter)	June to August
Short wet season (spring)	September to November
Short dry season (summer)	December to January
Long wet season (fall)	February to May

4 ⊕ TOPOGRAPHIC REGIONS

Burundi has three major natural regions: 1) the Rift Valley area in the west, which consists of the narrow plains along the Rusizi River and the shores of Lake Tanganyika, together with the belt of foothills on the western face of the divide between the Congo and Nile Rivers; 2) the mountains that form the Congo-Nile divide; and 3) the central and eastern plateaus and the warmer, drier plains near the country's eastern and southeastern borders.

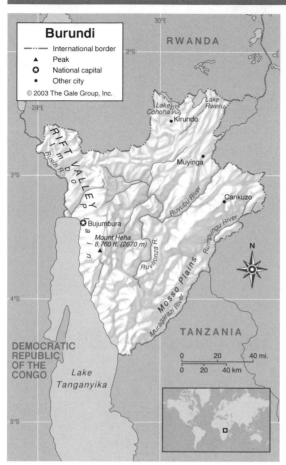

Burundi

- – – – International border
- ▲ Peak
- ✪ National capital
- • Other city

© 2003 The Gale Group, Inc.

RWANDA

Lake Cohoha
Lake Rweru
Kirundo

RIFT VALLEY

Muyinga

Ruvubu River

Cankuzo

Bujumbura

Mount Heha
8,760 ft. (2670 m) ▲

Ruvironza R.

Rumpungu River

Mosso Plains

Mungarazi River

TANZANIA

DEMOCRATIC
REPUBLIC
OF THE
CONGO

Lake
Tanganyika

N

0   20   40 mi.
0   20   40 km

5 ⊕ OCEANS AND SEAS

Burundi is landlocked.

6 ⊕ INLAND LAKES

Burundi shares Lake Tanganyika with Tanzania, Zambia, and the Democratic Republic of the Congo. Its shores form Burundi's southeastern border, extending for over 161 kilometers (100 miles). Burundi also has a number of smaller lakes located entirely within its borders, of which Lake Rweru in the north is among the largest.

7 ⊕ RIVERS AND WATERFALLS

West of the mountains that form the Congo-Nile divide, runoff waters drain down Burundi's narrow western plains into the Ru-

sizi River and Lake Tanganyika. This area is known as the western watershed (area where all the rainfall drains into a common river or lake system). The major rivers of the central plateaus include the Ruvironza (or Luvironza) and the Ruvubu; the latter is an extension of the White Nile River. In the east, the two principal rivers on the border with Tanzania are the Rumpungu and the Malagarasi, which forms most of Burundi's southern border.

8 ⊕ DESERTS

There are no desert areas in Burundi.

9 ⊕ FLAT AND ROLLING TERRAIN

Above the flat western plains that border the Rusizi River and Lake Tanganyika, a belt of foothills and steeper slopes forms the western face of the Congo-Nile divide. This region includes valleys and farmland. At the westernmost edge of the country, the narrow Imbo plain extends south along the Rusizi River from the Rwanda border through Bujumbura. It then continues southward for another 48 kilometers (30 miles) along the eastern shore of Lake Tanganyika. This plain, which belongs to the western branch of the Great Rift Valley, is entirely below 1,066 meters (3,500 feet) in elevation. On Burundi's southeastern border, the Mosso plains lie along the Malagarasi, Rumpungu, and Rugusi Rivers.

Most of Burundi's terrain (land surface) is a treeless plain, called savannah, covered with grasses. Burundi once had areas of forest, but most of the country's trees have been cut down.

10 ⊕ MOUNTAINS AND VOLCANOES

Burundi's mountains, located in the western part of the country, form part of the divide between the basins of the Nile and Congo Rivers. They extend the entire length of the country from north to south, forming a series of long, narrow ridges that are generally less than 16

EPD/Cynthia Bassett

Most of Burundi is savannah (treeless plain).

kilometers (10 miles) wide, with an average elevation of about 2,438 meters (8,000 feet).

11 ⊕ CANYONS AND CAVES

There are no significant caves or canyons in Burundi.

12 ⊕ PLATEAUS AND MONOLITHS

East of the rugged Congo-Nile divide lies a large central plateau with an average elevation of 1,525 to 2,000 meters (5,000 to 6,500 feet). This pleasant highland, inhabited by farmers and cattle herders, is heavily farmed and grazed.

13 ⊕ MAN-MADE FEATURES

Burundi, with help from international experts, is developing factories and methods for converting its natural peat (partially decomposed water plants) into fuel, since there is a shortage of wood to burn for cooking and heating.

14 ⊕ FURTHER READING

Books

Forster, Peter G., Michael Hitchcock, and Francis F. Lyimo. *Race and Ethnicity in East Africa.* New York: St. Martin's Press, 2000.

Nyankanzi, Edward L. *Genocide: Rwanda and Burundi.* Rochester, VT.: Schenkman Books, 1998.

Weinstein, Warren. *Historical Dictionary of Burundi.* Metuchen, NJ: Scarecrow Press, 1976.

Web Sites

University of Pennsylvania Web site. http://www.sas.upenn.edu/African_Studies/NEH/br-geog.html (accessed February 10, 2003).

World Atlas Website. http://www.worldatlas.com/atlas/africa/maps/burundi.htm (accessed June 13, 2003).

Cambodia

- **Official name:** Kingdom of Cambodia
- **Area:** 181,040 square kilometers (69,900 square miles)
- **Highest point on mainland:** Phnom Aural (1,810 meters/5,939 feet)
- **Lowest point on land:** Gulf of Thailand at sea level
- **Hemispheres:** Northern and Eastern
- **Time zone:** 7 P.M. = noon GMT
- **Longest distances:** 730 kilometers (454 miles) from northeast to southwest; 512 kilometers (318 miles) from northwest to southeast

- **Land boundaries:** 2,572 kilometers (1,598 miles) total boundary length; Laos, 541 kilometers (336 miles); Thailand, 803 kilometers (499 miles); Vietnam, 1,228 kilometers (763 miles)
- **Coastline:** 443 kilometers (275 miles)
- **Territorial sea limits:** 22 kilometers (12 nautical miles)

1 ⊕ LOCATION AND SIZE

Cambodia is located in the southwestern part of the Indochina peninsula. (Besides Cambodia, the countries of Myanmar, Thailand, Laos, Vietnam, and part of Malaysia make up the Indochina peninsula in Southeast Asia.) Cambodia lies completely within the tropics—its southernmost points are only a little more than ten degrees above the equator. Bordered by Laos, Thailand, and Vietnam, Cambodia also has a short but heavily indented coastline on the Gulf of Thailand. Cambodia has an area of 181,040 square kilometers (69,900 square miles), or slightly less than the state of Oklahoma.

2 ⊕ TERRITORIES AND DEPENDENCIES

Cambodia claims no territories or dependencies.

3 ⊕ CLIMATE

Cambodia has a humid, tropical climate. There is little seasonal variation in temperatures, which generally range from 20°C to 36°C (68°F to 97°F). The two seasons are determined by monsoons. Southwestern winds bring the rainy season, which lasts from April or May to November; northeast monsoon winds trigger a drier season for the remainder of the year, characterized by lower rainfall, less humidity, and variable skies. Rainfall varies from 127 to 140 centimeters (50 to 55 inches) in the great central basin to 508 centimeters (200 inches) or more in the southwestern mountains.

SEASON	MONTHS
Rainy (summer)	April to November
Dry (winter)	December to March

4 ⊕ TOPOGRAPHIC REGIONS

The heart of Cambodia, occupying three-quarters of the country, is the large drainage basin of the Tonle Sap Lake and the Mekong River. Located in the center of the country,

EPD/Cynthia Bassett

Tonle Sap is Cambodia's largest lake.

it consists mostly of plains with elevations generally less than 91 meters (300 feet) above sea level. It is bounded by highlands to the east and northeast and by the Cardamom Mountains and Elephant Mountains to the southwest. The mountain ranges that mark the southwestern edge of the central plains are bordered on the Gulf of Thailand side by a narrow coastal plain.

5 ⊕ OCEANS AND SEAS

Cambodia is bordered on the southwest by the Gulf of Thailand.

Seacoast and Undersea Features

Recreational snorkelers enjoy exploring the waters off Kâmpóng Saôm.

Sea Inlets and Straits

The most important feature of Cambodia's short coastline is the deep, irregularly shaped bay at the port of Kâmpóng Saôm.

Islands and Archipelagos

Numerous islands dot the waters off the Cambodian coast. The largest include Kaôh Kong and Kaôh Rung.

Coastal Features

Cambodia's coastline is heavily indented. The largest and deepest indentation is the bay at Kâmpóng Saôm.

6 ⊕ INLAND LAKES

Cambodia's largest lake is the Tonle Sap, or Great Lake. Connected to the Mekong River by the Tonle Sap River, it acts as a natural reservoir during the Mekong's flood period. During this time, the area of the lake is enlarged from a low of about 260 square kilometers (100 square miles) to nearly 2,100 square kilometers (800 square miles) at the height of the flooding.

7 ⊕ RIVERS AND WATERFALLS

The Mekong River, together with its drainage basin, is Cambodia's dominant physical feature. The Mekong flows southward in Cam-

CAMBODIA

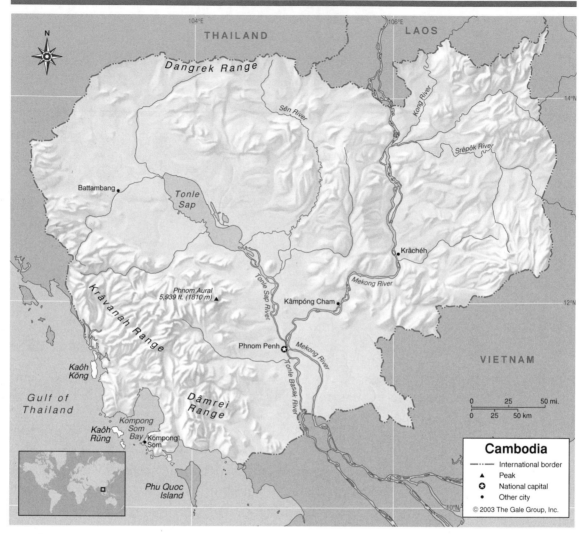

bodia for about 505 kilometers (315 miles), from the Cambodia-Laos border to below the provincial capital of Krâchéh, where it turns westward and then southwestward to Phnom Penh. From Phnom Penh, the river flows generally southeastward. It divides at this point into two principal channels. The new one is known as the Tonle Basak River, which flows independently from here on through the delta area into the South China Sea. In the southwest, the Cardamom and Elephant ranges form a separate drainage divide. To the east of this divide, the rivers flow into the Tonle Sap; those to the west drain into the

Gulf of Thailand. There are extensive rapids located just upstream of Krâchéh.

8 ⊕ DESERTS

There are no desert areas in Cambodia.

9 ⊕ FLAT AND ROLLING TERRAIN

The alluvial plain (area made up of soil deposited by a river) of the Mekong River and the Tonle Sap drainage basin occupies the center of the country, surrounded by a transitional zone of rolling land with elevations of up to several hundred feet above sea level. The regular flood-

EPD/Cynthia Bassett

*Cambodian countryside as viewed
from a mountain peak.*

ing of the central plain irrigates the land for the cultivation of rice and other crops.

10 ⊕ MOUNTAINS AND VOLCANOES

The Cardamom (Krâvanh) Mountains, extending in a northwest-southeast direction, have elevations rising to over 1,524 meters (5,000 feet); Phnom Aural, an eastern spur of this range, is the highest point in the country. The Elephant (Dâmrei) Mountains, running south and southeastward from the Cardamom, has elevations above 914 meters (3,000 feet). The Dangrek range at the northern rim of the basin consists of a steep cliff with an average elevation of about 487 meters (1,600 feet). Facing south, it constitutes the southern edge of the Khorat Plateau, which extends northward into Thailand.

11 ⊕ CANYONS AND CAVES

There are a few caves in Cambodia. At Phnom Proset, about 40 kilometers (25 miles) from

Phnom Penh, is Prasat Ruong, or Temple of the Mountain Cave. Prasat Ruong was built over the opening to a cave that may be explored for about 50 meters (160 feet).

12 ⊕ PLATEAUS AND MONOLITHS

East of the Mekong River, mountains and plateaus extend eastward at an average elevation of 360 meters (1,200 feet), continuing past the border as the central highlands of Vietnam.

13 ⊕ MAN-MADE FEATURES

Hydroelectric dams were being planned in 2001 and 2002, including one in Bokor National Park in southwest Cambodia.

14 ⊕ FURTHER READING

Books

Downie, Susan. *Down Highway One: Journeys Through Vietnam and Cambodia*. North Sydney: Allen & Unwin, 1993.

Livingston, Carol. *Gecko Tails: A Journey Through Cambodia*. London: Weidenfeld and Nicolson, 1996.

Wurlitzer, Rudolph. *Hard Travel to Sacred Places*. Boston: Shambhala, 1994.

Web Sites

Asian Studies Virtual Library Web site. http://www.iias.nl/wwwvl/southeas/cambodia.html (accessed February 26, 2003).

Internet Travel Guide. http://www.pmgeiser.ch/cambodia/ (accessed February 26, 2003).

Cameroon

- **Official name**: Republic of Cameroon
- **Area:** 475,440 square kilometers (183,568 square miles)
- **Highest point on mainland:** Mount Cameroon (4,095 meters/13,435 feet)
- **Lowest point on land:** Sea level
- **Hemispheres:** Northern and Eastern
- **Time zone:** 1 P.M. = noon GMT
- **Longest distances:** 1,206 kilometers (749 miles) from north to south; 717 kilometers (446 miles) from east to west
- **Land boundaries:** 4,591 kilometers (2,853 miles) total boundary length; Central African Republic, 797 kilometers (495 miles); Chad, 1,094 kilometers (680 miles); Republic of the Congo, 523 kilometers (325 miles); Equatorial Guinea, 189 kilometers (117 miles); Gabon, 298 kilometers (185 miles); Nigeria, 1,690 kilometers (1050 miles)
- **Coastline:** 402 kilometers (250 miles)
- **Territorial sea limits:** 91 kilometers (50 nautical miles)

1 ⊕ LOCATION AND SIZE

Cameroon is a triangle-shaped country located between West Africa and Central Africa. It has a western border on the waters of the Bight of Biafra in the Gulf of Guinea, between Equatorial Guinea (south) and Nigeria (north). It also shares borders with the countries of Gabon and Republic of the Congo to the south, and Central African Republic and Chad to the east. With a total area of 475,440 square kilometers (183,568 square miles), Cameroon is slightly larger than the state of California. The country is divided into ten provinces.

2 ⊕ TERRITORIES AND DEPENDENCIES

Cameroon claims no territories or dependencies.

3 ⊕ CLIMATE

Cameroon has a climate that varies from tropical along the coast to semiarid (little annual rainfall) and hot in the north. The average temperature range in Yaoundé is from 18 to 29°C (64 to 84°F). The north part of Cameroon has a wet season between April and September with an average annual precipitation between 100 and 175 centimeters (39 and 69 inches). The south alternates between wet and dry seasons. The two wet seasons are from March to June and again from August to November. Annual precipitation in the south reaches 403 centimeters (159 inches).

4 ⊕ TOPOGRAPHIC REGIONS

The terrain (surface of the land area) of Cameroon is diverse. The country has four basic geographic regions. The southwestern lowlands are located along the coast. The northwestern highlands run from the northern coast along the border with Nigeria.

The central region covers a majority of the country and includes the Adamawa Plateau. The northern plains run through the northern arm of the country that reaches up through Chad. This area is a part of the Sahel, the semiarid region that borders the Sahara Desert.

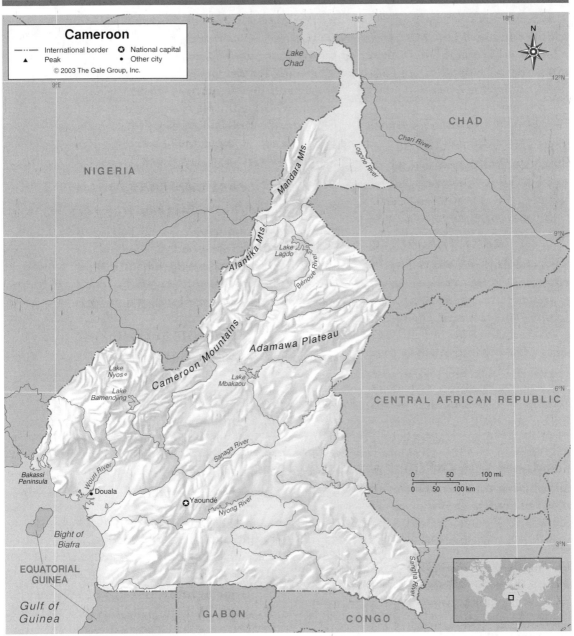

Cameroon
- - - International border ⊗ National capital
▲ Peak • Other city
© 2003 The Gale Group, Inc.

5 ⊕ OCEANS AND SEAS

Seacoast and Undersea Features

Along its west coast, Cameroon borders the Bight of Biafra, an eastern bay of the Gulf of Guinea.

Coastal Features

The Bakassi Peninsula is a 1,554-square-kilometer (600-square-mile) region that includes the northern edge of the Cameroon coast and a series of islands that are believed to contain rich oil reserves. The area is mostly a mangrove forest swampland. Currently, the

EPD/Evangelical Lutheran Church in America

Homes in Cameroon are typically built in the grassland regions.

governments of Cameroon and Nigeria both claim ownership of the Bakassi, as each hopes to profit from these potential oil reserves. As of 2002, both countries had filed suits with the International Court of Justice of the United Nations, but the dispute is not expected to be resolved quickly.

Most of the coastal zone is a flat area of sedimentary soils that stretch along the Gulf of Guinea for about 257 kilometers (160 miles). In the south, the coastal plain is covered by equatorial rain forests, with swamplands along its edges. The beaches near Limbe, at the base of Mount Cameroon, are known for their black volcanic sand.

6 ⊕ INLAND LAKES

The largest lake in Cameroon is Lake Chad, which is shared by the neighboring country of Chad. The size of the lake varies from season to season, depending on rainfall, with a total area of 10,360 to 25,900 square kilometers

(4,000 to 10,000 square miles). It is divided into north and south basins, reaching depths of only about 7.6 meters (25 feet). The lake has no outlets. Its chief tributary is the Chari River, which extends into Chad. Lake Chad is the largest inland body of water on the Sahel.

Freshwater Lake Nyos and Lake Monoun, in the northwestern highlands, formed in volcanic craters. Both lakes contain toxic levels of carbon dioxide gas. In 1986, a buildup of this gas erupted from Lake Nyos, spewing 80 meters (260 feet) into the air. It created a heavy poisonous cloud that eventually swept over an area of about 25 kilometers (16 miles), suffocating seventeen hundred villagers living in the valley below. In 1984, a similar eruption from Lake Monoun killed thirty-seven people. In 2001, scientists began a project to construct a pipeline ventilation system in the lakes. Through this system, the contaminated waters from the bottom of the lakes are pumped slowly and regularly to the surface in a gas-water fountain. This allows for the carbon dioxide to be released into the atmosphere at a slower, more controlled rate.

Other crater lakes include Barombi Mbo, Bermin, Dissoni (Soden), Benakouma, Kotto, and Mboandong.

7 ⊕ RIVERS AND WATERFALLS

The longest river in Cameroon is the Sanaga at 515 kilometers (325 miles). It is formed by headstreams from the center of the country and flows southwest to the Gulf of Guinea. Three other major rivers are the Djérem, Bénuoé, and Nyong.

8 ⊕ DESERTS

The northern plains between Maroua and Lake Chad are part of the region known as the Sahel. Sahel is an Arabic word meaning "shore." It refers to the 5,000-kilometer (3,125-mile) stretch of savannah that is the shore or edge of the Sahara Desert. The Sahel spreads

DID YOU KN⊕W?

Cameroon's exotic native wildlife is attractive to tourists. The government has created game reserves where animals can be observed first-hand, such as elephants, lions, giant eland (a large antelope), bongos (white-striped antelope), chimpanzees, crocodiles, and dozens of species of birds. Game reserves are located in the far north and in the southeast, which is home to a small population of lowland gorillas.

from Mauritania and Senegal in the west to Somalia in the east.

9 ⊕ FLAT AND ROLLING TERRAIN

Vast stretches of grassland are typical within the highlands near the city of Bamenda, while thorn trees and scrub cover the semi-arid northern plains. A few wooded savannah areas dot the east-central part of the country. Only 4 percent of the land in Cameroon is considered permanent pasture, and only 13 percent of the land is arable.

The Mandara Mountains of northern Cameroon extend northward from the town of Garoua and along the Nigerian border. They have a fairly low elevation, with most peaks under about 1,400 meters (4,593 feet)—much lower than the mountains of the northwestern highlands. The Mandara range is known for the ethnic diversity of its residents; more than fifty ethnic groups live there. Most of the mountain dwellers survive as farmers or cattle breeders.

10 ⊕ MOUNTAINS AND VOLCANOES

The highest mountain range in the country is the Cameroon Mountains, located in the northwest bulge of the country along the border with Nigeria. Elevations in this range are generally between 1,676 meters (5,500 feet) and 2,438 meters (8,000 feet).

These mountains were formed through the volcanic activity of the Cameroon Rift, but currently the only active volcano is Mount Cameroon, with its most recent eruption in May 2000.

The volcano is called Mount Faka in Cameroon. With an altitude of 4,095 meters (13,435 feet), it is the highest peak in West and Central Africa.

11 ⊕ CANYONS AND CAVES

There are no significant caves or canyons in Cameroon.

12 ⊕ PLATEAUS AND MONOLITHS

The Adamawa (Adamaoua) Plateau extends from the eastern to the western border of Cameroon and Nigeria at average elevations of about 1,371 meters (4,500 feet). Surface features in the central parts of this high plateau include small hills or mounds capped by granite or gneiss (a type of rock).

Along the western and eastern borders, old eruptions from fissures and volcanoes have covered the granite surface with lava rock. The Adamawa Plateau forms a barrier between the agricultural south and the pastoral north.

13 ⊕ MAN-MADE FEATURES

Cameroon relies on a system of river dams for hydropower and water reserves. The Edéa Dam on the Sanaga River provides the bulk of the country's electricity. A dam on the Bénoué River, built in 1986, formed Lake Lagdo, a large reservoir near Garoua. Other large reservoirs exist near Tibati and Bafoussam.

14 ⊕ FURTHER READING

Books

Africa South of the Sahara 2002: Cameroon. London: Europa Publications Ltd., 2002.

DeLancy, Mark W., and Mark Dike DeLancey. *Historical Dictionary of Cameroon.* African Historical Dictionaries, No. 81. Lanham, MD and London: The Scarecrow Press, Inc., 2000.

Europa World Yearbook 2000: Cameroon. London: Europa Publications, Ltd., 2000.

Web Sites

"Savage Planet: Volcanic Killers-Degassing Lake Nyos." PBS. http://www.pbs.wnet/savageplanet/01volcano (accessed June 23, 2003).

Wo Yaa! Cameroon. http://www.woyaa.com (accessed June 23, 2003).

Canada

- **Official name**: Canada
- **Area:** 9,976,185 square kilometers (3,851,809 square miles)
- **Highest point on mainland:** Mount Logan (5,959 meters/19,551 feet)
- **Lowest point on land:** Sea level
- **Hemispheres:** Northern and Western
- **Time zone:** Newfoundland: 8:30 A.M. = noon GMT; New Brunswick, Nova Scotia, Prince Edward Island, and eastern Quebec: 8 A.M. = noon GMT; Ontario east of 90° and western Quebec: 7 A.M. = noon GMT; western Ontario and Manitoba: 6 A.M. = noon GMT; Alberta and Saskatchewan: 5 A.M. = noon GMT; British Columbia and Yukon Territory: 4 A.M. = noon GMT

- **Longest distances:** 5,187 kilometers (3,223 miles) from east to west; 4,627 kilometers (2,875 miles) from north to south
- **Land boundaries:** 8,893 kilometers (5,526 miles) total boundary length; United States (mainland), 6,416 kilometers (3,987 miles); the state of Alaska, 2,477 kilometers (1,539 miles)
- **Coastline:** 243,791 kilometers (151,485 miles)
- **Territorial sea limits:** 22 kilometers (12 nautical miles)

1 ⊕ LOCATION AND SIZE

Canada is located on the northern portion of the North American continent, north of the mainland of the United States. Waters bordering the country include the North Atlantic Ocean to the east, the North Pacific Ocean to the west, and the Arctic Ocean to the north. With a total area of about 9,976,185 square kilometers (3,851,809 square miles), it is the largest country in the Western Hemisphere and the second-largest in the world, exceeded only by Russia. Canada's size is about the same as that of the continent of Europe. Canada is divided into ten provinces and three territories.

2 ⊕ TERRITORIES AND DEPENDENCIES

Canada has three territories: Yukon Territory, Northwest Territories, and Nunavut Territory. These lands are all located in the northwestern, tundra regions of Canada, and each of them has a relatively small population in comparison to the other provinces. The territories are primarily settled by native tribes; these indigenous peoples have obtained a certain level of self-government for each particular territory.

The Yukon Territory (pop. 31,070 as of 1999) was originally occupied by the Athapaskan tribe, which still has six distinct groups of peoples residing in the territory. In the Northwest Territories (pop. 39,672 as of 1996), about 28 percent of the population is descended from the Dene tribe. Other native groups include the Inuvialuit and the Métis.

The Nunavut Territory (pop. 27,700 as of 2000) was separated from the Northwest Territories in 1999. It is now the largest political subdivision in the country, covering

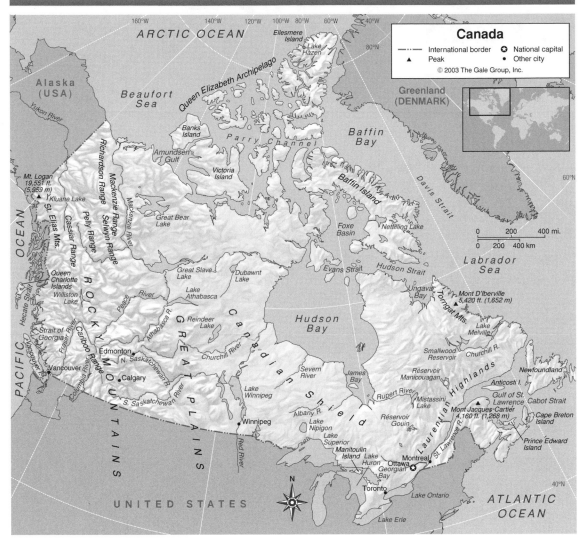

18 percent of the total land area– also the largest native land-claim settlement in the history of the country. About 84 percent of the residents claim ancestry from native tribes;the largest of these Nunavut tribes is the Inuit (83 percent), formerly known as the Eskimos (a derogatory term meaning "eaters of raw meat"). The remainder of the native population in Nunavut Territory is descended from the Dene and Métis tribes.

Each territory has only one senator and one representative in the national parliament, many fewer legislators than those representing the other provinces.

3 🌐 CLIMATE

Canada's continental climate is sub-arctic to arctic in the north, while near the U.S. border a narrow strip has a temperate climate with cold winters. The east and west coasts are maritime and more temperate. The north Canadian coast is permanently icebound, except for Hudson Bay, which is frozen for only nine months of the year. Canada's greatest temperature variation is found in the Northwest Territories, where at Fort Good

Hope temperatures range from -31°C (-24°F) in January to 16°C (61°F) in July.

Temperatures on the west coast of Canada range from about 4°C (39°F) in January to 16°C (61°F) in July. On the Atlantic coast, the winter temperatures are warmer than those of the interior, but the summer temperatures are lower. Much of the southern interior of Canada has high summer temperatures and long, cold winters. Average temperature ranges in Ottawa are -15° to -6°C (5° to 21° F) in January and 15° to 26°C (59° to 79°F) in July.

The west coast of the country and some inland valleys have mild winters and mild summers with rainfall occurring throughout the year. The west coast receives between 150 centimeters and 300 centimeters (60 and 120 inches) of rain annually while the maritime provinces receive 115 to 150 centimeters (45 to 60 inches) annually. The driest area is the central prairie, where fewer than 50 centimeters (20 inches) of rain fall each year. The region to the east of Winnipeg is considerably wetter than the western prairie, receiving 50 to 100 centimeters (20 to 40 inches) of rainfall yearly.

4 ⊕ TOPOGRAPHIC REGIONS

Topographically, Canada is divided into the Atlantic provinces, the Great Lakes-St. Lawrence Lowlands, the Canadian Shield, the Interior Plains, the Western Cordillera, and the Northwest Territories (including the political division of the Nunavut Territory). The Territories cover the region east of the Western Cordillera and north of the Interior Plains and the Canadian Shield. Within this large area, there are two distinct sub-regions: the sub-arctic Mackenzie River Valley to the west, and the arctic area of the islands and north-central mainland.

The Canadian Shield is surrounded by a series of lowlands: the Atlantic region and the Great Lakes-St. Lawrence Lowlands to the east, the Interior Plains to the west, and the Arctic Lowlands to the north. The Atlantic provinces have rugged, indented coasts. The Great Lakes-St. Lawrence Lowlands constitute the heartland of the country's population. This region has the largest area of level land easily accessible by water from the east.

Canada is located on the North American Tectonic Plate.

Because much of Canada has low population density (averaging just three people per square kilometer, or eight people per square mile), many species of wildlife thrive in large expanses of native habitat. The habitat of the northern Arctic region supports populations of Arctic fox, wolf, Arctic hare, ptarmigan, ookpik (a species of owl), musk ox, polar bear, seal, and caribou. The Rocky Mountain region supports species of bear (brown, black, and grizzly), cougar, elk, deer, moose, bighorn sheep, mountain goat, and coyote. The vast plains region supports coyote, deer, and hawk, among others. The ocean waters surrounding Canada support species of whale, and the country's many lakes support trout, salmon, and pike.

5 ⊕ OCEANS AND SEAS

Seacoast and Undersea Features

Canada borders three oceans: the Pacific on the west, the Arctic to the north, and the Atlantic on the east. The Beaufort Sea in the Arctic Ocean lies off the northwest border of the country, near the border shared with Alaska.

The Arctic Archipelago lies on a submerged plateau of the Arctic Ocean, with a floor that varies from flat to gently undulating. From the Alaskan border eastward to the mouth of the Mackenzie River, the continental shelf is shallow and continuous, with its outer edge

Iceberg in the waters of Nunavut territory.

at a depth of 64 meters (210 feet) at about 74 kilometers (46 miles) from the shore. The underwater Mackenzie Trough (formerly known as the Herschel Sea Canyon) is located near the western edge of the Mackenzie River Delta. The submerged portion of the Mackenzie Delta forms a pock-marked undersea plain, most of it less than 55 meters (180 feet) deep. A deeply submerged continental shelf runs along the entire western coast of the Arctic Archipelago, from Banks Island to Greenland.

Along the Atlantic coast, the submerged continental shelf has great width and diversity. From the coast of Nova Scotia, its width varies from 111 to 185 kilometers (69 to 115 miles), from Newfoundland 185 to 518 kilometers (115 to 322 miles) at the entrance of Hudson Strait, and northward from there it merges with the submerged shelf of the Arctic Ocean.

The outer edge varies in depth from 189 to 3,110 meters (620 to 10,201 feet). The overall gradient is slight, but the shelf is studded with shoals, ridges, and banks.

The Pacific coast is strikingly different and is characterized by bold, abrupt relief—a repetition of the mountainous landscape. From the islet-strewn coast, the continental shelf extends from 93 to 185 kilometers (58 to 115 miles), except on the western slopes of Vancouver Island and the Queen Charlotte Islands, where the seafloor drops rapidly.

Sea Inlets and Straits

Amundsen Gulf lies just east of the Beaufort Sea and separates Banks Islands from the mainland. A series of gulfs, straits, and channels surround the islands of the Arctic Archipelago. These include the Viscount Melville Sound, M'Clintock Channel, Queen Maud Gulf, the Gulf of Boothia, Lancaster Sound, Parry Channel, M'Clure Strait, Norwegian Bay, Jones Sound, and Smith Sound. These waters of the Arctic are locked in ice most of the year.

Baffin Bay, in the north, separates Baffin Island from Greenland, opening to the Davis Strait and then to the Labrador Sea, which lies off the southeastern tip of Greenland. Turning south around Newfoundland, the easternmost point of the North American continent, the Cabot Strait separates Newfoundland and Nova Scotia and provides a channel to the Atlantic for the Gulf of St. Lawrence. The Hudson Bay is a shallow inland sea which is 822,325 square kilometers (317,417 square miles) in area, having an average depth of 128 meters (422 feet). Hudson Bay, along with its southern arm James Bay and its northern arm Foxe Basin, connects to the Labrador Sea and the Atlantic Ocean through the Evans Strait and the Hudson Strait. The Hudson Strait, which also separates Baffin Island from the continental coast, is 796 kilometers (495 miles) long and from 69 to 222 kilometers (43 to 138 miles) wide.

On the west coast of Canada, fronting the North Pacific, is a labyrinth of straits and sounds extending from Vancouver Island in the south and winding through the Alexander Archipelago in the north. These waters include the relatively shallow Queen Charlotte Sound as well as two straits: Hecate Strait and the Strait of Georgia.

Islands and Archipelagos

Canada has more than fifty-two thousand islands, with all but a few hundred of them considered "minor" in size, defined as less than 129 square kilometers (49.81 square miles) in area. The largest islands are those in the Arc-

tic Archipelago, extending from James Bay to Ellesmere Island. Within the Arctic Archipelago, Baffin Island is larger than 500,000 square kilometers (193,050 square miles), Victoria Island contains 217,000 square kilometers (83,783 square miles), and Banks Island covers some 70,000 square kilometers (27,027 square miles).

The Queen Elizabeth Archipelago surrounding the north magnetic pole has thirty-five islands, each one larger than 129 square kilometers (49.81 square miles) in size. Ellesmere, the northernmost of Canada's islands, is the largest of the Elizabeth group, covering more than 196,000 square kilometers (75,675 square miles).

The largest islands on the western coast are Vancouver Island (31,285 square kilometers/ 12,079 square miles) and the Queen Charlotte Islands. Large islands on the eastern coast include: Newfoundland (108,860 square kilometers/42,030 square miles), Prince Ed-

DID YOU KN⊕W?

Visitors to Gros Morne National Park in Newfoundland can see plate tectonics in action. Geologists believe that, at least six hundred million years ago, North America and Europe were a single landmass. As the two continents pulled apart, magma from deep inside Earth oozed up between them. This solidified magma, as well as fossils preserved in the sedimentary rock, is on display at Gros Morne, which also contains some of eastern Canada's most dramatic scenery.

CANADA'S TEN LARGEST LAKES (LISTED IN DESCENDING ORDER OF SIZE)		
NAME	**AREA**	**PROVINCE**
Lake Superior	82,367 square kilometers (31,802 square miles)	Ontario (shared with U.S.)
Lake Huron	59,565 square kilometers (23,000 square miles)	Ontario (shared with U.S.)
Great Bear Lake	31,328 square kilometers (12,095 square miles)	Northwest Territories
Great Slave Lake	28,568 square kilometers (11,030 square miles)	Northwest Territories
Lake Erie	25,655 square kilometers (9,910 square miles)	Ontario (shared with U.S.)
Lake Winnipeg	23,760 square kilometers (9,174 square miles)	Manitoba
Lake Ontario	19,009 square kilometers (7,340 square miles)	Ontario (shared with U.S.)
Lake Athabasca	7,850 square kilometers (3,030 square miles)	Saskatchewan
Reindeer Lake	5,660 square kilometers (2,185 square miles)	Saskatchewan
Nettiling Lake	5,066 square kilometers (1,956 square miles)	Nunavut Territory

ward Island (5,620 square kilometers/2,170 square miles), Cape Breton Island (10,311 square kilometers/3,981 square miles), Grand Manan and Campobello Islands in New Brunswick, and Anticosti Island and the Ile de la Madeleine of Quebec. Manitoulin Island in Lake Huron is the world's largest island located within a freshwater lake; its land mass covers some 2,765 square kilometers (1,068 square miles).

Coastal Features

Canada's coastlines of nearly 244,000 kilometers (151,647 miles), including its mainland and offshore islands, are among the largest of any country in the world.

6 ⊕ INLAND LAKES

Canada has 31,752 lakes; more than a third of these are situated in the northern half of the country, in the Northwest Territories and Nunavut Territory. Lakes and rivers cover 7.6 percent of Canada's total area; consequently, surface water is the source of 90 percent of the fresh water used by residents. Indeed, Canada's lakes play a critical role in the country's eco-

system as natural regulators of river flow, smoothing out excess runoff during flooding and sustaining the waterways during dry seasons.

Thirty-six percent of the Great Lakes, the largest freshwater lakes in the world, are situated in Canada. Of the five Great Lakes, only Lake Michigan is completely outside of Canadian borders. Lake Superior, Canada's largest lake in terms of volume (and shared with the United States), has a surface area of 82,367 square kilometers (31,802 square miles) and is the world's largest freshwater lake. Lake Nipigon, in eastern Canada near Lake Superior, is famous for its towering cliffs and its greenish-black sand beaches.

In Canada's northern provinces lie two significant lakes. The Great Slave Lake, in the Northwest Territories, is the deepest and fourth-largest of Canada's lakes, reaching a depth of 614 meters (2,014 feet). Also in this region is the Great Bear Lake, located in a largely uninhabited part of northwestern Canada. It is third in size, but it is the largest lake wholly within Canada.

In the northeast, the Nunavut Territory contains two more notable lakes. Nettling Lake, the country's tenth-largest, receives run-off from the slightly smaller Amadjuak Lake, which in turn helps to drain Baffin Island into Foxe Basin. Nettling Lake is frozen most of the year. Far to the north, on Ellesmere Island, is Lake Hazen (540 square kilometers/210 square miles), the largest lake in the world to lie completely north of the Arctic Circle. This lake helps function as a "thermal oasis," catching the sun's energy and heating the surrounding land to moderate temperatures that are unusual at such an altitude. The lake itself, however, almost never thaws.

In the eastern coastal regions, the important lakes are Smallwood Reservoir (an artificial lake which covers 6,460 square kilometers/2,500 square miles) and Lake Melville (3,000 square kilometers/1,160 square miles). Churchill River connects Lake Melville to Smallwood Reservoir. Lake Melville is a large coastal lake that is linked to the Atlantic Ocean by Hamilton Inlet.

Canada's southern central and western regions include the rest of the country's largest lakes. Lake Winnipeg, in the province of Manitoba, is the country's sixth-largest lake. Not far to the northwest is Reindeer Lake. Farther northwest, on the way to the Great Slave Lake, is Lake Athabasca, famous for its plentiful trout. One lucky Canadian, fishing at this lake in 1961 with a gillnet, caught one of the world's largest lake trout: a 46-kilogram (102-pound) fish.

7 ⊕ RIVERS AND WATERFALLS

Canada's rivers drain into five major ocean outlets: the Pacific, Arctic, and Atlantic Oceans; Hudson Bay; and the Gulf of Mexico. The Yukon and Mackenzie Rivers in the west, the North Saskatchewan, South Saskatchewan, Saskatchewan, Peace, and Athabasca Rivers in central Canada, and the Ottawa and St. Lawrence Rivers in the east comprise Canada's main rivers.

The Central Canadian Shield is drained by the Nelson-Saskatchewan, Churchill, Severn, and Albany Rivers, all of which flow into Hudson Bay. The 4,290-kilometer-long (2,635-mile-long) Mackenzie River is the country's longest river. It is fed by several tributaries and by three large lakes (Great Bear Lake, Great Slave Lake, and Lake Athabasca), and it drains into the Arctic Ocean. The Columbia, Fraser, and Yukon Rivers are the principal drainage systems of western Canada. The Great Lakes drain into the broad St. Lawrence River, which flows into the Gulf of St. Lawrence.

In the prairies, groundwater is the principal source of water for streams during the frequent dry weather periods. In hot summer months, melting glaciers may contribute up to 25 percent of the flow of the Saskatchewan and Athabasca Rivers.

8 ⊕ DESERTS

There are no desert regions in Canada.

9 ⊕ FLAT AND ROLLING TERRAIN

Between the Western Cordillera and the Canadian Shield is the region broadly known as the West, including the Manitoba and Mackenzie Lowlands. The Manitoba Lowland (leading to the Saskatchewan and Alberta Plains) is one of only a few parts of Canada that is as flat as a tabletop. The Manitoba Escarpment forms the boundary between the Manitoba Lowland and the Saskatchewan Plain. In the south, the Missouri Couteau divides the Saskatchewan and Alberta Plains. The landscape of the two plains is similar to that of the U.S. Great Plains, with rolling prairie; deeply incised rivers; water-filled depressions (called sloughs); dry streambeds (called coulees); and, in the drier areas, mesas, buttes, and badlands.

EPD/Cynthia Bassett

Polar bears live in Canada's Arctic region.

To the south and southeast of the Shield lies a triangular, flat, and fertile plain bounded by Georgian Bay in Lake Huron, the St. Lawrence River, and Lake Ontario. Grasslands made up of many different types of stunted bushes and grasses extend over much of the southern Canadian Great Plains.

The Tundra is situated on the northern Canadian Shield. This is an area of Precambrian rock with moss-covered, frozen subsoil. Low-growing grasses and small bushes thrive in this arctic region.

Between the northern tundra and the southern grassland is the boreal forest. Canada's great boreal forest is the largest of its woodlands, occupying 35 percent of the total Canadian land area and 77 percent of Canada's total forest land. Named for the Greek god of the north wind, Boreas, this forest constitutes a band 1,000 kilometers (600 miles) wide.

The boreal forest is characterized by the predominance of coniferous trees, which first sprung up during the Miocene Epoch, twelve to fifteen million years ago; today, this forest is an important source of paper products, jack-pine railway ties, and logs.

Canada possesses 24 percent of the world's wetlands, covering more than 127 million hectares (314 million acres). Most of the wetlands are located in the boreal peat bogs in arctic and sub-arctic regions, or in the Prairie pothole region across south-central Canada and the northern United States, which contains more than four million wetlands and ponds.

10 ⊕ MOUNTAINS AND VOLCANOES

The principal mountainous region is the Western Cordillera (or Cordilleran) Mountain system located in the westernmost portion of Canada. The Cordilleran range, commonly known as the Canadian Rockies, is composed of relatively young, folded, and faulted mountains and plateaus. These Canadian Rockies include several smaller ranges, including the Richardson, Mackenzie, Selwyn, Pelly, Cassiar, and Cariboo Ranges. The chain is much narrower than the Rocky Mountains in the United States, with less extensive interior plateaus.

The individual summits, however, are much higher in Canada, and they contain some of the most beautiful scenery in the world, with magnificent forests of alpine fir, Engelmann spruce, lodgepole pine, aspen, and mountain hemlock. Most peaks in the Canadian Rockies exceed elevations of 4,500 meters (14,765 feet); twenty-four summits top 4,000 meters (13,123 feet). Canada's highest point is Mount Logan (5,959 meters/19,551 feet), located near the Alaskan border in the St. Elias Mountains of the Yukon Territory. The only other parts of Canada with comparable spectacular mountains are Baffin and Ellesmere Islands in the northeastern Arctic Ocean.

The Torngat Mountains stretch through Quebec, Newfoundland, and Labrador in eastern Canada. The highest point in Quebec is Mont D'Iberville, at 1,652 meters (5,420 feet), within the Torngat range. The Appalachian Chain crosses parts of eastern Canada. In the Appalachians, the highest peak is Mont Jacques-Cartier, at 1,268 meters (4,160 feet).

11 ⊕ CANYONS AND CAVES

Canada has caves in nearly every region. Vancouver Island is commonly called the "Island of Caves" because of the large number of caves located there, many of which have not been explored.

The longest cave in the country is Castleguard Cave in the Banff National Park of Alberta province. It runs about 20,122 meters (66,017 feet) long and about 390 meters (1,280 feet) deep. Banff National Park also contains the Cave and Basin, an area which boasts naturally occurring warm mineral springs. The discovery of the cave in 1883 prompted the government to choose the site as the center of its first national park, making the cave a national historic site as well as a protected area.

Arctomys Cave, in the Canadian Rockies of British Columbia, is the deepest cave in the country and one of the deepest in North America north of Mexico. It has a depth of 536 meters (1,759 feet).

There are a number of canyons throughout the Canadian Rockies, including Johnston, Marble, Cline River, Coral River, Thomson, and Fraser Canyons.

12 ⊕ PLATEAUS AND MONOLITHS

The most prominent geographic feature in the country is the Canadian Shield (sometimes called the Precambrian Shield or the Laurentian Plateau), which takes up almost half of Canada's total area. It extends beyond the Canadian boundary into the United States in two limited areas: at the head of Lake Superior and in the Adirondack Mountains. Structurally,

the shield may be thought of as a huge saucer, the center of which is occupied by Hudson Bay and James Bay, which have breached the northeastern rim to drain into the Atlantic Ocean through the Hudson Strait. Most of the shield is relatively level and less than 612 meters (2,000 feet) above sea level.

Only along the dissected rim of the saucer are there major hills and mountains: the Torngat Mountains. Except for the plains, the rest of the shield is composed of undulating terrain with rocky, knoblike hills; lakes interconnected by rapidly flowing streams occupy the hollows between these hills. A second and far less extensive plateau supports the Western Cordillera.

DID YOU KN⊕W?

The North Magnetic Pole is located at 78°N latitude and 104°W longitude, in the Queen Elizabeth Islands of northern Canada. The earth's magnetic poles represent the two nearly opposite ends of the planet where the earth's magnetic intensity is the greatest. These differ slightly in location from the geographic poles, which are designated as 90°N latitude/0° longitude (North Pole) and 90°S latitude/0° longitude (South Pole). The South Magnetic Pole is located at 66°S latitude and 139°E longitude, on the Adélie Coast of Antarctica.

13 ⊕ MAN-MADE FEATURES

As of 2002, the Syncrude Tailings Dam in Alberta was the largest in the world, based on the total amount of building material used in its construction. It is a barrage dam, created from piled-up dirt and residue (or tailings) left over from mining operations at Syncrude Canada Ltd. The Gardiner Dam in Saskatchewan is the twelfth-largest water-retaining dam in the world. Hydroelectric power from this dam is used across the province. The WAC Bennett Dam, on the Peace River in British Columbia, is responsible for the creation of Williston Lake, the largest artificial lake in Canada (1,761 square kilometers/680 square miles). The Churchill Falls Dam and its underground power station (in Newfoundland) make up the sixth largest hydroelectric plant in the world.

Yoho National Park of British Columbia contains the Spiral Tunnels, carved through the Canadian Rockies by the Canadian Pacific Railroad. The Hector Tunnel is 992 meters (3,255 feet) long and the Field Tunnel is 891 meters (2,922 feet) long.

14 ⊕ FURTHER READING

Books

Flashfield, Jean F. *Cartier: Jacques Cartier in Search of the Northwest Passage.* Minneapolis: Compass Point Books, 2002.

Kalman, Bobbie. *Canada.* New York: Crabtree, 2002.

Malcolm, Andres. *The Land and People of Canada.* New York: HarperCollins, 1988.

MacLean, Doug, comp. *Canadian Geographic Quizbook: Over 1000 Questions on All Aspects of Canadian Geography.* Markham, Ontario: Fitzhenry and Whiteside, Ltd., 2000.

Marx, David F. *Canada.* New York: Children's Press, 2000.

Sorensen, Lynda. *The Wonders of Canada.* Vero Beach, FL: Rourke Book Company, 1995.

Websites

The Atlas of Canada. Facts about Canada. http://www.atlas.gc.ca/site/english/facts/index.html (accessed June 13, 2003).

Canadian Council for Geographic Education. http://www.ccge.cecgeo.org/splash/splash.htm (accessed June 13, 2003).

Cape Verde

- **Official name**: Republic of Cape Verde
- **Area:** 4,033 square kilometers (1,557 square miles)
- **Highest point on mainland:** Mount Fogo (Pico de Cano) (2,829 meters/9,281 feet)
- **Lowest point on land:** Sea level
- **Hemispheres:** Northern and Western
- **Time zone:** 10 A.M. = noon GMT

- **Longest distances:** 332 kilometers (206 miles) from southeast to northwest and 299 kilometers (186 miles) from northeast to southwest
- **Land boundaries:** None
- **Coastline:** 965 kilometers (598 miles)
- **Territorial sea limits:** 22 kilometers (12 nautical miles)

1 ⊕ LOCATION AND SIZE

Cape Verde is an archipelago (chain of islands) off the coast of West Africa. The country consists of ten islands and five islets (small islands) located in the North Atlantic Ocean just west of Senegal. The islands are generally divided into northern (Barlavento) and southern (Sotavento) groups. With a total land area of 4,033 square kilometers (1,557 square miles), the country is slightly larger than the state of Rhode Island. The country is divided into fourteen districts.

2 ⊕ TERRITORIES AND DEPENDENCIES

Cape Verde claims no territories or dependencies.

3 ⊕ CLIMATE

The cold Atlantic Canary Current, in the Atlantic Ocean, creates an arid (almost no rain) atmosphere around the islands. Cape Verde has two seasons. Rainfall is scarce and generally occurs in the latter half of the year. Annual precipitation is only about 13 centimeters (5 inches) in the northern islands and 30 centimeters (12 inches) in the southern ones. Droughts (periodic lack of rainfall) often last for years and can devastate the environment.

SEASON	MONTHS	AVERAGE TEMPERATURE
Winter (dry)	December through June	21°C (70°F)
Summer (slightly rainier)	July through November	27°C (81°F)

4 ⊕ TOPOGRAPHIC REGIONS

Though the Cape Verde islands were formed by volcanic activity, there is currently only one active volcano (Mount Fogo, also called Pico de Cano) on the islands. Most of the islands are mountainous with steep cliffs and ravines. The two districts of Barlavento and Sotavento were determined by the direction of the prevailing northeasterly winds. Barlavento lies windward (closest to the direction from which the wind blows), while Sotavento is leeward (the direction to which the wind blows).

5 ⊕ OCEANS AND SEAS

Seacoast and Undersea Features

The islands of Cape Verde are completely surrounded by the waters of the North Atlantic Ocean. The cold Canary Current runs adjacent to the islands, providing an ideal environment

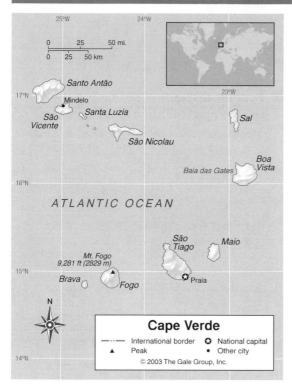

for a fishing industry. The Canary Current is so named because it flows southwestward from Spain through the Canary Islands. The waters around Cape Verde support vibrant colonies of aquatic life, including parrot fish, barracuda, moray eels, several species of whales, dolphins, porpoises, and turtles.

Sea Inlets and Straits

Cape Verde has several fine harbors, with Mindelo on São Vicente being the principal one.

Islands and Archipelagos

The Barlavento islands of Cape Verde include Santo Antão, São Vicente, Santa Luzia (uninhabited), São Nicolau, Sal, Boa Vista, plus two islets. The Sotavento islands include Brava, Fogo, São Tiago, Maio, and three islets.

Coastal Features

The beaches at Baia das Gates on Boa Vista are the most popular among tourists.

6 ⊕ INLAND LAKES

There are no significant lakes in Cape Verde.

7 ⊕ RIVERS AND WATERFALLS

Because of the general drought-like conditions of the islands, there are no significant rivers in Cape Verde. Several small temporary streams may form after heavier rainfalls. There are four islands that have year-round running streams, but these contain very little water.

8 ⊕ DESERTS

Because of Cape Verde's relatively cool climate, its barren, dry islands are not classified as desert.

9 ⊕ FLAT AND ROLLING TERRAIN

With drought, cyclones, volcanic activity, and problems with insect infestation, Cape Verde's land problems are recurrent. Only 11 percent of the land is arable (able to support agriculture) and excessive soil erosion has occurred from raising crops and grazing animals on land that is too arid for such purposes.

EPD/Saxifraga/Piet Zomerdijk

The island of São Vincente is typical of the Cape Verde islands.

CAPE VERDE

UNESCO/Dominique Roger

Coastal view of Cidade Velha on the island of Sao Tiago.

10 ⊕ MOUNTAINS AND VOLCANOES

Except for the low-lying islands of Sal, Boa Vista, and Maio, the Cape Verde islands are quite mountainous with both rugged cliffs and deep ravines. The highest areas receive the most moisture, not as rainfall, but from the condensation of moisture that accumulates off the slopes of the mountains from the Atlantic currents. The terrain is able to support lush vegetation and trees that are typical of both temperate and tropical climates.

The highest peak in Cape Verde is Mount Fogo (also called Pico de Cano), located on the island of Fogo. Mount Fogo stands 2,829 meters (9,281 feet) high and is the only active volcano on the islands, erupting most recently in 1995.

11 ⊕ CANYONS AND CAVES

Deep ravines interlace the cliffs and mountains of the country.

12 ⊕ PLATEAUS AND MONOLITHS

There are no plateau regions on Cape Verde.

13 ⊕ MAN-MADE FEATURES

There are no major man-made structures affecting the geography of Cape Verde.

14 ⊕ FURTHER READING

Irwin, Aisling, and Colum Wilson. *Cape Verde Islands: The Bradt Travel Guide.* Old Saybrook, CT: Globe Pequot Press, 1998.

U.S. Department of State. *Background Notes, Cape Verde.* http://www.state.gov (accessed June 13, 2003).

Central African Republic

- **Official name:** Central African Republic

- **Area:** 622,984 square kilometers (240,534 square miles)

- **Highest point on mainland:** Mount Ngaoui (1,420 meters /4,659 feet)

- **Lowest point on land:** Ubangi River (335 meters /1,099 feet)

- **Hemispheres:** Northern and Eastern

- **Time zone:** 1 P.M. = noon GMT

- **Longest distances:** 1,437 kilometers (893 miles) from east to west; 772 kilometers (480 miles) from north to south

- **Land boundaries:** 5,203 kilometers (3,233 miles) total boundary length; Cameroon, 797 kilometers (495 miles); Chad, 1,197 kilometers (744 miles); Democratic Republic of the Congo, 1,577 kilometers (980 miles); Republic of the Congo, 467 kilometers (290 miles); Sudan, 1,165 kilometers (724 miles)

- **Coastline:** None

- **Territorial sea limits:** None

1 ⊕ LOCATION AND SIZE

In accordance with its name, the landlocked Central African Republic lies roughly at the center of the African continent just north of the equator and more than 603 kilometers (375 miles) from the Atlantic Ocean. Bordered by five neighboring nations, it has an area of 622,984 square kilometers (240,534 square miles), or slightly less than the state of Texas.

2 ⊕ TERRITORIES AND DEPENDENCIES

Central African Republic claims no territories or dependencies.

3 ⊕ CLIMATE

The climate is tropical (hot, sunny, and humid), but is also moderated by rainfall and altitude.

Temperatures average around 27°C (80°F) all year. The harmattan—a hot, dry Saharan wind—affects the climate during the summer months. Rainfall varies, increasing from north to south. The northern part of the country is relatively dry, with an annual average rainfall of about 76 centimeters (30 inches). The northeast, with a semiarid climate, is the driest part of the country. The central plateau region receives up to 152 centimeters (60 inches) of rain per year. Annual rainfall in the southern part of the country averages at least 178 centimeters (70 inches).

SEASON	MONTHS	AVERAGE TEMPERATURE: °CELSIUS (°FAHRENHEIT)
Summer	July and August	21-29°C (70°-84°F)
Winter (dry)	November to April	21-34°C (70°-93°F)

4 ⊕ TOPOGRAPHIC REGIONS

Most of the country consists of a large plateau that separates the basin of Lake Chad to the north from that of the Congo River to the south. The dominant features of the landscape are the Bongo Mountains in the eastern part of the country and the Karre Mountains, otherwise known as Yadé Massif, to the west.

CENTRAL AFRICAN REPUBLIC

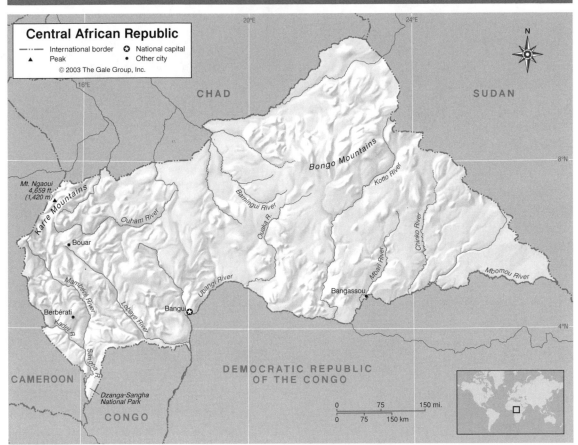

Central African Republic

— · — · — International border ✪ National capital
▲ Peak • Other city
© 2003 The Gale Group, Inc.

CHAD

SUDAN

Bongo Mountains

Kotto River

Mt. Ngaoui
4,659 ft.
(1,420 m)

Karre Mountains

Ouham River

Bamingui River

Ouaka R.

Chinko River

Bouar

Mbari River

Mbomou River

Mambéré River

Lobaye River

Ubangi River

Bangassou

Berbérati

Kadei R.

Bangui

Sangha R.

CAMEROON

DEMOCRATIC REPUBLIC
OF THE CONGO

Dzanga-Sangha
National Park

CONGO

0   75   150 mi.
0   75   150 km

5 ⊕ OCEANS AND SEAS

The Central African Republic is landlocked.

6 ⊕ INLAND LAKES

Many of the country's lakes are seasonal, filling during the rainy season and drying up when the rains stop.

7 ⊕ RIVERS AND WATERFALLS

Two river systems drain the Central African Republic, one flowing southward, the other flowing northward. The Chinko, Mbari, Kotto, Ouaka, and Lobaye Rivers flow south. They are tributaries of the Ubangi River, which forms most of the country's southern border with the Democratic Republic of the Congo. From the conjunction of the Uele and Mbomou Rivers, the Ubangi flows westward along the Congo border from Bangassou. It bends to the south past Bangui to form the border between the Republic of the Congo and the Democratic Republic of the Congo. The Mambéré and Kadei, which also flow south, are tributaries of the Congo River. They join in the southwest to form the Sangha River. The Ouham and Bamingui flow north to Chad to join the Chari River, which continues northward to the Chad Basin.

8 ⊕ DESERTS

The country's northeastern tip, which borders the Sahel, has a semiarid desert climate.

9 ⊕ FLAT AND ROLLING TERRAIN

The valleys of the Chari and Ubangi rivers break up the central plateau in the north and south, respectively.

AP Photo/Christine Nesbitt

Refugees carry their possessions onto a ferry to cross the Ubangi River from Bangui,
Central African Republic, to the Democratic Republic of the Congo in 2002.

10 ⊕ MOUNTAINS AND VOLCANOES

The country's central plateau rises to the Bongo Mountains near the border with Sudan in the northeast, and to the Yadé Massif near the borders with Cameroon and Chad in the northwest. The Bongo Mountains rise to elevations as high as 1,368 meters (4,488 feet) and extend into the Sudan. The granite escarpment (steep slope) of the Yadé Massif in the northwest is a continuation of Cameroon's Adamoua Plateau. It includes Mount Ngaoui, the Central African Republic's highest peak.

11 ⊕ CANYONS AND CAVES

There are no significant caves in the Central African Republic.

12 ⊕ PLATEAUS AND MONOLITHS

An undulating plateau, with elevations roughly between 610 meters and 762 meters (2,000 feet and 2,500 feet), extends across the center of the country. It is covered with grass and scattered groups of trees, crisscrossed by river valleys, ridges, and isolated granite peaks called *kaga*. The plateau's eastern section slopes southward toward the Mbomou and Ubangi Rivers. A large expanse of sandstone is located in the southwestern part of the country near Berbérati and Bouar.

13 ⊕ MAN-MADE FEATURES

National parks include the Bamingui-Bangoran National Park and Saint Floris National Park in the northeast, where the terrain is relatively flat and grassy. Here, visitors can observe

EPD/Evangelical Lutheran Church in America

Much of the terrain is dry in Central African Republic, with scrubby trees the only vegetation.

African "big game" animals—examples of species include elephant, lion, leopard, rhinoceros, giraffe, buffalo, hippopotamus, monkey, baboon, cheetah, crocodile, warthog, galago (also called bushbaby, a large-eyed, long-tailed furry animal), and many types of birds. Poachers have killed so many animals here that some of the species are now endangered. There were once huge herds of elephants in this region, but as of 2002, only a few thousand remained.

The Dzanga-Ndoki Park and Dzanga-Sangha Reserve, in the south, have the last areas of undisturbed rain forest in the country. Tourists may observe lowland gorillas and forest elephants that make the reserve their home. Several species of antelopes, chimpanzees, and monkeys may also be seen.

14 ⊕ FURTHER READING

Books

O'Toole, Thomas. *Central African Republic in Pictures.* Minneapolis: Lerner Publications, 1989.

Periodicals

Hagmann, Michael. "On the Track of Ebola's Hideout?" *Science,* Oct. 22, 1999, 654.

Sillery, Bob. "Urban Rainforest: An African Jungle Comes to Life on New York's West Side." *Popular Science,* March 1998, 70-71.

Web Sites

Africa South of the Sahara (Stanford University). http://www-sul.stanford.edu/depts/ ssrg/africa/centralafr.html (accessed March 4, 2003).

Chad

- **Official name**: Republic of Chad
- **Area:** 1,284,000 square kilometers (495,755 square miles)
- **Highest point on mainland:** Emi Koussi (3,415 meters/11,204 feet)
- **Lowest point on land:** Bodélé Depression (160 meters/525 feet)
- **Hemispheres:** Northern and Eastern
- **Time zone:** 1 P.M. = noon GMT
- **Longest distances:** 1,765 kilometers (1,097 miles) from north to south; 1,030 kilometers (640 miles) from east to west

- **Land boundaries:** 5,968 kilometers (3,708 miles) total boundary length; Libya, 1,055 kilometers (655 miles); Sudan, 1,360 kilometers (845 miles); Central African Republic, 1,195 kilometers (743 miles); Cameroon, 1,094 kilometers (680 miles); Nigeria, 87 kilometers (54 miles); Niger, 1,175 kilometers (730 miles)
- **Coastline:** None
- **Territorial sea limits:** None

1 ⊕ LOCATION AND SIZE

Chad is a landlocked country located in northern Central Africa, south of Libya. It extends north to south for more than 1,609 kilometers (1,000 miles) from the Tropic of Cancer, within the Sahara Desert. It is bordered by Libya to the north; Niger, Nigeria, and Cameroon to the west; and Sudan and the Central African Republic to the east. With an area of 1,284,000 square kilometers (495,755 square miles), Chad is slightly more than three times the size of the state of California. The country is divided into fourteen prefectures (districts).

2 ⊕ TERRITORIES AND DEPENDENCIES

Chad claims no territories or dependencies.

3 ⊕ CLIMATE

From north to south, Chad has three climate zones. In the north, the Sahara Desert swings between extreme temperatures from day to night. In the central Sahel region, where the capital city of N'Djamena is located, the average daily temperatures range from 28°C to 42°C (73°F to 108°F) in April and from 14°C to 33°C (57°F to 91°F) in December. In the southern Sudan region, temperatures are more moderate. The most extreme temperatures in the country range from -12°C (10°F) to 50°C (122°F).

Like the temperatures, rainfall varies considerably from north to south. In the Sahara Desert, annual rainfall averages only 2.5 centimeters (1 inch). In the Sahel, however, average annual rainfall is about 76 centimeters (30 inches). In the Sudan region, average rainfall can be as high as 122 centimeters (48 inches).

Because of sparse rainfall and northern harmattan (hot, dry) winds, the country suffers from periodic droughts (periods with almost no rainfall). Locust plagues (large swarms of grasshoppers which destroy vegetation) are also a problem.

CHAD

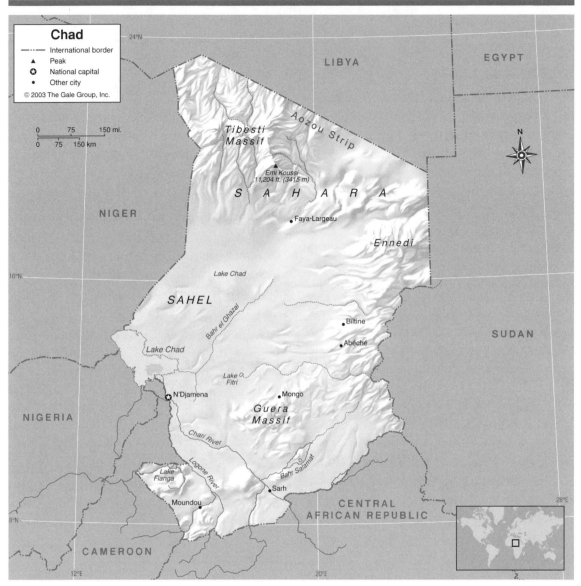

0 75 150 mi.

0 75 150 km

LIBYA

EGYPT

24°N

Tibesti Massif

Aozou Strip

▲ Emi Koussi
11,204 ft. (3415 m)

S A H A R A

NIGER

• Faya-Largeau

Ennedi

16°N

Lake Chad

SAHEL

Bahr el Ghazal

• Biltine

SUDAN

• Abéché

Lake Chad

Lake Fitri

• Mongo

✪ N'Djamena

Guera Massif

NIGERIA

Chari River

Logone River

Lake Fianga

Bahr Salamat

• Sarh

• Moundou

CENTRAL AFRICAN REPUBLIC

28°E

8°N

CAMEROON

12°E

20°E

4 ⊕ TOPOGRAPHIC REGIONS

From the swamp-like regions surrounding Lake Chad and the Chari River system in western Chad, the central portion of the country dips into the shallow bowl of the Bodélé Depression. This basin extends for more than 804 kilometers (500 miles) to the plateaus, mountain ranges, and extinct volcanoes associated with the Tibesti Massif in northern Chad, a major landmark of the Sahara Desert.

Southeast of Lake Chad, an area of relatively flat, sedimentary land extends for several hundred miles before rising gently to the rolling plateaus and scattered low mountains of the eastern and southern border areas.

5 ⊕ OCEANS AND SEAS

Chad is a landlocked country.

6 ⊕ INLAND LAKES

Lake Chad is the country's largest lake, shared by the bordering country of Cameroon. The size of the lake varies from season to season, depending on rainfall, from 10,360 to 25,900 square kilometers (4,000 to 10,000 square miles). It is divided into north and south basins with maximum depths of only about 7.6 meters (25 feet). Its chief tributary, the Chari River, extends southeastward to the Central African Republic. Lake Chad is the largest inland body of water on the Sahel.

A number of very shallow lakes are scattered across the flat plains surrounding Lake Chad. Lake Fitri to the southeast holds water year-round and is a major supplier of fish in the area. Most of the others, however, are temporary lakes that fill with rain or flood waters from the river system. By the end of the annual dry season, their waters have usually evaporated. One of the largest, the Bahr el Ghazal, receives some overflow from Lake Chad during its flood stage. The Lake Chad basin region contains great rolling dunes separated by very deep depressions. In some of these are found oases with groves of date palms.

7 ⊕ RIVERS AND WATERFALLS

The longest river in Chad is the Chari River (also called the Shari). At 1,200 kilometers (720 miles) long, it is also the longest river of interior drainage in Africa. It forms at the junction of the Gubingui and Bamingui Rivers, located at the border with the Central African Republic, and the Chari River then flows northwest into Lake Chad. The Logone River is its chief tributary. The Chari and Logone join near the city of N'Djamena.

Seasonal flooding of the rivers creates swamp-like wetlands in the surrounding areas. These wetlands are often used for irrigation.

There are no permanent streams in northern or central Chad. Summer rainfall collected by the various shallow wadis (seasonally dry streambeds) flows toward inland basins, but most of these streams disappear soon after the end of the brief rainy season.

8 ⊕ DESERTS

Desert covers roughly one-half of the country, beginning with the Saharan Aozou strip along the northern border with Libya and extending into the central and southern Sahel and Sudan regions, which include the Lake Chad basin.

The Sahara Desert, which covers an area of 9,065,000 square kilometers (3,500,000 square miles) is the largest desert in the world. It covers the entire region of North Africa, from the Atlantic coast on the west to the Red Sea on the east. It borders the Mediterranean Sea and the Atlas Mountains in the north and extends into the southern region known as the Sahel.

Sahel is an Arabic word that means "shore." It refers to the 5,000-kilometer-long (3,125-mile-long) stretch of savannah that forms the shore, or edge, of the Sahara Desert. The Sahel spreads west to Mauritania and Senegal and east to Somalia.

Just beyond the Sahel is a region known as the Sudan Desert, south of the Sahara but still north of the equator. It extends from the Atlantic coast of the continent to the mountains of Ethiopia.

9 ⊕ FLAT AND ROLLING TERRAIN

The southern Sudanic climate supports wide areas of savannah grasslands or prairies. Though only 3 percent of the land in Chad is considered arable, 36 percent supports permanent pastures. The Sahel region is covered with

EPD/Robert J. Groelsema

Chadian fishermen use nets to haul in their daily catch.

a carpet of brilliant green grass following the first rains of the season. These grasses, with thorn trees interspersed throughout, often exist for several months of the year before disappearing in the dry season. Palms and acacia trees also grow in this region.

Isolated hills found in the southwest region of the country do not generally exceed elevations of 457 meters (1,500 feet). These rocky outcroppings, which resemble piles of boulders, rise unexpectedly over the flat and gently rolling landscape, but they support only sparse vegetation.

The low-lying area of the Bodélé Depression is within the Sahel region. This area dips to 160 meters (525 feet) above sea level, the lowest point in the country. The basin was probably a part of Lake Chad in prehistoric times.

10 ⊕ MOUNTAINS AND VOLCANOES

The highest mountains in Chad are found in the Tibesti Massif, located at the northern border of the country. This volcanic mountain range covers an area that is about 563 kilometers (350 miles) long. It is the highest mountain range in the Sahara Desert and includes seven main volcanoes. Of these, Emi Koussi is the highest peak in Chad.

Emi Koussi rises to an altitude of 3,415 meters (11,204 feet). Now an extinct volcano, it has a crater that is 19 kilometers (12 miles) wide and 1,219 meters (4,000 feet) deep.

11 ⊕ CANYONS AND CAVES

There are no significant canyons or caves in Chad.

12 ⊕ PLATEAUS AND MONOLITHS

From the central bowl to southern Chad, the land slopes upward almost imperceptibly to rolling plateaus, which for the most part are less than 610 meters (2,000 feet) above sea level. The plateaus are marked here and there by mountains, such as the Guera Massif near Mongo, which has at least one peak above 1,493 meters (4,900 feet).

13 ⊕ MAN-MADE FEATURES

In 2000, the petroleum producers ExxonMobil and Chevron of the United States and Petronas of Malaysia began to develop the oil resources of southern Chad. The pipeline under construction will stretch 1,070 kilometers (670 miles) from the fields in Chad to a port on the Cameroon coast. It is scheduled to become operational in 2003.

14 ⊕ FURTHER READING

Books

Birmingham, David, and Phyllis Martin, eds. *History of Central Africa*. London: Longman, 1983.

Collelo, Thomas. *Chad: A Country Study*. Washington, DC: General Printing Office, 1990.

Decalo, Samuel. *Historical Dictionary of Chad*. 2nd ed. Metuchen, NJ: Scarecrow Press, 1987.

Web Sites

National Geographic. http://www.national geographic.com (accessed June 17, 2003).

Volcano World - The University of North Dakota. http://www.volcano.und.nodak.edu (accessed June 17, 2003).

Chile

- **Official name:** Republic of Chile
- **Area:** 756,950 square kilometers (292,260 square miles)
- **Highest point on mainland:** Ojos del Salado (6,880 meters/22,573 feet)
- **Lowest point on land:** Sea level
- **Hemispheres:** Southern and Western
- **Time zone:** 8 A.M. = noon GMT
- **Longest distances:** 356 kilometers (221 miles) from east to west; 4,270 kilometers (2,653 miles) from north to south

- **Land boundaries:** 6,171 kilometers (3,835 miles) total boundary length; Argentina, 5,150 kilometers (3,200 miles); Bolivia, 861 kilometers (535 miles); Peru, 160 kilometers (99 miles)
- **Coastline:** 6,435 kilometers (3,999 miles)
- **Territorial sea limits:** 22 kilometers (12 nautical miles)

1 ⊕ LOCATION AND SIZE

Chile is a long, narrow country fringing the southwestern edge of South America, between the Pacific Ocean to the west and the Andes Mountains to the east. It reaches to Cape Horn, the southernmost tip of the continent, and it touches the Atlantic Ocean at the Strait of Magellan. It also extends beyond the Strait of Magellan to include part of Tierra del Fuego, an archipelago that it shares with Argentina. The Andes Mountains span almost the full length of the country, which has an area of 756,950 square kilometers (292,260 square miles), or slightly less than the state of Montana. Measuring 4,270 kilometers (2,653 miles) between its northern and southern extremities, Chile has an average width of not much more than 161 kilometers (100 miles), making it the world's longest and narrowest country. Its 38-degree latitude span gives it an extremely varied climate and vegetation.

2 ⊕ TERRITORIES AND DEPENDENCIES

Chile has several island dependencies in the Pacific Ocean, including Easter Island, which is situated more than 3,218 kilometers (2,000 miles) west of the mainland. The most remote possession of any Latin American country, Easter Island is volcanic land mass with an area of 117 kilometers (45 miles) and a subtropical climate. Chile's other island possessions are Sala y Gómez, San Felix, San Ambrosio, and the Juan Fernandez Islands. Like Easter Island, these islands are preserved as part of a national park. Chile is also one of several nations that claim land in Antarctica.

3 ⊕ CLIMATE

Due to its great length, Chile covers a wide range of latitudes, so its climate varies considerably. Temperatures steadily cool as the country extends southward, away from the equator and toward Antarctica. The mean temperature at Arica, in the far north, is 18°C (64°F), while that of Santiago, in the center of the country, is 14°C (57°F), and

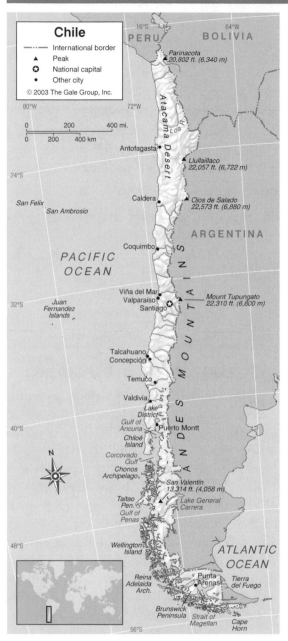

Chile

- ----- International border
- ▲ Peak
- ✪ National capital
- • Other city

© 2003 The Gale Group, Inc.

PERU
BOLIVIA
Parinacota
20,802 ft. (6,340 m)
Atacama Desert
Antofagasta
Llullaillaco
22,057 ft. (6,722 m)
Caldera
Ojos de Salado
22,573 ft. (6,880 m)
San Felix
San Ambrosio
ARGENTINA
Coquimbo
PACIFIC OCEAN
Juan Fernandez Islands
Viña del Mar
Valparaíso
Santiago
Mount Tupungato
22,310 ft. (6,800 m)
ANDES MOUNTAINS
Talcahuano
Concepción
Temuco
Valdivia
Lake District
Gulf of Ancuna
Puerto Montt
Chiloé Island
Corcovado Gulf
Chonos Archipelago
San Valentin
13,314 ft. (4,058 m)
Taitao Pen.
Lake General Carrera
Gulf of Penas
Wellington Island
ATLANTIC OCEAN
Reina Adelaida Arch.
Punta Arenas
Tierra del Fuego
Brunswick Peninsula
Strait of Magellan
Cape Horn

ated seasons; its winters are mild, and its summers are warm and dry.

The southern part of the country is subject to frequent storms.

While average temperatures in Chile steadily drop with increasing southerly latitude, the amount of rainfall gradually rises. It ranges from virtually no precipitation north of 27°S latitude to around 406 centimeters (160 inches) annually at 48°S latitude (the heaviest precipitation in any region outside the tropics). Between these extremes are Copiapó at 3 centimeters (1 inch), Santiago at 33 centimeters (13 inches), and Puerto Montt at 185 centimeters (73 inches). In the far south, precipitation once again decreases, to 46 centimeters (18 inches) at Punta Arenas. Snow and sleet are common in the southern third of the country. The coastal archipelagos are among the world's rainiest regions.

4 ⊕ TOPOGRAPHIC REGIONS

Chile is commonly divided into regions by latitude from north to south. Major regions are: the Norte Grande (a desert); the Norte Chico (a semiarid region); the Central Valley (a temperate heartland); the south-central region (a dense rain forest and the picturesque Lake District); and the southern region (a cold and windswept landscape). The coastline of the southern region includes thousands of islands, extending down to Cape Horn.

5 ⊕ OCEANS AND SEAS

Chile borders the South Pacific Ocean, and the curved southernmost portion of its coast reaches to the Atlantic Ocean at the Strait of Magellan. The Humboldt Current, an ocean current flowing northward from Antarctica, chills the waters of the Pacific off the Chilean coast.

Punta Arenas in the extreme south averages 6°C (43°F). Winter temperatures are moderated by winds off the Pacific Ocean, and sea winds also temper the heat in summer.

Central Chile, where most of the country's population is concentrated, has a pleasant Mediterranean climate, with well-differenti-

Mountain peaks in Lauca National Park in northern Chile.

Seacoast and Undersea Features

Chile's offshore islands consist of submerged mountaintops that are a continuation of the Andes Mountains.

Sea Inlets and Straits

At the southern tip of the country, the Strait of Magellan lies between Tierra del Fuego and the rest of Chile, providing Chile with an opening to the Atlantic Ocean. Numerous other inlets separate the islands of Chile's southern coast, including the Gulf of Corcovado, the Gulf of Penas, and the Nelson Strait.

Islands and Archipelagos

The southern third of the Chilean coast consists of an extensive series of islands and archipelagos stretching for some 1,130 kilometers (700 miles). Separated by thin channels and fjords, they form a long chain from Chiloé Island slightly south of Puerto Montt to Tierra del Fuego. Cape Horn, located on an island to the south of Tierra del Fuego, is the southernmost point in South America.

Coastal Features

There are few beaches and natural harbors along Chile's long, narrow coast. In the north, the coastal mountains rise close to the shoreline in steep cliffs; however, rocky outcroppings do provide good protection from the sea at the harbors of Valparaíso and Talcahuano. The Brunswick Peninsula, separated from Tierra del Fuego by the Strait of Magellan, is the southernmost point on mainland South America.

6 ⊕ INLAND LAKES

There is a picturesque district of lakes, hills, and waterfalls at the eastern edge of the Central Valley, between Concepción and Puerto Montt. In the southern part of this district lies

EPD/Saxifraga/Wiel Poelmans

Mountainous landscape of northern Chile.

Lake Llanquihue, the country's largest lake, and the third-largest natural lake in South America. It has a maximum length of 35 kilometers (22 miles), a maximum width of 40 kilometers (25 miles), and maximum depths of 1,500 meters (5,000 feet).

7 ⊕ RIVERS AND WATERFALLS

Because most of Chile's rivers flow across the narrow country in a westward direction—down the Andes and into the Pacific—they are short. Nevertheless, their steep path down the mountainsides makes them a good source for hydroelectric power. There are around thirty rivers, including the Loa, Aconcagua, Huasco, Coquimbo, Limari, Mapocho, Maule, Maipo, Bío-Bío, Copiapó, and Toltén. The longest is the Loa River in the north.

8 ⊕ DESERTS

The Atacama Desert, which extends from the northern border to the Aconcagua River,

consists largely of dry river basins and salt flats, with a few rivers and oases. It is both the warmest and driest part of the country, and is said to be the world's driest desert. The region immediately to the south of the Atacama Desert is semiarid.

9 ⊕ FLAT AND ROLLING TERRAIN

Chile has no notable flat or rolling terrain.

10 ⊕ MOUNTAINS AND VOLCANOES

The Andes Mountains reach their greatest elevations in Chile, where they span nearly the entire length of the country, starting with the peaks of the Atacama Desert in the north. The Andes chain forms most of Chile's border with Argentina to the east. The crests of the Andean range are higher in the northern half of the country. In this northern sector is Ojos del Salado, Chile's loftiest peak, and—at more than 6,857 meters (22,500 feet)—the second-highest point in the Western Hemisphere. Chile's tallest volcano, Guallatiri (6,060 meters/19,882 feet) lies in the far north, near the borders with Bolivia and Peru. A little to the south, near the borders with Bolivia and Argentina, lies Lascar (5,990/19,652), another volcano.

South of Santiago, the peaks of the Andes become progressively lower. In the far south, the Andes continue to decline in elevation, merging into the lowlands of Chilean Patagonia on both sides of the Strait of Magellan. The mountain system makes a final appearance at Cape Horn, which is also the crest of a submerged mountain.

By contrast, the peaks and plateaus of the coastal mountain range in the west are lower than those of the Andes, with elevations ranging from 300 to 2,100 meters (1,000 to 7,000 feet) in the northern half of the country. The system declines in elevation south of Valparaíso and plunges into the sea in the far south. Its peaks reappear as the islands of the southern archipelagos.

DID YOU KN🌐W?

Chile has experienced many earthquakes throughout history, including the worst earthquake ever to occur anywhere on Earth since 1960, as measured by the U.S. Geological Service. This earthquake, centered just off the Chilean coast on May 22, 1960, registered 8.6 on the Richter scale. On July 30, 1995, an earthquake measuring 8.0 on the Richter scale struck near the northern coast of Chile, causing three deaths and leaving hundreds of people homeless.

11 ⊕ CANYONS AND CAVES

The Cueva del Milodon (Cave of the Milodon) National Park features a 30-meter-deep (100-foot-deep) cave. The milodon is a mythical prehistoric animal believed to have been a plant-eating mammal that was twice the size of a human. The caves in the park also house remnants of human settlements. Archaeologists believe ancient humans lived in these caves thousands of years ago.

12 ⊕ PLATEAUS AND MONOLITHS

In northern Chile, there are dry, barren plateau basins at elevations of 610 to 1,219 meters (2,000 to 4,000 feet) between the eastern and western mountain ranges. In the north-central part of the country, much of this plateau land gives way to spurs of the Andes, with fertile valleys in between.

13 ⊕ MAN-MADE FEATURES

Chile has no significant man-made features affecting its geography.

14 ⊕ FURTHER READING

Books

Bernhardson, Wayne. *Chile & Easter Island: A Lonely Planet Travel Atlas.* Hawthorn, Victoria, Australia: Lonely Planet Publications, 1997.

Hickman, John. *News from the End of the Earth: A Portrait of Chile.* New York: St. Martin's Press, 1998.

Wheeler, Sara. *Travels in a Thin Country: A Journey Through Chile.* New York: Modern Library, 1999.

Web Sites

Chile Online. http://www. chile-online.com/ (accessed March 10, 2003).

Lonely Planet World Guide. http://www.lonely planet.com/destinations/south_america/chile_and_easter_island/ (accessed June 29, 2003).

China

- **Official name**: People's Republic of China
- **Area:** 9,596,960 square kilometers (3,705,407 square miles)
- **Highest point on mainland:** Mount Everest (8,850 meters/29,035 feet)
- **Lowest point on land:** Turpan Pendi (154 meters/505 feet below sea level)
- **Hemispheres:** Northern and Eastern
- **Time zone:** 8 P.M. = noon GMT in East; 5 p.m. = noon GMT in West.
- **Longest distances:** 845 kilometers (525 miles) from east-southeast to west-southwest; 3,350 kilometers (2,082 miles) from south-southeast to north-northwest
- **Land boundaries:** 22,147 kilometers (13,762 miles) total boundary length; Afghanistan, 76 kilometers (47 miles); Bhutan, 470 kilometers (292 miles); Myanmar, 2,185 kilometers (1,358 miles); Hong Kong, 30 kilometers (19 miles); India, 3,380 kilometers (2,100 miles); Kazakhstan, 1,533 kilometers (953 miles); Kyrgyzstan, 858 kilometers (533 miles); Laos, 423 kilometers (263 miles); Mongolia, 4,677 kilometers (2,906 miles); Nepal, 1,236 kilometers (768 miles); North Korea, 1,416 kilometers (880 miles); Pakistan, 523 kilometers (325 miles); Russia, 3,645 kilometers (2,265 miles); Tajikistan, 414 kilometers (257 miles); Vietnam, 1,281 kilometers (796 miles)
- **Coastline:** 14,500 kilometers (9,010 miles)
- **Territorial sea limits:** 22 kilometers (12 nautical miles)

1 ⊕ LOCATION AND SIZE

China is located in eastern Asia, west of the East China Sea, Korea Bay, Yellow Sea, and South China Sea. The country is bordered by fourteen other nations. With a total area of about 9,596,960 square kilometers (3,705,407 square miles), the country is slightly smaller than the United States. China is administratively divided into twenty-three provinces, five autonomous (self-governing) regions, and four municipalities.

2 ⊕ TERRITORIES AND DEPENDENCIES

Most international governments recognize Taiwan as an independent country; China, however, strongly disagrees with the rest of the world. It claims Taiwan as one of its provinces. The Special Administrative Regions of Hong Kong and Macau, located near the southeast edge of China, both maintain largely independent political and economic government structures; they are governed by China, however, in matters of foreign affairs and defense.

3 ⊕ CLIMATE

Most of the country enjoys a temperate climate, but since the country is so large with such variations in altitude, many extremes in climate do exist. At the highest elevations in southwestern China, there are only fifty frost-free days per year. The hottest spot in China is in northwestern China in the Turpan Pendi, where summer highs can reach 47°C (116°F). Winter temperatures in northern China often drop to as low as -27°C (-17°F), and even in summer, they reach just 12°C (54°F). In the

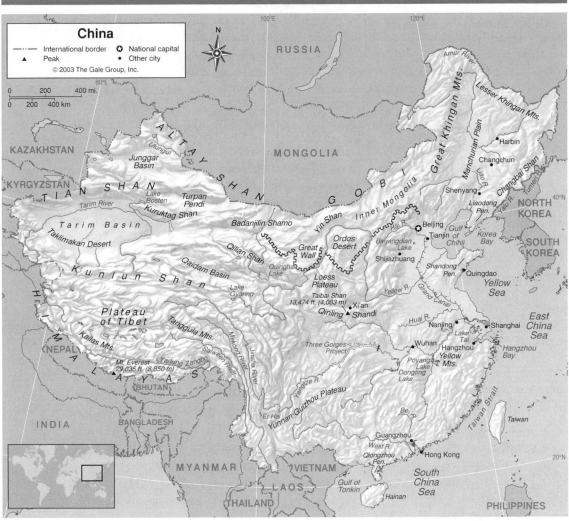

Yangtze River valley, the mean temperature in summer is 29°C (85°F).

Most of the country's rainfall occurs during the summer months. Rainfall is heaviest in the southeast, averaging 200 centimeters (80 inches) per year. In the northeastern region near Beijing, annual rainfall averages about 60 centimeters (25 inches). In the far northwest, the annual rainfall averages 10 centimeters (4 inches), although some desert regions may go a year or longer with no precipitation. Along the southern coast, severe storms are common, with destructive typhoons occasionally occurring.

4 ⊕ TOPOGRAPHIC REGIONS

The vast territory of China exhibits great variation in terrain and vegetation. The highest elevations are found in the far southwest in the Plateau of Tibet (Xizang Gaoyuan) and the Himalayas. The high elevations of the western portion of the country, which cover more than half of the overall territory, have cold temperatures and generally arid conditions that prevent the development of agriculture. As a result, the

EPD/Cynthia Bassett

Chinese farmers carve terraces into the land to grow rice.

western region is more isolated and much more sparsely populated than the eastern areas.

The eastern quarter of the country is mostly lowlands and may be divided into northern China and the slightly larger southern China, separated from each other by the Yellow River and the Qinling Shandi (Ch'in Ling Shan) mountain range. In the northeastern region is the large Manchurian Plain. The Gobi Desert is separated from the Manchurian Plain by the Great Khingan Mountains, which occupy a northeastern region of China straddling the China-Mongolia border. To the southeast, the heavily populated Loess Plateau stretches from Beijing to Nanjing across the valley of the Yellow River.

China lies entirely on the Eurasian Tectonic Plate. The Tibetan region in the southwest, however, straddles the boundary of the Indian and Eurasian Tectonic Plates. Seismic fault lines also run north to south through the

eastern region of China and the Manchurian Plain. Consequently, both the northeast and southwest regions are centers of seismic activity and experience periodic earthquakes, some of which have been devastating.

China's varied terrain supports diverse populations of plants, birds, reptiles, amphibians, and mammals. China's more than one hundred unique wildlife species include the giant panda, the golden-haired monkey, the South China tiger, the Chinese alligator, the freshwater white-flag dolphin, and the red-crowned crane. The metasequoia, found only in China, is believed to be one of the oldest tree species in the world.

5 ⊕ OCEANS AND SEAS

Seacoast and Undersea Features

The waters surrounding China are principally seas of the Pacific Ocean. From north to south along the western coast, they include the

Yellow Sea (Huang Hai), East China Sea (Dong Hai), and the South China Sea (Nan Hai). The South China Sea features a deep ocean floor. Elsewhere, the continental shelf supports coastal fish farms and also contains substantial oil deposits.

Sea Inlets and Straits

Korea Bay and the Gulf of Chihli (Bo Hai), both inlets of the Yellow Sea, have substantial amounts of sea ice. Korea Bay separates the Liaodong Peninsula from North Korea. The turbulent waters of the Gulf of Chihli are relatively shallow, at 20 meters (70 feet). Also, the coastal area of the Gulf of Chihli has extensive wetlands, including riverine wetland, marshes, and salt marshes. The Taiwan Strait lies between the mainland and the island of

---

DID YOU KN🌐W?

The Silk Road is an ancient, seven-thousand-mile-long trading route that extended from east-central China through the present day countries of India, Pakistan, Iran, Iraq, and Syria. It essentially connected the region of the Yellow River Valley to the Mediterranean Sea. From there, costly Chinese silk could be transported throughout the Roman Empire. The Silk Road served not only as a transportation route for trade but also as a route of cultural exchange; travelers and traders from different regions shared their religious, political, and social beliefs and customs with one another.

Taiwan. The Gulf of Tonkin lies off the coast of Guangxi, the extreme southeastern province of China, located between Hainan Island and Vietnam.

Islands and Archipelagos

There are more than five thousand islands lying off the eastern coast of China. Taiwan (with an area of 36,000 square kilometers/ 22,500 square miles) is the largest. Hainan Island (about 34,000 square kilometers /21,250 square miles) is the second-largest island, but it is the largest which is fully under the jurisdiction of China. Other neighboring islands include the Spratly Islands, the Diaoyutai Islands, the Paracel Islands, and the Pescadores. The ownership of all of these islands groups is under dispute.

Coastal Features

China's coastline extends more than 14,500 kilometers (9,010 miles). More than half the coastline (predominantly in the south) is rocky, while most of the remainder is sandy. The Hangzhou Bay (Hangzhou Wan), just south of Shanghai, roughly divides the two types of shoreline.

The Shandong Peninsula juts out at the northernmost reach of the Yellow Sea. It features the dramatic and sacred peak, Tai Shan (1,530 meters/5,069 feet). North of the Shandong Peninsula, the coastline curves around another land mass: the Liaodong Peninsula. This peninsula separates Korea Bay from the Gulf of Chihli. In the south, separating the Gulf of Tonkin from the South China Sea, the narrow Qiongzhou Peninsula extends out from the mainland at China's southernmost point and almost touches Hainan Island.

The coastal areas of China are the most densely populated regions, containing more than 400 people per square kilometer (1,036 people per square mile). Bustling port cities lie along the coast, from Shanghai near the Yangtze Delta to Guangzhou (Canton), where the West River and Bei River join to become the Pearl River.

6 ⊕ INLAND LAKES

Qinghai Lake is currently China's largest lake and the third-largest salt lake in the world, with an area of 4,209 square kilometers (1,625 square miles). The lake is slowly drying up, however, shrinking a little bit each year. It is located in the Qaidam Basin, a sandy and swampy basin that contains many other salt lakes, including Lakes Ngoring and Gyaring.

Poyang Hu is the largest freshwater lake in China with a surface area of 2,779 square kilometers (1,073 square miles). It is found on the south Yangtze River in southeast China.

Dongting Hu is a large, shallow lake also south of the Yangtze. About 40 percent of the Yangtze's water travels through several channels into the lake. Lake Tai is located at the base of Mount Yu Shan on the other side of the Great Canal, just inland from Shanghai. Baiyangdian Lake (360 square kilometers/140 square miles) is used as a water source for the region just to the southwest of Beijing, which is home to hundreds of thousands of people. The lake is drying up due to overuse for industrial and agricultural production and drinking water, as well as a result of recurring drought.

There are several other notable lakes in China, many of which are located in the various mountain ranges, catching water from the many mountain streams. Erhai Lake is a freshwater lake on the plateau of Yunnan. Tianchi Lake (Heavenly Lake) lies in the Tian Shan Mountains in the northwest, about 115 kilometers (70 miles) northeast of Ürümqi. Also in the northwest between the Tian Shan and Kuruktag Shan Mountains is Lake Bosten, which receives the Kaidu River and other streams.

EPD/Cynthia Bassett

The giant panda is one of the many unique animal species found in China.

7 ⊕ RIVERS AND WATERFALLS

China's most important rivers lie in the eastern and northeastern part of the country. The three major river systems here are the Yangtze River (Chang Jiang), the Yellow River (Huang He), and the Hai River. The Yangtze is found south of the Kunlun and Qinling Mountains. It is the longest river in China—5,525 kilometers (3,434 miles)—and is navigable over much of its length. The Yangtze begins on the Plateau of Tibet and flows east through the heart of the country, draining an area of 1.8 million square kilometers (694,000 million square miles) before emptying into the East China Sea. The large Jinsha River is a major tributary of the upper Yangtze. The Hai River rises southwest of Beijing and flows through several lakes before joining the Yangtze.

Flowing initially northeast from its source in the Kunlun Shan, the Yellow River follows a winding path, measuring 4,671 kilometers (2,903 miles), as it courses toward the sea through the Loess Plateau. It is China's second-longest river. Over the centuries, the Yellow River has become choked with silt as it brings down a heavy load of sand and mud from its upper reaches, much of which is deposited on the flat plain. The water travels through artificial embankments that require constant repair. After years of these repairs, the river now actually flows on a raised ridge, the riverbed having risen 50 meters (164 feet) or more above the plain.

The Hai River flows west to east and is located north of the Yellow River. Its upper course consists of five rivers that converge near Tianjin, then flow 70 kilometers (43 miles) before emptying into the Gulf of Chihli.

Other significant rivers in northeastern China include the Amur River (Heilong Jiang), which flows a total 4,350 kilometers (2,719 miles) through Russia and China; the Liao River; and the Yalu River, which, along with the Tumen River, forms the border with North Korea. The largest river flowing in the southeast is the Pearl River (Zhu Jiang). The Pearl River flows to form the large Boca Tigris estuary between Hong Kong and Macau, linking Guangzhou to the South China Sea. The West River in southeastern China is an important commercial waterway. All of these rivers drain into the Pacific Seas.

Between the high mountains of the north and northwest, the rivers have no outlet to the sea. Many such waterways terminate in lakes or else diminish in the desert. A few are useful for irrigation. The largest of these rivers are the Konqi, the Kaidu, the Ulungur, and the Tarim.

Its length of 2,179 kilometers (1,354 miles) makes the Tarim River China's longest river without an outlet to the sea.

8 ⊕ DESERTS

One of the significant problems facing China is desertification. Currently, the total desert area comprises more than 2.6 million square kilometers (1 million square miles), or about 30 percent of the country's total land area. In the extreme west of the country, between two east-west mountain ranges, lies the Tarim Basin, where Asia's driest desert, the Taklimakan Desert, is found. Brutal sandstorms, arid conditions, extreme temperatures, and the remoteness of the area have prevented any significant exploitation of the vast petroleum reserves of this desert region. The Gobi Desert lies along the northern border with Mongolia. In China, the Badanjilin Shamo forms the southern limit of the Gobi. Much of the Gobi is mountainous, stark terrain. The Ordos (or Mu Us) Desert is the extension of the Gobi that lies along the southern edge of Inner Mongolia (Nei Mongol).

9 ⊕ FLAT AND ROLLING TERRAIN

Only about 12 percent of China's land area may be classified as grasslands. Because of the country's size, however, there are still some significant plains regions. A principal feature of the south-central part of China is the fertile plain that is home to the Yangtze River. To the south of the river, a large plate-shaped section of the plain surrounds Lake Tai.

The Loess Plateau is mainly a large plain, also known as the North China Plain. It is actually a continuation of the central Manchurian Plain to the northeast, but is separated from it by the Gulf of Chihli. The Han people, China's largest ethnic group, have farmed the rich alluvial soils of the plain since ancient times, constructing the Grand Canal (Dayun He) for north-south transport.

EPD/Cynthia Bassett

Animals graze in a wide valley in Guizhou Province in southern China.

There are also grasslands in the massive Tarim Basin and the Junggar Basin in China's northwest corridor. Rich deposits of coal, oil, and metallic ores lie in this area. The Tarim is China's largest inland basin, measuring 1,500 kilometers (932 miles) from east to west and 600 kilometers (373 miles) from north to south at its widest parts.

Being so mountainous, China has many hill regions between and at the feet of the various ranges. There are also some notable hilly regions in the south, along the coastline of the South China Sea, where farmers must carve terraces into the land to grow rice.

10 ⊕ MOUNTAINS AND VOLCANOES

Mountains cover more than two-thirds of the nation's territory, impeding communication and leaving only limited areas of level land for agriculture. The Himalayas form a natural boundary with countries on the southwest. Similarly, the Altay Shan Mountains form the extreme northwest border with Mongolia.

The Himalayas are the highest mountains on Earth. They extend along a 2,414-kilometer (1,500-mile) arc from Jammu and Kashmir in the northwest to where the Brahmaputra River cuts south through the mountains near the Myanmar border. This range forms much of China's western and all of its southwestern international borders. Mount Everest, the world's highest mountain—8,850 meters (29,035 feet)—is found in this region on the border between Nepal and China. Seven of the world's nineteen peaks with summit elevations greater than 7,000 meters (23,000 feet) are also located here.

CHINA

SACRED MOUNTAIN PEAKS IN CHINA			
Name	**Location**	**Height**	**Religion**
Bei Heng Shan	Shanxi Province	3,060 meters (10,095 feet)	Taoism
Nan Heng Shan	Hunan Province	1,282 meters (4,232 feet)	Taoism
Hua Shan	Shanxi Province (along the Yellow River)	1,985 meters (6,552 feet)	Taoism
Song Shan	Henan Province (along the Yellow River)	1,485 meters (4,900 feet)	Taoism
Tai Shan	Shandong Province	1,530 meters (5,069 feet)	Taoism
Emei Shan	Sichuan Provnice	3,060 meters (10,095 feet)	Buddhism
Jiuhua Shan	Anhui Province	1,322 meters (4,340 feet)	Buddhism
Putuo Shan	Zhejiang Province	282 meters (932 feet)	Buddhism

Moving north from the Himalayas, several ranges also run west to east, including the Kailas Mountains (Gangdisê Shan), Tanggula Mountains, the Kunlun Shan, the Kuruktag Shan, the Qilian Shan, and the Tian Shan. The Tian Shan stretch across China between Kyrgyzstan and Mongolia. The Qinling Shandi (Ch'in Ling Shan), a continuation of the Kunlun Shan, divides the Loess Plateau from the Yangtze River Delta. The Qinling Shandi forms both geographic and cultural boundaries between the two great parts of China. To the south lie the densely populated and highly developed areas of the lower and middle plains of the Yangtze. To the north are the more remote, more sparsely populated areas.

In the far northeast, north of the Great Wall, the Great Khingan Mountains (Da Hinggan Ling) form a barrier along the border with Mongolia, extending from the Amur to the Liao River in a north-south orientation, with elevations reaching 1,715 meters (5,660 feet). The Lesser Khingan Mountains (Xiao Hinggan Ling) line the northeastern border with Russia. To the east, along the border with Korea, lie the Changbai Shan (Forever White Mountains), where snow covers the peaks year-round.

The Yellow Mountains (Huang Shan), southwest of Shanghai, contain seventy-two peaks, the tallest of which is Lianhua Feng (Lotus Flower Peak) at 1,864 meters (6,151 feet). The Yellow Mountains region also includes hot mineral springs, where the water temperature is constant at 42°C (108°F).

11 ⊕ CANYONS AND CAVES

The Grand Yarlung Zangbo Canyon in the Tibet autonomous region is the largest canyon in the world at 505 kilometers (316 miles) long and 6,009 meters (10,830 feet) deep. The Yarlung Zangbo, the river that eventually becomes the Bramaputra, carved this canyon.

The Three Gorges, a famous 322-kilometer-deep (200-mile-deep) canyon on the Yangtze, will be submerged when the Three Gorges Dam becomes operational in 2009. The Hutiaojian ("Tiger Leaping") Canyon, located along the Jinsha River, an upper tributary of the Yangtze, is one of the world's deepest canyons at 3,000 meters (9,900 feet) deep.

There are a large number of natural and hand-carved caves in China that were created and used by religious monks and followers. The Longmen Grottoes in the city of Luoyang contain one of the largest collections of Chinese and Buddhist art of the late Northern Wei and Tang Dynasties (c. 316-907 A.D.), including statues carved into rock, sculptured walls and ceilings, and rock paintings. The site has about 2,345 caves.

The Yungang Grottoes, in Datong city, contain similar Chinese and Buddhist art, including about 51,000 statues in 252 caves. The Magao Grottoes in Dunhuang (also called the Dunhuang Grottoes) are located along the old Silk Road of China. This region features 492 caves with an estimated 45,000 square meters of frescos and 2,415 painted statues. Nearly fifty thousand artifacts were found in Magao, including Buddhist scriptures, historical documents, textiles, and other relics. All of these cave sites have been designated as United Nations Educational, Scientific, and Cultural Organization (UNESCO) World Heritage Sites.

12 ⊕ PLATEAUS AND MONOLITHS

About 25 percent of China's total area may be characterized as plateau. The Plateau of Tibet is in China's southwest, enclosed by the Himalayas and the Kunlun Shan. It is the highest and most extensive plateau in the world, incorporating some 2.3 million square kilometers (888,000 square miles) with elevations that average more than 4,000 meters (13,123 feet) above sea level. The loftiest summits rise to over 7,200 meters (23,622 feet). It is referred to as the "roof of the world," and the land there continues to rise, gaining an average of 10 millimeters (0.04 inches) per year in elevation. North of Tibet rise two more plateaus : the Tarim Basin and the Junggar Basin. In these regions, the elevation averages 4,600 meters (15,000 feet). The Tian Shan range separates the two plateaus.

The Inner Mongolia (Nei Mongol) Plateau, China's second-largest plateau, lies in the northeast near the border with Mongolia. It covers an area of about 1,000,000 square ki-lometers (386,100 square miles), with 2,000 kilometers (1,250 miles) stretching from east to west and 500 kilometers (300 miles) from north to south. The elevation averages between 1,000 and 2,000 meters (3,300 to 6,600 feet).

To the south is Loess Plateau, the third largest plateau in China, covering 600,000 square kilometers (308,881 square miles). The plateau is covered by a layer of loess, a yellowish soil blown in from the deserts of Inner Mongolia. The loess layer ranges from 100 to 200 meters (330 to 660 feet) in depth and rises to elevations that range from 800 to 2,000

DID YOU KN⊕W?

The Great Wall of China is one of the largest structures ever built by humans. Construction began around the seventh and eighth centuries B.C. Most of the Great Wall along the country's northern flank, the east-west extent of which is more than 3,300 kilometers (2,050 miles), was completed about 220 B.C. The wall was built as a barrier against invaders and became, for a time, the world's largest military structure. In its most complete stage, it stretched across 6,000 kilometers (3,729 miles) of mountainous and desert terrain in northeastern China. Today, some of the sections are in ruins or seriously decayed. Several segments remain intact and are visited by tourists, however, including guard towers.

meters (2,640 to 6,600 feet). The Loess Plateau experiences some of the most severe soil erosion conditions of anywhere in the world.

The last notable plateau in China is the Yunnan-Guizhou plateau in the southwest. The smallest plateau in China, it features unusual geology with dramatic stone outcroppings and overhangs.

13 ⊕ MAN-MADE FEATURES

In 1994, work began on the seventeen-year-long project to construct the world's largest dam on the Yangtze. The Three Gorges Dam will be the largest hydroelectric dam in the world, measuring just over 2 kilometers (about a mile) across and 185 meters (610 feet) high when it is completed (projected for 2009). Its reservoir is expected to extend more than 560 kilometers (350 miles) upstream, flooding the towns and villages that are home to an estimated two million people, all of whom will be forced to relocate when the dam is completed.

The Grand Canal (Dayun He), running from Beijing in the north to Hangzhou in the south, is the longest (1,801 kilometers/1,126 feet) and oldest artificial canal in the world. It links five rivers: the Hai River, Yellow River, Huai River, the Yangtze River, and the Qian-

tang River. It was dug by hand over a period that stretched from 486 B.C. to 1293 A.D.

14 ⊕ FURTHER READING

Books

Dramer, Kim. *People's Republic of China.* New York: Children's Press, 1999.

Harper, Damian. *The National Geographic Traveler: China.* Washington, D.C.: National Geographic Society, 2001.

Leeming, Frank. *The Changing Geography of China.* Cambridge, MA: Blackwell, 1993.

Smith, Christopher J. *China: People and Places in the Land of One Billion.* Boulder, CO: Westview Press, 1991.

Periodicals

Riboud, Marc. "China's Magic Mountain." *Life,* 7 (March 1984): 48ff.

Web Sites

"China in Brief." *China Guide.* http://www.chinaguide.org/e-china/index.htm (accessed June 4, 2003).

Gray, Martin. "Sacred Mountains of China." *Places of Peace and Power.* http://www.sacredsites.com/2nd56/3343640.html (accessed June 13, 2003).

NOVA: Everest. http://www.pbs.org/wgbh/nova/everest/earth/ (accessed June 13, 2003).

Colombia

- **Official name**: Republic of Colombia
- **Area:** 1,138,910 square kilometers (439,736 square miles)
- **Highest point on mainland:** Pico Cristóbal Colón (5,775 meters/18,947 feet)
- **Lowest point on land:** Sea level
- **Hemispheres:** Northern and Western
- **Time zone:** 7 A.M. = noon GMT
- **Longest distances:** 1,700 kilometers (1,056 miles) from north-northwest to south-southeast; 1,210 kilometers (752 miles) from north-northeast to south-southwest

- **Land boundaries:** 6,004 kilometers (3,731 miles) total boundary length; Brazil, 1,643 kilometers (1,021 miles); Ecuador, 590 kilometers (367 miles); Panama, 225 kilometers (140 miles); Peru, 1,496 kilometers (930 miles); Venezuela, 2,050 kilometers (1,274 miles)
- **Coastline:** Total: 3,208 kilometers (1,993 miles); Caribbean Sea, 1,760 kilometers (1,100 miles); North Pacific Ocean, 1,448 kilometers (905 miles)
- **Territorial sea limits:** 22 kilometers 12 nautical miles

1 ⊕ LOCATION AND SIZE

Located in the northwest corner of the South American continent, Colombia is the only country in South America with both Atlantic (Caribbean) and Pacific Ocean coastlines. It is the fifth-largest in size of the Latin American countries. It shares borders with Panama, Venezuela, Brazil, Peru, and Ecuador. With an area of about 1,138,910 square kilometers (439,736 square miles), the country is slightly less than three times the size of Montana. Colombia is divided into thirty-two departments and one federal district.

2 ⊕ TERRITORIES AND DEPENDENCIES

Colombia has no outside dependencies or territories.

3 ⊕ CLIMATE

Temperatures throughout the country are dependent more on altitude than on a change in seasons. The hottest area, also known as *tierra caliente*, is a tropical zone that extends vertically from sea level to about 1,100 meters (3,500 feet). In this area, the temperature is usually between 24 and 27°C (75°F and 81°F), with a maximum near 38°C (100°F) and a minimum of 18°C (64°F). A temperate zone, or *tierra templada,* exists at elevations between 1,100 and 2,000 meters (3,500 and 6,500 feet), with an average temperature of 18°C (64°F). Rising to elevations between 2,000 and 3,000 meters (6,500 and 10,000 feet), one encounters the *tierra fría,* or cold country, which has yearly temperatures averaging 13°C (55°F). Above 3,000 meters (10,000 feet), one encounters more frigid temperatures, often between -17°C and 13°C (1°F and 55°F).

The seasons are determined by changes in rainfall. Areas in the north generally experience only one rainy season, lasting from May through October. Other areas of the country, particularly on the western coast and near the

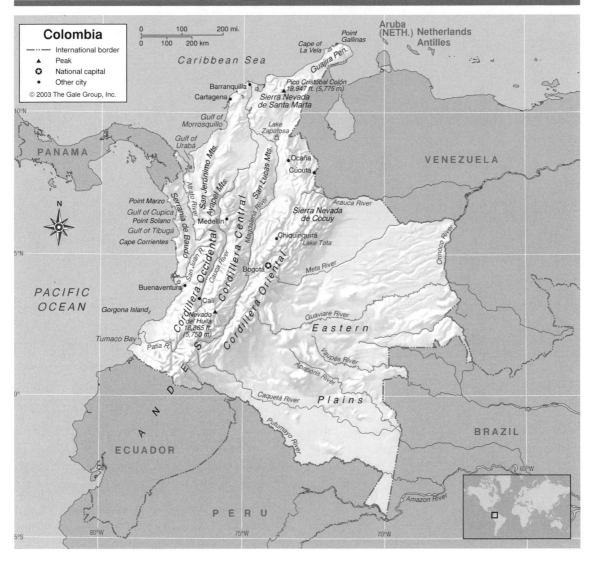

Andes, experience alternating three-month cycles of wet and dry seasons. Annual rainfall averages 107 centimeters (42 inches).

4 ⊕ TOPOGRAPHIC REGIONS

The country consists of four main geographic regions: the Central Highlands (including the three Andean ranges and the lowlands between them), the Atlantic Lowlands, the Pacific Lowlands and their coastal regions, and the Eastern Plain. Among the unusual animals that thrive in Colombia are the jaguar, puma, ocelot, peccary (a small hog-like animal), and armadillo. Native birds include the colorful red-billed emerald hummingbird, found along the coast and in the forested lower slopes of the mountains, and various species of eagle, hawk, falcon, vulture, and condor. Several species of poisonous snake inhabit the tropical forests, including the South American rattlesnake, the anaconda, and various coral snakes.

A missionary complex lies on a Colombian hilltop.

Colombia sits on the extreme edge of the South American Tectonic Plate. Just to the east is the Nazca Plate, and immediately to the north is the Caribbean Plate. Subduction (one plate pushing under another) at these plate boundaries has pushed up the rock, resulting in the mountains that exist on Colombia's coasts. This process also formed volcanoes, and many of them remain active. Folding and faulting of Earth's crust resulted in seismic fault lines between the mountain ranges, and the continued movement of the plates subjects Colombia to frequent earthquakes, some of which are very destructive.

5 ⊕ OCEANS AND SEAS

Seacoast and Undersea Features

The Caribbean Sea, an arm of the Atlantic Ocean, lies northwest of Colombia. The waters along the Caribbean coast are attractive to snorkelers and scuba divers from around the world, since the water is clear and the coastal areas are lined with extensive coral reefs. Colombia has a southwestern coastline along the Pacific Ocean, which is separated from the Caribbean Sea by the Isthmus of Panama.

Rich marine life fills the Pacific Ocean waters along Colombia's western coast, influenced by the Humbolt Current. It is common to see dolphins here, and deep-sea fishing is a popular tourist activity. From July through September, humpback whales populate the waters during their mating season.

Sea Inlets and Straits

The Gulf of Morrosquillo is located on the Caribbean coast, south of Cartegena. Further south, the Gulf of Urabá cuts sharply into the mainland just before the Isthmus of Panama.

The Pacific coast is very irregular, featuring many alternating bays and capes. From north to south, the sea inlets are the Gulf of Cupica, the Gulf of Tibugá, and at the southernmost point, Tumaco Bay.

Islands and Archipelagos

Colombia possesses a few islands in the Caribbean Sea and some in the Pacific Ocean. The combined area of these islands does not exceed 65 square kilometers (25 square miles). Off Nicaragua, about 644 kilometers (400 miles) northwest of the Colombian coast, lies the San Andrés y Providencia Intendency, an archipelago of thirteen small cays grouped around the two larger islands of San Andrés and Providencia. Other islands in the same area—the ownership of which has been in dispute— are the small islands, cays, or banks of Santa Catalina, Roncador, Quita Sueno, Serrana, and Serranilla. Off the coast south of Cartagena are several small islands, among them the islands of Rosario, San Bernardo, and Fuerte.

The island of Malpelo lies in the Pacific Ocean about 434 kilometers (270 miles) west of Buenaventura. Nearer the coast, a prison colony is located on Gorgona Island. Gorgonilla Cay is off its southern shore.

Coastal Features

The Atlantic Lowlands consist of all land in Colombia north of an imaginary line extending northeastward from the Gulf of Urabá to the Venezuelan frontier at the northern extremity of the Cordillera Oriental. The region corresponds generally to one that is often referred to as the Caribbean Lowland or Coastal Plain. This Atlantic Lowland region is roughly the shape of a triangle, the longest side of which is the coastline. Inland from the coastal cities are swamps, hidden streams, and shallow lakes that support banana and cotton plantations, countless small farms and, in higher places, cattle ranches. The northernmost extension of the Atlantic Coast is Point Gallinas.

The Pacific Lowlands are a thinly populated region of jungle and swamp with considerable but little-exploited potential wealth in minerals and other resources. Buenaventura, at about the midpoint of the 1,287-kilometer-long (800-mile-long) coast, is the only port of any size. On the east, the Pacific Lowlands are bounded by the Cordillera Occidental, from which run numerous streams. The peaks of the Cordillera Occidental provide a barrier to rainclouds; as a result, the rainfall along the coast is heavy. The rainforest that lines the coast is dense, with a rich diversity of plant, animal, and bird life. From north to south along the Pacific Coast are Point Marzo, Point Solano, and Cape Corrientes.

6 ⊕ INLAND LAKES

While Colombia has several lakes, none of them are very large and data concerning the area of each lake is scarce. Laguna de la Cocha, a volcanic lake located in the department of Nariño, and Lake Fúquene (with an area of 30 square kilometers/11 square miles), a shallow lake that lies in the Cordillera Oriental, are both being considered by the international organization RAMSAR as wetlands of international significance.

Lake Tota near Bogotá supports tourism with abundant resources for fishing and boating. The largest lake in the north is Laguna de la Plaza. It is located in the Sierra Nevada de Cocuy Mountain Range near the border with Venezuela and has a shore lined with rock formations. Another lake in the area is Laguna Grande de los Verdes. Lake Zapatosa is the largest of the many lakes of northern Colombia.

7 ⊕ RIVERS AND WATERFALLS

The Amazon River is the longest river in South America and the second-longest river in the world. The Amazon starts in Peru and touches the southernmost part of Colombia before coursing through Brazil to flow eastward to the Atlantic Ocean. The total length of the

Residents of Cartagena in northwest Colombia can enjoy sunsets over the Caribbean Sea.

Amazon is about 6,570 kilometers (4,080 miles). It has a total of eighteen major tributaries, including ten that are larger than the Mississippi River. The river is also known as having the world's largest flow of water, with about eighty million gallons of water per second emptying into the Atlantic Ocean. The main Colombian rivers that serve as tributaries to the Amazon are the Vaupés, Apaporis, Caquetá, and the Putumayo.

The Magdalena River rises near a point some 177 kilometers (110 miles) north of Ecuador, where the Cordillera Oriental and the Cordillera Central diverge. It is fed by numerous mountain torrents originating high in the snowfields, where for millennia glaciers have planed the surface of folded and stratified rocks. The Magdalena is navigable from the Caribbean Sea as far as the town of Neiva, deep in the interior, but is interrupted at the midpoint of the country by rapids at the town of Honda.

Running parallel to the Magdalena and separated from it by the Cordillera Central, the Cauca River has headwaters not far from those of the Magdalena. The Cauca eventually joins the Magdalena in swamplands of the Atlantic (Caribbean) coastal region. Further west, the navigable Atrato River flows northward to the Gulf of Urabá.

There are no great rivers in western Colombia, as the mountains lie too close to the coastline. The longest rivers in this region are the San Juan and the Patia. East of the Andes, however, there are many large rivers, including several that are navigable. The Orinoco River flows north along part of the border with Venezuela. Many of Colombia's eastern rivers flow into it. The Guaviare River and two rivers to its north, the Arauca and the Meta,

EPD/Peter Langer

The region around Medellín in north-central Colombia averages 1,500 meters (5,000 feet) in elevation.

are the Orinoco's major Colombian tributaries. The Guaviare serves as a border for five political subdivisions, and it divides eastern Colombia into the Eastern Plains subregion in the north and the Amazonas subregion in the south.

8 ⊕ DESERTS

In the plains region of the northeast, between the Meta River and the Cordillera Oriental, some of the terrain is dry. This region may resemble desert during periods of drought, but there is no true desert terrain in Colombia.

9 ⊕ FLAT AND ROLLING TERRAIN

The Eastern Plains lie east of the Andes and are crisscrossed from east to west by many large rivers. The Spanish term for plains (*llanos*) can be applied only to the open plains in the northern part where cattle are raised, particularly in piedmont areas near the Cordillera Oriental.

The narrow region along the Pacific coast, known as the Pacific Lowlands, is swampy, heavily forested, and sparsely populated. Along the Atlantic coast, the Atlantic Lowlands also consist largely of open, swampy land, but there are cattle ranches and plantations there, and settlements centered on the port cities.

The Cordillera Occidental is separated from the Cordillera Central by the deep rift of the Cauca River Valley. This tropical valley follows the course of the Cauca River for about 241 kilometers (150 miles) southward from a narrow gorge at about its midpoint near the town of Cartago. The cities of Cali and Palmira are situated on low terraces above the floodplain of the Cauca Valley. It is a fertile sugar agricultural zone that includes the best farmland in the country.

10 ⊕ MOUNTAINS AND VOLCANOES

Beginning near the border with Ecuador, the Andes Mountains divide into three distinct cordilleras (mountain chains) that extend northward almost to the Caribbean Sea. The Cordillera Occidental in the west roughly follows the Pacific coast. Slightly inland, the Cordillera Central extends parallel to the Cordillera Occidental, while the Cordillera Oriental lies furthest east. Altitudes in these ranges reach almost 5,791 meters (19,000 feet) and the mountain peaks are permanently covered with snow. Below the summits, the elevated basins and plateaus of these ranges have a moderate climate that provides pleasant living conditions and enables farmers in many places to harvest twice a year.

The Cordillera Occidental range is the lowest and the least populated of the three and supports little economic activity. It is separated from the Cordillera Central by the deep rift of the Cauca River Valley. A pass about 1,524 meters (5,000 feet) above sea level provides the major city of Cali with an outlet to the Pacific Ocean. The relatively low elevation of the cordillera permits dense vegetation, which on the western slopes is truly tropical.

The Cordillera Central, also called the Cordillera del Quindío, is the loftiest of the mountain systems. Its crystalline peaks form a 805-kilometer-long (500-mile-long) towering wall dotted with snow-covered volcanoes, several of which reach elevations greater than 5,500 meters (18,000 feet). There are no plateaus in this range and no passes below 3,352 meters (11,000 feet). The highest peak, the Nevado del Huila, rises 5,750 meters (18,865 feet) above sea level. Toward its northern end, this cordillera separates into several branches that descend toward the Atlantic coast, including the San Jerónimo Mountains, the Ayapel Mountains, and the San Lucas Mountains.

DID YOU KN⊕W?

In the volcanic mountains of the Sierra Nevada de Santa Marta, the town of Arboletes is especially known for its pungent mud volcanoes, which, instead of spewing molten rock, bubble and spatter a mixture of hot water and clay or mud from deep within Earth. One of its volcanoes has a large crater that is filled with a lake of mud. Locals and tourists alike enjoy swimming and soaking in the lake.

The Cordillera Oriental is the longest of the three systems, extending more than 1,200 kilometers (745 miles). In the far north, where the Cordillera Oriental makes an abrupt turn to the northwest near the Venezuela border, lies the Sierra Nevada de Cocuy.

The Sierra Nevada de Santa Marta is an isolated mountain system near the Caribbean coast in the northern, semiarid Guajira Peninsula. It is the tallest coastal mountain range in the world. The range includes many tall peaks, as well as some active volcanoes. Its slopes are generally too steep for cultivation. In the southern part of the peninsula, the Sierra Nevada de Santa Marta rise to a height of 5,775 meters (18,947 feet) at Pico Cristóbal Colón, the highest peak in Colombia.

To the west of the Atrato River, along the Pacific Coast and the Panama border, rises the Serranía de Baudó, an isolated chain that occupies a large part of the coastal plain. Its highest elevation is less than 1,829 meters (6,000 feet).

DID YOU KN🌐W?

Colombia has two archeological sites that are designated as World Heritage Sites by UNESCO (United Nations Educational, Scientific, and Cultural Organization). Tierradentro is a complex of hypogea (underground chambers) located in the town of San Andrés de Pisimbalá in the southern Andes. The underground structures are ancient burial chambers that have been decorated with black and red geometric figures representing the decorations of homes from the time period in which they were created (between the sixth and tenth centuries). There are a number of large animal-like statues surrounding the chambers, which were most likely meant to serve as guards to the tombs.

San Agustin, located in the mountains and canyons just to the south of Tierradentro, is a similar site that also contains a number of burial mounds, tombs, small temples, and large monolithic animal sculptures. Researchers believe that this area was a ceremonial site where natives worshipped nature and death as symbols of continuity and evolution.

11 🌐 CANYONS AND CAVES

There are no major caves or canyons in Colombia.

12 🌐 PLATEAUS AND MONOLITHS

North of Bogotá, the densely populated plateaus of Chiquinquirá and Boyacá feature fertile fields, rich mines, and large industrial establishments. The average elevation in this area is about 2,438 meters (8,000 feet).

13 🌐 MAN-MADE FEATURES

There are two major dams in Colombia, both of which are built on fairly small but fast-flowing rivers. The Guavio Dam, on the Guavio River near Bogotá, is the tenth-highest dam in the world at 243 meters (797 feet). This hydroelectric dam produces most of the electricity for the surrounding areas. The Urrá Multipurpose Dam Project is located on the Sinú River, which flows south of the town of Montería in northwest Colombia. Besides serving as a source of hydroelectric power, this dam is expected to regulate the annual downstream flooding.

14 🌐 FURTHER READING

Books

Dydynski, Krzysztof. *Colombia: A Travel Survival Kit.* Hawthorn, Australia: Lonely Planet Publications, 1995.

Lessard, Marc. *Colombia.* Montréal, Canada: Ulysse, 1999.

Morrison, Marion. *Colombia.* New York: Children's Press, 1999.

Pollard, Peter. *Colombia Handbook.* Lincolnwood, IL: Passport Books, 1998.

Williams, Raymond L., et al. *Culture and Customs of Colombia.* Westport, CT: Greenwood Press, 1999.

Web Site

UNESCO World Heritage Sites in Colombia. http://www.geo.ya.com/travelimages/unesco-colombia.html (accessed June 13, 2003).

Comoros

- **Official name**: Federal Islamic Republic of Comoros

- **Area:** 2,170 square kilometers (838 square miles)

- **Highest point on mainland:** Mount Karthala (2,360 meters/7,743 feet)

- **Lowest point on land:** Sea level

- **Hemispheres:** Southern and Eastern

- **Time zone:** 3 P.M. = noon GMT

- **Longest distances:** 180 kilometers (110 miles) from east-southeast to west-northwest; 110 kilometers (60 miles) from north-northeast to south-southwest

- **Land boundaries:** None

- **Coastline:** 340 kilometers (211 miles)

- **Territorial sea limits:** 22 kilometers 12 nautical miles

1 ⊕ LOCATION AND SIZE

Comoros is a group of three islands located in the northern edge of the Mozambique Channel, between the eastern shore of Mozambique and the island of Madagascar. With an area of 2,170 square kilometers (838 square miles), the country is a little more than twelve times the size of Washington, D.C.

2 ⊕ TERRITORIES AND DEPENDENCIES

Comoros has no territories or dependencies.

3 ⊕ CLIMATE

The islands of Comoros have a tropical marine climate. The temperature averages 28°C (82°F) in March, the hottest month. From May to September, southerly winds bring cooler and drier conditions with temperatures averaging around 19°C (66°F). The rainy season is from December to April with January rainfall averaging about 42 centimeters (16.5 inches). Rainfall and temperature vary from island to island during any given month and even vary throughout an island due to the topography. The central, higher areas of an island are often cooler and moister than the coastal regions.

4 ⊕ TOPOGRAPHIC REGIONS

Comoros is composed of three islands: Grande Comore (Ngazidja), Anjouan (Nzwani) and Mohéli (Mwali). The islands were created by the volcanic action along a fissure in the underlying seabed running west-northwest to east-southeast. The center of Grande Comore is a desert lava field. Hilly, black basalt relief formations rise 1,200 to 1,600 meters (3,950 to 5,250 feet) on Anjouan and 500 to 800 meters (1,650 to 2,600 feet) on Mohéli.

5 ⊕ OCEANS AND SEAS

Seacoast and Undersea Features

The islands of Comoros are completely surrounded by the waters of the Mozambique Channel, an arm of the Indian Ocean set apart by the island of Madagascar.

Islands and Archipelagos

The northernmost and largest island in Comoros is Grande Comore (Ngazidja), with an area of 1,148 square kilometers (443 square miles). Next in size and to the south of Grande Comore is Mohéli (Mwali) at 290 square kilo-

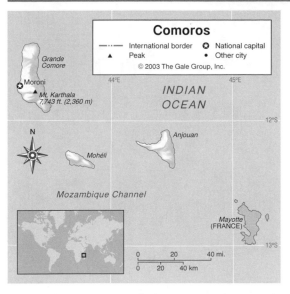

Comoros

--- ---- International border   ⊙ National capital
▲ Peak   • Other city
© 2003 The Gale Group, Inc.

Grande Comore

Moroni

▲ Mt. Karthala
7,743 ft. (2,360 m)

44°E   45°E

INDIAN OCEAN

12°S

N

Anjouan

Mohéli

Mozambique Channel

Mayotte (FRANCE)

13°S

0   20   40 mi.
0   20   40 km

meters (112 square miles). Anjouan (Nzwani), which is east of Mohéli, is 424 square kilometers (164 square miles) in area.

The island of Mayotte (Maore), southeast of Anjouan, is claimed by Comoros but remains under French administrative control.

There are also several smaller islands surrounding the main land areas.

Coastal Features

Mangrove swamps can be found along the coastal zones of the islands. The sandy beaches of the islands have the potential to become an important resource for the tourism industry in Comoros. In places, rocky cliffs rise dramatically from the sea.

6 ⊕ INLAND LAKES

There are no major lakes in Comoros.

7 ⊕ RIVERS AND WATERFALLS

There are no major rivers in Comoros.

8 ⊕ DESERTS

A desert lava field lies in the central interior of the island of Grande Comore.

9 ⊕ FLAT AND ROLLING TERRAIN

There are large tracts of fertile soil on the volcanic islands, but because of the dense population, farming has been forced upwards on the hills, leading to deforestation and erosion. The rich volcanic soils enable the growth of plentiful vegetation. Mangroves predominate in the coastal areas, with palms, bananas, and mangoes further inland.

The island of Anjouan has steep hills that rise nearly 1,500 meters (5,000 feet) from a volcanic massif in the center of the island. On Mohéli there is a ridge in the center of a plain that reaches 580 meters (1,900 feet) above sea level.

10 ⊕ MOUNTAINS AND VOLCANOES

The highest peak of the Comoros is Mount Karthala (2,360 meters/7,743 feet), located

ARAMCO/Ilene Perlman

*Domoni on the island of Anjouan (Nzwani)
is an important trading center.*

ARAMCO/Ilene Perlman

Dramatic cliffs rise from the sea on the coast of Comoros.

on the southern tip of the island of Grande Comore. It is also an active volcano. Lush forest areas grow around the hills and volcanic peaks of the islands.

11 ⊕ CANYONS AND CAVES

There are no notable canyons or caves on Comoros.

12 ⊕ PLATEAUS AND MONOLITHS

The plateau on Grande Comore rises nearly 600 meters (2,000 feet).

13 ⊕ MAN-MADE FEATURES

While there are no notable man-made features on the Comoros Islands, humans have been living on the volcanic islands for centuries.

14 ⊕ FURTHER READING

Books

Madagascar and Comoros: A Travel Survival Kit. Berkeley, CA: Lonely Planet Publications, 1989.

Ottenheimer, Martin, and Harriet Ottenheimer. *Historical Dictionary Islands.* Metuchen, NJ: Scarecrow Press, 1994.

Websites

ArabNet. http://www.arab.net/comoros/comoros_contents.html (accessed March 5, 2003).

U.S. Department of State, Bureau of Public Affairs. "Background Notes, Comoros." http://www.state.gov (accessed March 5, 2003).

A ⊕ CONTINENTS BY AREA, FROM LARGEST TO SMALLEST

Rank	Continent	Area (sq mi)	Area (sq km)
1	Asia	17,139,445	44,391,162
2	Africa	11,677,239	30,244,049
3	North America	9,361,791	24,247,039
4	South America	6,880,706	17,821,029
5	Antarctica	5,500,000	14,245,000
6	Europe	3,997,929	10,345,636
7	Australia	2,967,909	7,686,884

B ⊕ COUNTRIES OF THE WORLD BY LAND AREA, FROM LARGEST TO SMALLEST

Rank	Country	Area (sq mi)	Area (sq km)	Percent of World Land Area
1	Russia	6,592,735	17,075,200	11.0
2	Antarctica	5,405,000	14,000,000	9.4
3	Canada	3,851,788	9,976,140	6.7
4	United States of America	3,717,792	9,629,091	6.4
5	China	3,705,386	9,596,960	6.4
6	Brazil	3,286,470	8,511,965	5.7
7	Australia	2,967,893	7,686,850	5.1
8	India	1,269,338	3,287,590	2.3
9	Argentina	1,072,157	2,776,890	1.9
10	Kazakhstan	1,049,150	2,717,300	1.8
11	Sudan	967,493	2,505,810	1.7
12	Algeria	919,590	2,381,740	1.6
13	Congo, Democratic Republic of the	905,563	2,345,410	1.6
15	Mexico	761,606	1,972,550	1.3
16	Saudi Arabia	756,984	1,960,582	1.3
17	Indonesia	741,096	1,919,440	1.3
18	Libya	679,358	1,759,540	1.2
19	Iran	636,293	1,648,000	1.1
20	Mongolia	604,247	1,565,000	1.0
21	Peru	496,223	1,285,220	0.9
22	Chad	495,755	1,284,000	0.9
23	Niger	489,189	1,267,000	0.8
24	Angola	481,350	1,246,700	0.8
25	Mali	478,764	1,240,000	0.8

	B ⊕ COUNTRIES OF THE WORLD BY LAND AREA, FROM LARGEST TO SMALLEST *(continued)*			
RANK	**COUNTRY**	**AREA (SQ MI)**	**AREA (SQ KM)**	**PERCENT OF WORLD LAND AREA**
26	South Africa	471,008	1,219,912	0.8
27	Colombia	439,733	1,138,910	0.8
28	Ethiopia	435,184	1,127,127	0.8
29	Bolivia	424,162	1,098,580	0.7
30	Mauritania	397,953	1,030,700	0.7
31	Egypt	386,660	1,001,450	0.7
32	Tanzania	364,879	945,037	0.6
33	Nigeria	356,667	923,768	0.6
34	Venezuela	352,143	912,050	0.6
35	Namibia	318,694	825,418	0.6
36	Pakistan	310,401	803,940	0.5
37	Mozambique	309,494	801,590	0.5
38	Turkey	301,382	780,580	0.5
39	Chile	292,258	756,950	0.5
40	Zambia	290,584	752,614	0.5
41	Myanmar	261,969	678,500	0.5
42	Afghanistan	250,000	647,500	0.4
43	Somalia	246,199	637,657	0.4
44	Central African Republic	240,534	622,984	0.4
45	Ukraine	233,089	603,700	0.4
46	Botswana	231,803	600,370	0.4
47	Madagascar	226,656	587,040	0.4
48	Kenya	224,961	582,650	0.4
49	France	211,208	547,030	0.4
50	Yemen	203,849	527,970	0.4
51	Thailand	198,455	514,000	0.3
52	Spain	194,896	504,782	0.3
53	Turkmenistan	188,455	488,100	0.3
54	Cameroon	183,567	475,440	0.3
55	Papua New Guinea	178,703	462,840	0.3
56	Sweden	173,731	449,964	0.3
57	Uzbekistan	172,741	447,400	0.3
58	Morocco	172,413	446,550	0.3
59	Iraq	168,753	437,072	0.3

RANK	COUNTRY	AREA (SQ MI)	AREA (SQ KM)	PERCENT OF WORLD LAND AREA
	B ⊕ COUNTRIES OF THE WORLD BY LAND AREA, FROM LARGEST TO SMALLEST (continued)			
60	Paraguay	157,046	406,750	0.3
61	Zimbabwe	150,803	390,580	0.3
62	Japan	145,882	377,835	0.3
63	Germany	137,846	357,021	0.2
64	Congo, Republic of	132,047	342,000	0.2
65	Finland	130,127	337,030	0.2
66	Malaysia	127,316	329,750	0.2
67	Vietnam	127,243	329,560	0.2
68	Norway	125,181	324,220	0.2
69	Côte d'Ivoire	124,502	322,460	0.2
70	Poland	120,728	312,685	0.2
71	Italy	116,305	301,230	0.2
72	Philippines	115,830	300,000	0.2
73	Ecuador	109,483	283,560	0.2
74	Burkina Faso	105,869	274,200	0.2
75	New Zealand	103,737	268,680	0.2
76	Gabon	103,347	267,667	0.2
77	Guinea	94,926	245,857	0.2
78	United Kingdom	94,525	244,820	0.2
79	Ghana	92,100	238,540	0.2
80	Romania	91,699	237,500	0.2
81	Laos	91,428	236,800	0.2
82	Uganda	91,135	236,040	0.2
83	Guyana	83,000	214,970	0.1
84	Oman	82,031	212,460	0.1
85	Belarus	80,154	207,600	0.1
86	Kyrgyzstan	76,640	198,500	0.1
87	Senegal	75,749	196,190	0.1
88	Syria	71,498	185,180	0.1
89	Cambodia	69,900	181,040	0.1
90	Uruguay	68,039	176,220	0.1
91	Tunisia	63,170	163,610	0.1
92	Suriname	63,039	163,270	0.1
93	Bangladesh	55,598	144,000	0.1

RANK	COUNTRY	AREA (SQ MI)	AREA (SQ KM)	PERCENT OF WORLD LAND AREA
	**B ⊕ COUNTRIES OF THE WORLD BY LAND AREA, FROM LARGEST TO SMALLEST** *(continued)*			
94	Tajikistan	55,251	143,100	0.1
95	Nepal	54,363	140,800	0.1
96	Greece	50,942	131,940	0.1
97	Nicaragua	49,998	129,494	0.1
98	Eritrea	46,842	121,320	0.1
99	Korea, North (Democratic People's Republic of)	46,540	120,540	0.1
100	Malawi	45,745	118,480	0.1
101	Benin	43,483	112,620	0.1
102	Honduras	43,278	112,090	0.1
103	Liberia	43,000	111,370	0.1
104	Bulgaria	42,822	110,910	0.1
105	Cuba	42,803	110,860	0.1
106	Guatemala	42,042	108,890	0.1
107	Iceland	39,769	103,000	0.1
108	Serbia and Montenegro	39,517	102,350	0.1
109	Korea, South (Republic of)	38,023	98,480	0.1
110	Hungary	35,919	93,030	0.1
111	Portugal	35,672	92,391	0.1
112	Jordan	35,637	92,300	0.1
114	Azerbaijan	33,436	86,600	0.1
115	Austria	32,378	83,858	0.1
116	United Arab Emirates	32,000	82,880	0.1
117	Czech Republic	30,450	78,866	0.1
118	Panama	30,193	78,200	0.1
119	Sierra Leone	27,699	71,740	0.05
120	Ireland	27,135	70,280	0.05
121	Georgia	26,911	69,700	0.05
122	Sri Lanka	25,332	65,610	0.04
123	Lithuania	25,174	65,200	0.04
124	Latvia	24,938	64,589	0.04
125	Togo	21,925	56,785	0.04
126	Croatia	21,831	56,542	0.04
127	Bosnia and Herzegovina	19,741	51,129	0.03

RANK	COUNTRY	AREA (SQ MI)	AREA (SQ KM)	PERCENT OF WORLD LAND AREA
B ⊕ COUNTRIES OF THE WORLD BY LAND AREA, FROM LARGEST TO SMALLEST *(continued)*				
128	Costa Rica	19,730	51,100	0.03
129	Slovakia	18,859	48,845	0.03
130	Dominican Republic	18,815	48,730	0.03
131	Bhutan	18,147	47,000	0.03
132	Estonia	17,462	45,226	0.03
133	Denmark	16,638	43,094	0.03
134	Netherlands	16,033	41,526	0.03
135	Switzerland	15,942	41,290	0.03
136	Guinea-Bissau	13,946	36,120	0.02
137	Moldova	13,067	33,843	0.02
137	Taiwan	13,892	35,980	0.02
138	Belgium	11,780	30,510	0.02
139	Lesotho	11,720	30,355	0.02
140	Armenia	11,506	29,800	0.02
141	Albania	11,100	28,748	0.02
142	Solomon Islands	10,985	28,450	0.02
143	Equatorial Guinea	10,831	28,051	0.02
144	Burundi	10,745	27,830	0.02
145	Haiti	10,714	27,750	0.02
146	Rwanda	10,169	26,338	0.02
147	Macedonia	9,781	25,333	0.02
148	Belize	8,867	22,966	0.02
149	Djibouti	8,494	22,000	0.01
150	El Salvador	8,124	21,040	0.01
151	Israel	8,019	20,770	0.01
152	Slovenia	7,820	20,253	0.01
153	Fiji	7,054	18,270	0.01
154	Kuwait	6,880	17,820	0.01
155	Swaziland	6,704	17,363	0.01
156	East Timor	5,640	14,609	0.01
157	Bahamas	5,382	13,940	0.01
158	Vanuatu	4,710	12,200	0.01
159	Qatar	4,416	11,437	0.01
160	Gambia, The	4,363	11,300	0.01

	B ⊕ COUNTRIES OF THE WORLD BY LAND AREA, FROM LARGEST TO SMALLEST *(continued)*			
RANK	COUNTRY	AREA (SQ MI)	AREA (SQ KM)	PERCENT OF WORLD LAND AREA
161	Jamaica	4,243	10,990	0.01
162	Lebanon	4,015	10,400	0.01
163	Cyprus	3,571	9,250	0.01
164	Brunei	2,228	5,770	0.004
164	Puerto Rico	3,515	9,104	0.01
165	Trinidad and Tobago	1,980	5,128	0.003
166	Cape Verde	1,557	4,033	0.003
167	Samoa	1,104	2,860	0.002
168	Luxembourg	998	2,586	0.002
169	Comoros	838	2,170	0.001
170	Mauritius	718	1,860	0.001
171	São Tomé and Príncipe	386	1,001	0.0007
172	Dominica	291	754	0.0005
173	Tonga	289	748	0.0005
174	Kiribati	277	717	0.0005
175	Micronesia	271	702	0.0005
176	Palau	177	458	0.0003
177	Bahrain	239	620	0.0004
178	Saint Lucia	239	620	0.0004
179	Andorra	181	468	0.0003
181	Singapore	250	647.5	0.0004
181	Seychelles	176	455	0.0003
182	Antigua and Barbuda	171	442	0.0003
183	Barbados	166	430	0.0003
184	Saint Vincent and the Grenadines	150	389	0.0003
185	Malta	122	316	0.0002
186	Maldives	115	300	0.0002
187	Saint Kitts and Nevis	101	261	0.0002
188	Marshall Islands	70	181.3	0.0001
189	Liechtenstein	62	160	0.0001
190	San Marino	24	61.2	--
191	Tuvalu	10	26	--
192	Nauru	8.1	21	--
193	Monaco	0.7	1.95	--
194	Vatican City	0.17	0.44	--

C ⊕ COUNTRIES OF THE WORLD, BY POPULATION

RANK	COUNTRY	CONTINENT	POPULATION (JULY 2002)
1	China	Asia	1,284,303,705
2	India	Asia	1,045,845,226
3	United States of America	North America	280,562,489
4	Indonesia	Asia	231,328,092
5	Brazil	South America	176,029,560
6	Pakistan	Asia	147,663,429
7	Russia	Europe	144,978,573
8	Bangladesh	Asia	133,376,684
9	Nigeria	Africa	129,934,911
10	Japan	Asia	126,974,628
11	Mexico	North America	103,400,165
12	Philippines	Asia	84,525,639
13	Germany	Europe	83,251,851
14	Vietnam	Asia	81,098,416
15	Egypt	Africa	70,712,345
16	Ethiopia	Africa	67,673,031
17	Turkey	Asia	67,308,928
18	Iran	Asia	66,622,704
19	Thailand	Asia	62,354,402
20	United Kingdom	Europe	59,778,002
21	France	Europe	59,765,983
22	Italy	Europe	57,715,625
23	Congo, Democratic Republic of the	Africa	55,225,478
24	Ukraine	Europe	48,396,470
25	Korea, South (Republic of)	Asia	48,324,000
26	South Africa	Africa	43,647,658
27	Myanmar	Asia	42,238,224
28	Colombia	South America	41,008,227
29	Spain	Europe	40,077,100
30	Poland	Europe	38,625,478
31	Argentina	South America	37,812,817
32	Tanzania	Africa	37,187,939
33	Sudan	Africa	37,090,298

C ⊕ COUNTRIES OF THE WORLD, BY POPULATION (continued)

RANK	COUNTRY	CONTINENT	POPULATION (JULY 2002)
34	Algeria	Africa	32,277,942
35	Canada	North America	31,902,268
36	Morocco	Africa	31,167,783
37	Kenya	Africa	31,138,735
38	Peru	South America	27,949,639
39	Afghanistan	Asia	27,755,775
40	Nepal	Asia	25,873,917
41	Uzbekistan	Asia	25,563,441
42	Uganda	Africa	24,699,073
43	Venezuela	South America	24,287,670
44	Iraq	Asia	24,001,816
45	Saudi Arabia	Asia	23,513,330
46	Malaysia	Asia	22,662,365
47	Taiwan	Asia	22,548,009
48	Romania	Europe	22,317,730
49	Korea, North (Democratic People's Republic of)	Asia	22,224,195
50	Ghana	Africa	20,244,154
51	Mozambique	Africa	19,607,519
52	Sri Lanka	Asia	19,576,783
53	Australia	Australia	19,546,792
54	Yemen	Asia	18,701,257
55	Syria	Asia	17,155,814
56	Côte d'Ivoire	Africa	16,804,784
57	Kazakhstan	Asia	16,741,519
58	Madagascar	Africa	16,473,477
59	Cameroon	Africa	16,184,748
60	Netherlands	Europe	16,067,754
61	Chile	South America	15,498,930
62	Ecuador	South America	13,447,494
63	Guatemala	North America	13,314,079
64	Cambodia	Asia	12,775,324
65	Burkina Faso	Africa	12,603,185

C ⊕ COUNTRIES OF THE WORLD, BY POPULATION (continued)

RANK	COUNTRY	CONTINENT	POPULATION (JULY 2002)
66	Zimbabwe	Africa	11,376,676
67	Mali	Africa	11,340,480
68	Cuba	North America	11,224,321
69	Malawi	Africa	10,701,824
70	Serbia and Montenegro	Europe	10,656,929
71	Greece	Europe	10,645,343
72	Niger	Africa	10,639,744
73	Angola	Africa	10,593,171
74	Senegal	Africa	10,589,571
75	Belarus	Europe	10,335,382
76	Belgium	Europe	10,274,595
77	Czech Republic	Europe	10,256,760
78	Portugal	Europe	10,084,245
79	Hungary	Europe	10,075,034
80	Zambia	Africa	9,959,037
81	Tunisia	Africa	9,815,644
82	Chad	Africa	8,997,237
83	Sweden	Europe	8,876,744
84	Dominican Republic	North America	8,721,594
85	Bolivia	South America	8,445,134
86	Austria	Europe	8,169,929
87	Azerbaijan	Asia	7,798,497
88	Guinea	Africa	7,775,065
89	Somalia	Africa	7,753,310
90	Bulgaria	Europe	7,621,337
91	Rwanda	Africa	7,398,074
92	Switzerland	Europe	7,301,994
93	Haiti	North America	7,063,722
94	Benin	Africa	6,787,625
95	Tajikistan	Asia	6,719,567
96	Honduras	North America	6,560,608
97	El Salvador	North America	6,353,681
98	Burundi	Africa	6,373,002

C ⊕ COUNTRIES OF THE WORLD, BY POPULATION (continued)

Rank	Country	Continent	Population (July 2002)
99	Israel	Asia	6,029,529
100	Paraguay	South America	5,884,491
101	Laos	Asia	5,777,180
102	Sierra Leone	Africa	5,614,743
103	Slovakia	Europe	5,422,366
104	Denmark	Europe	5,368,854
105	Libya	Africa	5,368,585
106	Jordan	Asia	5,307,470
107	Togo	Africa	5,285,501
108	Finland	Europe	5,183,545
109	Papua New Guinea	Asia	5,172,033
110	Nicaragua	North America	5,023,818
111	Georgia	Asia	4,960,951
112	Kyrgyzstan	Asia	4,822,166
113	Turkmenistan	Asia	4,688,963
114	Norway	Europe	4,525,116
115	Eritrea	Africa	4,465,651
116	Singapore	Asia	4,452,732
117	Moldova	Europe	4,434,547
118	Croatia	Europe	4,390,751
119	Bosnia and Herzegovina	Europe	3,964,388
120	Puerto Rico	North America	3,957,988
121	New Zealand	Asia	3,908,037
122	Ireland	Europe	3,883,159
123	Costa Rica	North America	3,834,934
124	Lebanon	Asia	3,677,780
125	Central African Republic	Africa	3,642,739
126	Lithuania	Europe	3,601,138
127	Albania	Europe	3,544,841
128	Uruguay	South America	3,386,575
129	Armenia	Europe	3,330,099
130	Liberia	Africa	3,288,198
131	Congo, Republic of the	Africa	2,958,448

RANK	COUNTRY	CONTINENT	POPULATION (JULY 2002)
	C ⊕ COUNTRIES OF THE WORLD, BY POPULATION *(continued)*		
132	Panama	North America	2,882,329
133	Mauritania	Africa	2,828,858
134	Mongolia	Asia	2,694,432
135	Jamaica	North America	2,680,029
136	Oman	Asia	2,713,462
137	United Arab Emirates	Asia	2,445,989
138	Latvia	Europe	2,366,515
139	Kuwait	Asia	2,111,561
140	Lesotho	Africa	2,207,954
141	Bhutan	Asia	2,094,176
142	Macedonia, The Former Yugoslav Republic of	Europe	2,054,800
143	Slovenia	Europe	1,932,917
144	Namibia	Africa	1,820,916
145	Botswana	Africa	1,591,232
146	Estonia	Europe	1,415,681
147	Gambia, The	Africa	1,455,842
148	Guinea-Bissau	Africa	1,345,479
149	Gabon	Africa	1,233,353
150	Mauritius	Africa	1,200,206
151	Trinidad and Tobago	South America	1,163,724
152	Swaziland	Africa	1,123,605
153	East Timor	Asia	952,618
154	Fiji	Asia	856,346
155	Qatar	Asia	793,341
156	Cyprus	Asia	767,314
157	Guyana	South America	698,209
158	Bahrain	Asia	656,397
159	Comoros	Africa	614,382
160	Equatorial Guinea	Africa	498,144
161	Solomon Islands	Asia	494,786
162	Djibouti	Africa	472,810
163	Luxembourg	Europe	448,569
164	Suriname	South America	436,494

RANK	COUNTRY	CONTINENT	POPULATION (JULY 2002)
	**C ⊕ COUNTRIES OF THE WORLD, BY POPULATION** *(continued)*		

C ⊕ COUNTRIES OF THE WORLD, BY POPULATION *(continued)*

RANK	COUNTRY	CONTINENT	POPULATION (JULY 2002)
165	Cape Verde	Africa	408,760
166	Malta	Europe	397,499
167	Brunei Darussalam	Asia	350,898
168	Maldives	Asia	320,165
169	Bahamas, The	North America	300,529
170	Iceland	Europe	279,384
171	Barbados	North America	276,607
172	Belize	North America	262,999
173	Vanuatu	Asia	196,178
174	Samoa	Asia	178,631
175	São Tomé and Príncipe	Africa	170,372
176	Saint Lucia	North America	160,145
177	Micronesia, Federated States of	Asia	135,869
178	Saint Vincent and the Grenadines	North America	116,394
179	Tonga	Asia	106,137
180	Kiribati	Asia	96,335
181	Grenada	North America	89,211
182	Seychelles	Africa	80,098
183	Marshall Islands	Asia	73,630
184	Dominica	North America	70,158
185	Andorra	Europe	68,403
186	Antigua and Barbuda	North America	67,448
187	Saint Kitts and Nevis	North America	38,736
188	Liechtenstein	Europe	32,842
189	Monaco	Europe	31,987
190	San Marino	Europe	27,730
191	Palau	Asia	19,409
192	Nauru	Asia	12,329
193	Tuvalu	Asia	11,146
194	Holy See	Europe	900
195	Antarctica	Antarctica	No permanent population

D 🌐 OCEANS AND SEAS OF THE WORLD, BY AREA

All measurements are approximate and are rounded to the nearest thousand.

RANK	NAME	AREA (SQ MI)	AREA (SQ KM)
1	Pacific Ocean	60,060,000	155,557,000
2	Atlantic Ocean	29,638,000	76,762,000
3	Indian Ocean	26,469,000	68,556,000
4	Southern Ocean	7,848,000	20,327,000
5	Arctic Ocean	5,427,000	14,056,000
6	Coral Sea	1,850,000	4,791,000
7	Arabian Sea	1,492,000	3,864,000
8	South China Sea (Nan Hai)	1,423,000	3,685,000
9	Weddell Sea	1,080,000	2,796,000
10	Caribbean Sea	1,063,000	2,753,000
11	Mediterranean Sea	971,000	2,515,000
12	Tasman Sea	900,000	2,331,000
13	Bering Sea	890,000	2,305,000
14	Bay of Bengal	839,000	2,173,000
15	Sea of Okhotsk	614,000	1,590,000
16	Gulf of Mexico	596,000	1,544,000
17	Gulf of Guinea	592,000	1,533,000
18	Barents Sea	542,000	1,405,000
19	Norwegian Sea	534,000	1,383,000
20	Gulf of Alaska	512,000	1,327,000
21	Hudson Bay	476,000	1,233,000
22	Greenland Sea	465,000	1,205,000
23	Bellinghausen Sea	430,000	1,110,000
24	Amundsen Sea	400,000	1,036,000
25	Arafura Sea	400,000	1,036,000
26	Philippine Sea	400,000	1,036,000
27	Sea of Japan	378,000	979,000
28	Mozambique Channel	376,000	975,000
29	Ross Sea	370,000	958,000
30	East Siberian Sea	361,000	936,000
31	Scotia Sea	347,000	900,000

D ⊕ OCEANS AND SEAS OF THE WORLD, BY AREA (continued)

All measurements are rounded to the nearest thousand.

Rank	Name	Area (sq mi)	Area (sq km)
32	Kara Sea	341,000	883,000
33	Labrador Sea	309,000	800,000
34	East China Sea (Dong Hai / Tung Hai)	290,000	752,000
35	Solomon Sea	278,000	720,000
36	Laptev Sea	270,000	700,000
37	Baffin Bay	268,000	695,000
38	Banda Sea	268,000	695,000
39	Drake Passage	240,000	620,000
40	Timor Sea	237,000	615,000
41	Andaman Sea	232,000	601,000
42	North Sea	232,000	601,000
43	Davis Strait	230,000	596,000
44	Chukchi Sea	225,000	582,000
45	Great Australian Bight	187,000	484,000
46	Beaufort Sea	184,000	476,000
47	Celebes Sea	182,000	472,000
48	Black Sea	178,000	461,000
49	Red Sea	175,000	453,000
50	Java Sea	167,000	433,000
51	Sulu Sea	162,000	420,000
52	Yellow Sea (Huang Hai)	161,000	417,000
53	Baltic Sea	147,000	382,000
54	Gulf of Carpentaria	120,000	310,000
55	Molucca Sea	119,000	307,000
56	Persian Gulf	93,000	241,000
57	Gulf of Thailand	92,000	239,000
58	Gulf of St. Lawrence	92,000	239,000
59	Bismarck Sea	87,000	225,000
60	Gulf of Aden	85,000	220,000
61	Makassar Strait	75,000	194,000
62	Ceram Sea	72,000	187,000

RANK	NAME	OCEAN	DEPTH (FT)	DEPTH (M)
1	Mariana Trench	Pacific	38,635	11,784
2	Philippine Trench	Pacific	37,720	11,505
3	Tonga Trench	Pacific	37,166	11,336
4	Izu Trench	Pacific	36,850	11,239
5	Kermadec Trench	Pacific	34,728	10,592
6	Kuril Trench	Pacific	34,678	10,577
7	New Britain Trench	Pacific	31,657	9,655
8	Puerto Rico Trench	Atlantic	31,037	9,466
9	Bonin Trench	Pacific	29,816	9,094
10	Japan Trench	Pacific	29,157	8,893
11	South Sandwich Trench	Atlantic	28,406	8,664
12	Palau Trench	Pacific	27,972	8,531
13	Peru-Chile Trench	Pacific	27,687	8,445
14	Yap Trench	Pacific	27,552	8,403
15	Aleutian Trench	Pacific	26,775	8,166
16	Roanche Gap	Atlantic	26,542	8,095
17	Cayman Trench	Atlantic	26,519	8,088
18	New Hebrides Trench	Pacific	25,971	7,921
19	Ryukyu Trench	Pacific	25,597	7,807
20	Java Trench	Indian	24,744	7,547
21	Diamantina Trench	Indian	24,249	7,396
22	Mid America Trench	Pacific	22,297	6,801
23	Brazil Basin	Atlantic	22,274	6,794
24	Ob Trench	Indian	21,785	6,644
25	Vema Trench	Indian	19,482	5,942
26	Agulhas Basin	Indian	19,380	5,911
27	Ionian Basin	Mediterranean Sea	17,306	5,278
28	Eurasia Basin	Arctic	16,122	4,917

E ⊕ OCEAN DEPTH

All measurements are approximate.

F ⊕ MAJOR ISLANDS OF THE WORLD, BY AREA

All measurements are approximate.

Rank	Island	Continent	Body of Water	Area (sq mi)	Area (sq km)
1	Greenland	North America	Atlantic Ocean	840,000	2,175,600
2	New Guinea	Oceania	Pacific Ocean	305,000	790,000
3	Borneo	Asia	South China Sea	285,000	737,000
4	Madagascar	Africa	Indian Ocean	226,657	587,040
5	Baffin	North America	Baffin Bay	196,000	507,000
6	Sumatra	Asia	Andaman Sea	164,000	425,000
7	Honshu	Asia	Pacific Ocean	88,000	228,000
8	Great Britain	Europe	North Sea	84,400	219,000
9	Victoria	North America	Viscount Melville Sound	83,900	217,000
10	Ellesmere	North America	Arctic Ocean	75,800	196,000
11	Sulawesi (Celebes)	Asia	Celebes Sea	67,400	174,000
12	South Island (New Zealand)	Oceania	Pacific Ocean	58,200	151,000
13	Java	Asia	Indian Ocean	50,000	129,000
14	North Island (New Zealand)	Oceania	Pacific Ocean	44,200	114,000
15	Newfoundland	North America	Atlantic Ocean	42,000	109,000
16	Cuba	North America	Caribbean Sea	40,500	105,000
17	Luzon	Asia	Pacific Ocean	40,400	105,000
18	Iceland	Europe	Atlantic Ocean	39,769	103,000
19	Mindanao	Asia	Pacific Ocean	36,500	94,600
20	Ireland	Europe	Atlantic Ocean	32,500	84,100
21	Hokkaido	Asia	Pacific Ocean	30,100	78,000
22	Sakhalin	Asia	Sea of Okhotsk	29,500	76,400
23	Hispaniola	North America	Atlantic Ocean	29,200	75,600
24	Banks	North America	Arctic Ocean	27,000	70,000
25	Sri Lanka	Asia	Indian Ocean	25,332	65,610
26	Tasmania	Australia	Indian Ocean	24,900	64,400
27	Devon	North America	Baffin Bay	21,300	55,200
28	Novaya Zemlya	Europe	North Kara Sea	18,900	48,900
29	Grande de Tierra del Fuego	South America	Atlantic Ocean	18,700	48,400
30	Marajo	South America	Atlantic Ocean	18,500	48,000
31	Alexander	Antarctica	Bellingshausen Sea	16,700	43,200
32	Axel Heiberg	North America	Arctic Ocean	16,700	43,200
33	Melville	North America	Viscount Melville Sound	16,300	42,100

RANK	ISLAND	CONTINENT	BODY OF WATER	AREA (SQ MI)	AREA (SQ KM)
34	Southampton	North America	Husdon Bay	15,900	41,200
35	West Spitsbergen	Europe	Arctic Ocean	15,300	39,500
36	New Britain	Oceania	Bismarck Sea	14,600	37,800
37	Taiwan	Asia	Pacific Ocean	13,892	35,980
38	Kyushu	Asia	Pacific Ocean	13,800	35,700
39	Hainan	Asia	South China Sea	13,100	34,000
40	Prince of Wales	North America	Viscount Melville Sound	12,900	33,300
41	Novaya Zemlya	Europe	Barents Sea	12,800	33,300
42	Vancouver	North America	Pacific Ocean	12,100	31,300
43	Timor	Asia	Timor Sea	10,200	26,300
44	Sicily	Europe	Mediterranean	9,810	25,400
45	Somerset	North America	Lancaster Sound	9,570	24,800
46	Sardinia	Europe	Mediterranean	9,190	23,800
47	Bananal	South America	Araguaia River	7,720	20,000
48	Halmahera	Asia	Molucca Sea	6,950	18,000
49	Shikoku	Asia	Pacific Ocean	6,860	17,800
50	Ceram	Asia	Banda Sea	6,620	17,200
51	New Caledonia	Oceania	Coral Sea	6,470	16,700
52	Bathurst	North America	Viscount Melville Sound	6,190	16,000
53	Prince Patrick	North America	Arctic Ocean	6,120	15,800
54	North East Land	Europe	Barents Sea	5,790	15,000
55	Flores	Asia	Flores Sea	5,520	14,300
56	Oktyabrskoy Revolyutsii	Asia	Arctic Ocean	5,470	14,170
57	Sumbawa	Asia	Indian Ocean	5,160	13,400
58	King William	North America	Queen Maud Gulf	5,060	13,100
59	Samar	Asia	Pacific Ocean	5,050	13,100
60	Negros	Asia	Sulu Sea	4,900	12,700
61	Palawan	Asia	South China Sea	4,550	11,800
62	Kotelnyy	Asia	Arctic Ocean	4,500	11,700
63	Panay	Asia	Sulu Sea	4,450	11,500
64	Bangka	Asia	Java Sea	4,370	11,320
65	Ellef Ringnes	North America	Arctic Ocean	4,360	11,300
66	Bolshevik	Asia	Arctic Ocean	4,350	11,270
67	Sumba	Asia	Indian Ocean	4,310	11,200

Table title: **F ⊕ MAJOR ISLANDS OF THE WORLD, BY AREA** (continued)
All measurements are approximate.

F ⊕ MAJOR ISLANDS OF THE WORLD, BY AREA (continued)

All measurements are approximate.

Rank	Island	Continent	Body of Water	Area (sq mi)	Area (sq km)
68	Bylot	North America	Baffin Bay	4,270	11,100
69	Jamaica	North America	Caribbean Sea	4,243	10,990
70	Dolak	Asia	Arafura Sea	4,160	10,800
71	Hawaii	Oceania	Pacific Ocean	4,040	10,500
72	Viti Levu	Oceania	Pacific Ocean	4,010	10,400
73	Cape Breton	North America	Atlantic Ocean	3,980	10,300
74	Bougainville	Oceania	Pacific Ocean	3,880	10,000
75	Mindoro	Asia	South China Sea	3,760	9,730
76	Prince Charles	North America	Foxe Basin	3,680	9,520
77	Kodiak	North America	Pacific Ocean	3,670	9,510
78	Cyprus	Asia	Mediterranean	3,571	9,250
79	Komsomolets	Asia	Arctic Ocean	3,480	9,010
80	Buru	Asia	Banda Sea	3,470	9,000
81	Corsica	Europe	Mediterranean	3,370	8,720
82	Puerto Rico	North America	Atlantic Ocean	3,350	8,680
83	New Ireland	Oceania	Pacific Ocean	3,340	8,650
84	Disco	North America	Davis Strait	3,310	8,580
85	Chiloe	South America	Pacific Ocean	3,240	8,390
86	Crete	Europe	Mediterranean	3,190	8,260
87	Anticosti	North America	Gulf of St. Lawrence	3,070	7,940
88	Wrangel	Asia	Chukchi Sea	2,820	7,300
89	Leyte	Asia	Visayan Sea	2,780	7,210
90	Zealand	Europe	Baltic Sea	2,710	7,020
91	Cornwallis	North America	Barrow Strait	2,700	7,000
92	Wellington	South America	Trinidad Gulf	2,610	6,750
93	Iturup (Etorofu)	Asia	Pacific Ocean	2,600	6,720
94	Prince of Wales	North America	Pacific Ocean	2,590	6,700
95	Graham	North America	Pacific Ocean	2,460	6,360
96	East Falkland	South America	Atlantic Ocean	2,440	6,310
97	Melville	Asia	Timor Sea	2,400	6,220
98	Novaya Sibir	Asia	East Siberian Sea	2,390	6,200
99	Kerguelen	Antarctica	Indian Ocean	2,320	6,000
100	Andros	North America	Grand Bahama Bank	2,300	5,960

G ⊕ DESERTS OF THE WORLD, BY AREA

All measurements are approximate.

RANK	NAME	CONTINENT	COUNTRY	AREA (SQ MI)	AREA (SQ KM)
1	Sahara	Africa	Algeria, Chad, Egypt, Libya, Mali, Mauritania, Morocco, Niger, Sudan, and Tunisia	3,475,000	9,000,000
2	Arabian*	Asia	Saudi Arabia, Kuwait, Qatar, the United Arab Emirates, Oman, Yemen, Jordan, Syria, Iraq	900,000	2,330,000
3	Gobi	Asia	China, Mongolia	500,000	1,300,000
4	Kalahari	Africa	Botswana, Namibia, South Africa	360,000	930,000
5	Great Victoria	Australia	Australia	134,652	348,750
6	Taklimakan (Takla Makan)	Asia	China	125,000	320,000
7	Sonoran	North America	United States of America, Mexico	120,000	310,000
8	Kara-Kum	Asia	Kazakhstan, Turkmenistan	115,830	300,000
9	Kyzyl Kum	Asia	Kazakhstan, Uzbekistan	115,000	297,850
10	Namib	Africa	Namibia, South Africa	110,000	285,000
11	Great Sandy	Australia	Australia	103,185	267,250
12	Somali	Africa	Somalia	100,000	260,000
13	Thar	Asia	India, Pakistan	90,000	233,000
14	Tanami	Australia	Australia	71,235	184,500
15	Atacama	South America	Chile, Peru	70,000	180,000
16	Simpson	Australia	Australia	68,150	176,500
17	Gibson	Australia	Australia	60,230	156,000
18	Little Sandy	Australia	Australia	43,050	111,500

* Two deserts are commonly referred to by this name. This entry refers to the deserts of the Arabian Peninsula and not the Arabian Desert of Egypt, which is part of the Sahara.

H ⊕ HIGHEST MOUNTAIN PEAKS, BY CONTINENT

All measurements are approximate.
Note that many mountains have multiple peaks, which will appear separately in the table.

AFRICA

RANK	NAME	COUNTRY	ELEVATION (FT)	ELEVATION (M)
1	Kibo (Mt. Kilimanjaro)	Tanzania	19,341	5,895
2	Mawensi (Mt. Kilimanjaro)	Tanzania	17,100	5,210
3	Batian (Mt. Kenya)	Kenya	17,058	5,203
4	Nelion (Mt. Kenya)	Kenya	17,020	5,190
5	Margherita Peak (Mt. Stanley)	Dem. Rep. of the Congo, Uganda	16,756	5,110
6	Alexandra Peak (Mt. Stanley)	Dem. Rep. of the Congo, Uganda	16,700	5,094
7	Albert Peak (Mt. Stanley)	Dem. Rep. of the Congo	16,690	5,090
8	Savoia Peak (Mt. Stanley)	Uganda	16,330	4,981
9	Elena Peak (Mt. Stanley)	Uganda	16,300	4,972
10	Elizabeth Peak (Mt. Stanley)	Uganda	16,170	4,932
11	Phillip Peak (Mt. Stanley)	Uganda	16,140	4,923
12	Moebius Peak (Mt. Stanley)	Uganda	16,130	4,920
13	Vittorio Emanuele (Mt. Speke)	Uganda	16,040	4,892
14	Ensonga (Mt. Speke)	Uganda	15,960	4,868
15	Johnston (Mt. Speke)	Uganda	15,860	4,834
16	Edward (Mt. Baker)	Uganda	15,890	4,846
17	Umberto (Mt. Emin)	Dem. Rep. of the Congo	15,740	4,798
18	Semper (Mt. Baker)	Uganda	15,730	4,795
19	Kraepelin (Mt. Emin)	Dem. Rep. of the Congo	15,720	4,791
20	Iolanda (Mt. Gessi)	Dem. Rep. of the Congo	15,470	4,751
21	Bottego (Mt. Gesi)	Dem. Rep. of the Congo	15,418	4,699
22	Sella (Mt. Luigi)	Dem. Rep. of the Congo	15,178	4,626
23	Ras Deshen	Ethiopia	15,157	4,620
24	Weismann (Mt. Luigi)	Dem. Rep. of the Congo	15,157	4,620
25	Okusoma (Mt. Luigi)	Dem. Rep. of the Congo	15,020	4,578

ANTARCTICA

RANK	NAME	COUNTRY	ELEVATION (FT)	ELEVATION (M)
1	Vinson	Antarctica	16,860	5,142
2	Tyree	Antarctica	16,290	4,968
3	Shinn	Antarctica	15,750	4,800
4	Gardner	Antarctica	15,370	4,690
5	Epperly	Antarctica	15,100	4,600

H ⊕ HIGHEST MOUNTAIN PEAKS, BY CONTINENT *(continued)*

ASIA

Rank	Name	Country	Elevation (ft)	Elevation (m)
1	Everest (Zhumulangma Feng)	Nepal, China	29,030	8,850
2	K2	China, Pakistan	28,251	8,611
3	Kanchenjunga	India, Nepal	28,169	8,586
4	Lhotse	China, Nepal	27,890	8,500
5	Makalu	China, Nepal	27,824	8,481
6	Kanchenjunga, south peak	India, Nepal	27,800	8,479
7	Kanchenjunga, west peak	India, Nepal	27,620	8,424
8	Lhotse Shar	China, Nepal	27,500	8,388
9	Dhaulagiri	Nepal	26,813	8,172
10	Man slu	Nepal	26,775	8,155
11	Cho Oyu	China, Nepal	26,750	8,150
12	Nanga Parbat I	Pakistan	26,660	8,130
13	Masherbrum I	Pakistan	26,610	7,810
14	Annapurna I	Nepal	26,500	8,080
15	Gasherbrum I	Pakistan	26,470	8,070
16	Broad, highest peak	Pakistan	26,400	8,050
17	Gasherbrum II	Pakistan	26,360	8,030
18	Gosainthan	China	26,290	8,010
19	Broad, middle peak	Pakistan	26,250	8,000
20	Gasherbrum III	Pakistan	26,090	7,950
21	Annapurna II	Nepal	26,040	7,940
22	Gasherbrum IV	Pakistan	26,000	7,930
23	Gyachung Kang	China, Nepal	25,990	7,927
24	Nanga Parbat II	Pakistan	25,950	7,910
25	Kangbachen	India, Nepal	25,930	7,909
26	Man slu, east pinnacle	Nepal	25,900	7,900
27	Distaghil Sar	Pakistan	25,870	7,890
28	Nuptse	Nepal	25,850	7,880
29	Himachuh	Nepal	25,800	7,860
30	Khiangyang Kish	Pakistan	25,760	7,850

H ⊕ HIGHEST MOUNTAIN PEAKS, BY CONTINENT (continued)

ASIA (continued)

Rank	Name	Country	Elevation (ft)	Elevation (m)
31	Ngojumba Ri	China, Nepal	25,720	7,847
32	Dakura	Nepal	25,710	7,842
33	Masherbrum II	Pakistan	25,660	7,826
34	Nanda Devi, west peak	India	25,650	7,823
35	Nanga Parbat III	Pakistan	25,650	7,823
36	Rakaposhi	Pakistan	25,550	7,793
37	Batura Mustagh I	Pakistan	25,540	7,790
38	GasherbrumV	Pakistan	25,500	7,770
39	Kamet	China, India	25,440	7,760

EUROPE

Rank	Name	Country	Elevation (ft)	Elevation (m)
1	El'brus (Elborus), west peak	Russia	18,481	5,633
2	El'brus (Elborus), east peak	Russia	18,360	5,590
3	Shkhara	Georgia, Russia	17,064	5,205
4	Dykh, west peak	Russia	17,050	5,200
5	Dykh, east peak	Russia	16,900	5,150
6	Koshtan	Russia	16,880	5,148
7	Pushkina	Russia	16,730	5,100
8	Kazbek, east peak	Georgia	16,526	5,040
9	Dzhangi	Georgia	16,520	5,039
10	Katyn	Georgia, Russia	16,310	4,975
11	Shota Rustaveli	Georgia, Russia	16,270	4,962
12	Mizhirgi, west peak	Russia	16,170	4,932
13	Mizhirgi, east peak	Russia	16,140	4,923
14	Kundyum-Mizhirgi	Russia	16,010	4,880
15	Gestola	Georgia, Russia	15,930	4,860
16	Tetnuld	Georgia, Russia	15,920	4,850
17	Mont Blanc, main peak	France, Italy	15,772	4,810
18	Dzhimariy	Georgia	15,680	4,780
19	Adish	Georgia, Russia	15,570	4,749
20	Courmayer (Mont Blanc)	France, Italy	15,577	4,748
21	Ushba	Georgia	15,450	4,710

H ⊕ HIGHEST MOUNTAIN PEAKS, BY CONTINENT *(continued)*				
NORTH AMERICA				
RANK	**NAME**	**COUNTRY**	**ELEVATION (FT)**	**ELEVATION (M)**
1	McKinley (Denali), south peak	U.S.A.	20,323	6,194
2	Logan, central peak	Canada	19,550	5,959
3	Logan, west peak	Canada	19,470	5,930
4	McKinley (Denali), north peak	U.S.A.	19,470	5,930
5	Logan, east peak	Canada	19,420	5,920
6	Pico de Orizaba	Mexico	18,701	5,700
7	Logan, north peak	Canada	18,270	5,570
8	Saint Elias	U.S.A., Canada	18,010	5,490
9	Popocatepetl	Mexico	17,887	5,452
10	Foraker	U.S.A.	17,400	5,300
11	Ixtacihuatl	Mexico	17,342	5,286
12	Queen	Canada	17,300	5,270
13	Lucania	Canada	17,150	5,230
14	King	Canada	16,970	5,170
15	Steele	Canada	16,640	5,070
16	Bona	U.S.A.	16,500	5,033
17	Blackburn, highest peak	U.S.A.	16,390	5,000
18	Blackburn, southeast peak	U.S.A.	16,290	4,968
19	Sanford	U.S.A.	16,240	4,950
20	Wood	Canada	15,880	4,840
OCEANIA				
RANK	**NAME**	**COUNTRY**	**ELEVATION (FT)**	**ELEVATION (M)**
1	Puncak Jaya	Indonesia	16,503	5,033
2	Daam	Indonesia	16,150	4,926
3	Pilimsit	Indonesia	15,750	4,800
4	Trikora	Indonesia	15,580	4,752
5	Mandala	Indonesia	15,420	4,700

H ⊕ HIGHEST MOUNTAIN PEAKS, BY CONTINENT (continued)

OCEANIA (continued)

RANK	NAME	COUNTRY	ELEVATION (FT)	ELEVATION (M)
6	Wisnumurti	Indonesia	15,080	4,590
7	Yamin	Indonesia	14,860	4,530
8	Wilhelm	Papua New Guinea	14,793	4,509
9	Kubor	Papua New Guinea	14,300	4,360
10	Herbert	Papua New Guinea	14,000	4,270

SOUTH AMERICA

RANK	NAME	COUNTRY	ELEVATION (FT)	ELEVATION (M)
1	Aconcagua	Argentina	22,835	6,960
2	Ojos del Salado, southeast peak	Argentina, Chile	22,573	6,880
3	Bonete	Argentina	22,550	6,870
4	Tupungato	Argentina, Chile	22,310	6,800
5	Pissis	Argentina	22,240	6,780
6	Mercedario	Argentina	22,210	6,770
7	Huascarán, south peak	Peru	22,204	6,768
8	Llullaillaco	Argentina, Chile	22,100	6,730
9	Libertador	Argentina	22,050	6,720
10	Ojos del Salado, northwest peak	Argentina, Chile	22,050	6,720
11	Gonzalez, highest peak	Argentina, Chile	21,850	6,664
12	Huascarán, north peak	Peru	21,840	6,661
13	Muerto	Argentina, Chile	21,820	6,655
14	Yerupaja, north peak	Peru	21,760	6,630
15	Incahuasi	Argentina, Chile	21,700	6,610
16	Galan	Argentina	21,650	6,600
17	Tres Cruces	Argentina, Chile	21,540	6,560
18	Gonzalez, north peak	Argentina, Chile	21,490	6,550
19	Sajama	Bolivia	21,463	6,542
20	Yerupaja, south peak	Peru	21,380	6,510
21	Chimborazo	Ecuador	20,681	6,267

I ⊕ HIGHEST VOLCANOES OF THE WORLD, BY HEIGHT

All measurements are approximate.

Rank	Name	Continent	Country	Elevation (ft)	Elevation (m)
1	Tupungato	South America	Chile	22,310	6,800
2	Tipas	South America	Argentina	21,845	6,660
3	Cerro el Condor	South America	Argentina	21,425	6,532
4	Antofallo	South America	Argentina	20,008	6,100
5	Guallatiri	South America	Chile	19,882	6,060
6	Lascar	South America	Chile	19,652	5,990
7	Cotopaxi	South America	Ecuador	19,344	5,896
8	Kilimanjaro	Africa	Tanzania	19,341	5,895
9	El Misti	South America	Peru	19,031	5,801
10	Pico de Orizaba	North America	Mexico	18,701	5,700
11	Tolima	South America	Colombia	18,425	5,616
12	Popocatépetl	North America	Mexico	17,887	5,452
13	Yucamani	South America	Peru	17,860	5,444
14	Sangay	South America	Ecuador	17,159	5,230
15	Tungurahua	South America	Ecuador	16,684	5,085
16	Cotacachi	South America	Ecuador	16,250	4,939
17	Purace	South America	Colombia	15,604	4,756
18	Klyuchevskaya	Asia	Russia	15,584	4,750
19	Kronotskaya	Asia	Russia	15,580	4,749
20	Shiveluch	Asia	Russia	15,580	4,749
21	Pichincha	South America	Ecuador	15,173	4,625
22	Karasimbi	Africa	Dem. Rep. of the Congo	14,873	4,507
23	Rainier	North America	USA	14,410	4,395
24	Wrangell	North America	USA (Alaska)	14,163	4,317
25	Colima	North America	Mexico	13,993	4,265
26	Tajumulco	North America	Guatemala	13,845	4,220
27	Mauna Kea	North America	USA (Hawaii)	13,796	4,205
28	Mauna Loa	North America	USA (Hawaii)	13,680	4,170
29	Cameroon	Africa	Cameroon	13,353	4,070
30	Tacana	North America	Guatemala	13,300	4,053
31	Kerintji	Asia	Indonesia	12,483	3,805
32	Erebus	Antarctica	Antarctica	12,448	3,794
33	Fuji	Asia	Japan	12,388	3,776
34	Fuego	North America	Guatemala	12,346	3,763

	I ⊕ HIGHEST VOLCANOES OF THE WORLD, BY HEIGHT *(continued)*				
All measurements are approximate.					
RANK	**NAME**	**CONTINENT**	**COUNTRY**	**ELEVATION (FT)**	**ELEVATION (M)**
35	Agua	North America	Guatemala	12,307	3,751
36	Rindjani	Asia	Indonesia	12,224	3,726
37	Pico de Teide	Africa	Spain (Canary Is.)	12,198	3,718
38	Tolbachik	Asia	Russia	12,077	3,682
39	Semeru	Asia	Indonesia	12,060	3,676
40	Ichinskaya	Asia	Russia	11,800	3,621
41	Atitlan	North America	Guatemala	11,650	3,551
42	Torbert	North America	USA (Alaska)	11,450	3,480
43	Nyirangongo	Africa	Dem. Rep. of the Congo	11,365	3,465
44	Kroyakskaya	Asia	Russia	11,336	3,456
45	Irazu	South America	Costa Rica	11,260	3,432
46	Slamet	Asia	Indonesia	11,247	3,428
47	Spurr	North America	USA (Alaska)	11,137	3,385
48	Lautaro	South America	Chile	11,120	3,380
49	Sumbing	Asia	Indonesia	11,060	3,371
50	Raung	Asia	Indonesia	10,932	3,332
51	Etna	Europe	Italy	10,902	3,323
52	Baker	North America	USA	10,778	3,285
53	Lassen	North America	USA	10,492	3,187
54	Dempo	Asia	Indonesia	10,390	3,158
55	Sundoro	Asia	Indonesia	10,367	3,151
56	Agung	Asia	Indonesia	10,337	3,142
57	Prahu	Asia	Indonesia	10,285	3,137
58	Llaima	South America	Chile	10,245	3,125
59	Redoubt	North America	USA (Alaska)	10,197	3,108
60	Tjiremai	Asia	Indonesia	10,098	3,078
61	One-Take	Asia	Japan	10,056	3,067
62	Nyamulagira	Africa	Dem. Rep. of the Congo	10,026	3,056
63	Iliamna	North America	USA (Alaska)	10,016	3,053
64	Ardjuno-Welirang	Asia	Indonesia	9,968	3,038
65	San Pedro	North America	Guatemala	9,902	3,020
66	Gede	Asia	Indonesia	9,705	2,958
67	Zhupanovsky	Asia	Russia	9,705	2,958
68	Apo	Asia	Philippines	9,692	2,954

I ⊕ HIGHEST VOLCANOES OF THE WORLD, BY HEIGHT *(continued)*					
All measurements are approximate.					
RANK	**NAME**	**CONTINENT**	**COUNTRY**	**ELEVATION (FT)**	**ELEVATION (M)**
69	Merapi	Asia	Indonesia	9,551	2,911
70	Marapi	Asia	Indonesia	9,479	2,891
71	Geureudong	Asia	Indonesia	9,459	2,885
72	Bezymianny	Asia	Russia	9,449	2,882
73	Shishaldin	North America	USA (Alaska)	9,372	2,856
74	Tambora	Asia	Indonesia	9,350	2,850
75	Villarrica	South America	Chile	9,318	2,840
76	Fogo	Africa	Cape Verde	9,281	2,829
77	Ruapehu	Oceania	New Zealand	9,175	2,796
78	Peuetsagoe	Asia	Indonesia	9,115	2,780
79	Paricutin	North America	Mexico	9,100	2,775
80	Big Ben	Antarctica	Heard Island (dependency of Australia)	9,006	2,745
81	Balbi	Oceania	Papua New Guinea	8,999	2,743
82	Avachinskaya	Asia	Russia	8,987	2,741
83	Melbourne	Antarctica	Antarctica	8,957	2,732
84	Poas	North America	Costa Rica	8,872	2,704
85	Papandajan	Asia	Indonesia	8,744	2,665
86	Piton de la Faournaise	Africa	Reunion (dependency of France)	8,626	2,631
87	Pacaya	North America	Guatemala	8,367	2,552
88	Mt. St. Helens	North America	USA	8,366	2,550
89	Asama	Asia	Japan	8,300	2,530
90	Pavlof	North America	USA (Alaska)	8,261	2,518
91	Veniaminof	North America	USA (Alaska)	8,220	2,507
92	Mayon	Asia	Philippines	8,077	2,462
93	Sinabung	Asia	Indonesia	8,066	2,460
94	Yake Dake	Asia	Japan	8,049	2,455
95	Tandikat	Asia	Indonesia	7,993	2,438
96	Canalaon	Asia	Philippines	7,984	2,435
97	Shoshuenco	South America	Chile	7,941	2,422
98	Idjen	Asia	Indonesia	7,823	2,386
99	Izalco	North America	El Salvador	7,828	2,386
100	Karthala	Africa	Comoros	7,746	2,361

J ⊕ RIVERS OF THE WORLD 1,000 MILES (1,600 KILOMETERS) OR LONGER

All measurements are approximate.

RANK	NAME	CONTINENT	COUNTRY	LENGTH (MI)	LENGTH (KM)
1	Nile	Africa	Egypt, Sudan, Uganda	4,160	6,693
2	Amazon	South America	Brazil, Colombia, Peru, Venezuela	3,900	6,280
3	Mississippi-Missouri	North America	U.S.A.	3,860	6,211
4	Chang Jiang (Yangtze or Yangtse)	Asia	China	3,434	5,525
5	Ob'-Irtysh	Asia	Kazakhstan, Russia	3,335	5,380
6	Paraná	South America	Argentina, Brazil, Paraguay	3,030	4,870
7	Huang He (Huang-ho or Yellow)	Asia	China	2,903	4,671
8	Irtysh	Asia	Kazakhstan, Russia	2,760	4,441
9	Lena	Asia	Russia	2,734	4,400
10	Amur	Asia	China, Russia	2,719	4,350
11	Congo (Zaire)	Africa	Angola, Dem. Rep. of the Congo, Rep. of the Congo	2,700	4,344
12	Mackenzie	North America	Canada	2,635	4,290
13	Mekong River (Lan ts'ang chiang or Lancang Jiang)	Asia	Cambodia, China, Laos, Myanmar, Thailand, Vietnam	2,600	4,200
14	Niger	Africa	Benin, Guinea, Mali, Niger, Nigeria	2,594	4,184
15	Yenisey	Asia	Russia	2,566	4,129
16	Missouri	North America	U.S.A.	2,466	3,968
17	Mississippi	North America	U.S.A.	2,348	3,787
18	Volga	Europe	Russia	2,293	3,689
19	Ob'	Asia	Russia	2,270	3,650
20	Euphrates	Asia	Iraq, Syria, Turkey	2,235	3,596
21	Purus	South America	Brazil, Peru	2,100	3,380
22	Madeira	South America	Brazil	2,013	3,241
23	Lower Tunguska	Asia	Russia	2,000	3,220
24	Indus	Asia	Pakistan	1,988	3,200
25	São Francisco	South America	Brazil	1,988	3,199
26	Yukon	North America	Canada, U.S.A.	1,980	3,180
27	Rio Grande	North America	Mexico, U.S.A.	1,885	3,034

	J ⊕ RIVERS OF THE WORLD 1,000 MILES (1,600 KILOMETERS) OR LONGER *(continued)*				
All measurements are approximate.					
Rank	**Name**	**Continent**	**Country**	**Length (mi)**	**Length (km)**
28	Brahmaputra (Jamuna)	Asia	Bangladesh, China, India	1,800	2,900
29	Danube	Europe	Austria, Bulgaria, Croatia, Germany, Hungary, Romania, Ukraine, Slovakia, Serbia-Montenegro	1,775	2,857
30	Salween	Asia	China, Myanmar	1,770	2,849
31	Darling	Australia	Australia	1,702	2,739
32	Tocantins	South America	Brazil	1,677	2,698
33	Nelson	North America	Canada	1,660	2,671
34	Vilyuy	Asia	Russia	1,650	2,650
35	Zambezi	Africa	Angola, Mozambique, Namibia, Zambia, Zimbabwe	1,650	2,650
36	Murray	Australia	Australia	1,609	2,589
37	Paraguay	South America	Argentina, Brazil, Paraguay	1,584	2,549
38	Amu Dar'ya	Asia	Afghanistan, Tajikistan, Turkmenistan, Uzbekistan	1,580	2,540
39	Kolyma	Asia	Russia	1,562	2,513
40	Ganges	Asia	Bangladesh, India	1,560	2,510
41	Ishim	Asia	Kazakhstan, Russia	1,520	2,450
42	Ural	Asia	Kazakhstan, Russia	1,510	2,430
43	Japurá	South America	Brazil, Colombia	1,500	2,414
44	Arkansas	North America	U.S.A.	1,460	2,350
45	Colorado	North America	U.S.A.	1,450	2,330
46	Dnieper	Europe	Belarus, Russia, Ukraine	1,420	2,290
47	Negro	South America	Brazil, Colombia, Venezuela	1,400	2,250
48	Ubangi	Africa	Central African Rep., Dem. Rep. of the Congo, Rep. of the Congo	1,400	2,253
49	Aldan	Asia	Russia	1,390	2,240
50	Columbia-Snake	North America	Canada, U.S.A.	1,390	2,240
51	Syr Dar'ya	Asia	Kazakhstan, Kyrgyzstan, Uzbekistan	1,370	2,200

	J ⊕ RIVERS OF THE WORLD 1,000 MILES (1,600 KILOMETERS) OR LONGER (continued)				
	All measurements are approximate.				
RANK	**NAME**	**CONTINENT**	**COUNTRY**	**LENGTH (MI)**	**LENGTH (KM)**
52	Araguaia	South America	Brazil	1,366	2,198
53	Olenek	Asia	Russia	1,350	2,170
54	Irrawaddy	Asia	Myanmar	1,350	2,170
55	Kasai	Africa	Angola, Dem. Rep of the Congo	1,338	2,153
56	Ohio-Allegheny	North America	U.S.A.	1,310	2,109
57	Tarim	Asia	China	1,300	2,090
58	Orange	Africa	Lesotho, Namibia, South Africa	1,300	2,090
59	Orinoco	South America	Venezuela	1,281	2,061
60	Shabeelle	Africa	Ethiopia, Somalia	1,250	2,011
61	Xingu	South America	Brazil	1,230	1,979
62	Columbia	North America	Canada, U.S.A.	1,214	1,953
63	Mamoré	South America	Bolivia	1,200	1,931
64	Tigris	Asia	Iraq, Turkey	1,180	1,900
65	Northern Dvina	Europe	Russia	1,160	1,870
66	Don	Europe	Russia	1,153	1,860
67	Angara	Asia	Russia	1,151	1,852
68	Kama	Europe	Russia	1,120	1,800
69	Indigirka	Asia	Russia	1,112	1,789
70	Pechora	Europe	Russia	1,112	1,789
71	Limpopo	Africa	Botswana, South Africa, Mozambique	1,100	1,770
72	Sénégal	Africa	Guinea, Mali, Mauritania, Senegal	1,015	1,663
73	Salado	South America	Argentina	1,110	1,770
74	Guaporé	South America	Bolivia, Brazil	1,087	1,749
75	Tobol	Asia	Kazakhstan, Russia	1,042	1,677
76	Snake	North America	U.S.A.	1,038	1,670
77	Red	North America	U.S.A.	1,018	1,638
78	Churchill	North America	Canada	1,000	1,613
79	Jubba	Africa	Ethiopia, Somalia	1,000	1,613
80	Okavango	Africa	Angola, Botswana	1,000	1,613
81	Pilcomayo	South America	Argentina, Bolivia, Paraguay	1,000	1,613
82	Uruguay	South America	Uruguay	1,000	1,613

K ⊕ WATERFALLS OF THE WORLD, BY HEIGHT

All measurements are approximate. If a waterfall has multiple cascades they are listed separately.

Rank	Name	Continent	Country	Height (ft)	Height (m)
1	Angel (upper falls)	South America	Venezuela	2,648	807
2	Utigord	Europe	Norway	2,625	800
3	Monge	Europe	Norway	2,539	774
4	Mtarazi (Mutarazi)	Africa	Mozambique, Zimbabwe	2,500	760
5	Itatinga	South America	Brazil	2,060	628
6	Cuquenán (Kukenaam)	South America	Guyana, Venezuela	2,000	610
7	Kahiwa	North America	U.S.A. (Hawaii)	1,750	533
8	Tysse (Tusse)	Europe	Norway	1,749	533
9	Maradalsfos	Europe	Norway	1,696	517
10	Ribbon	North America	U.S.A.	1,612	491
11	Roraima	South America	Guyana	1,500	457
12	Della	North America	Canada	1,445	440
13	Yosemite, Upper	North America	U.S.A.	1,430	436
14	Gavarnie	Europe	France	1,385	422
15	Tugela (highest falls in chain)	Africa	South Africa	1,350	411
16	Krimml	Europe	Austria	1,250	380
17	Silver Strand	North America	U.S.A.	1,170	357
18	Basaseachic	North America	Mexico	1,020	311
19	Staubbach	Europe	Switzerland	980	299
20	Vettis	Europe	Norway	902	275
21	King George VI	South America	Guyana	850	260
22	Wallaman	Oceania	Australia	850	260
23	Takakkaw	North America	Canada	838	254
24	Hunlen	North America	Canada	830	253
25	Jog (Gersoppa)	Asia	India	830	253

K ⊕ WATERFALLS OF THE WORLD, BY HEIGHT (continued)

All measurements are approximate. If a waterfall has multiple cascades they are listed separately.

Rank	Name	Continent	Country	Height (ft)	Height (m)
26	Skykje	Europe	Norway	820	250
27	Sutherland, Upper	Oceania	New Zealand	815	248
28	Sutherland, Middle	Oceania	New Zealand	751	229
29	Kaieteur	South America	Guyana	741	226
30	Wollomombi	Oceania	Australia	726	220
31	Kalambo	Africa	Tanzania, Zambia	704	215
32	Fairy	North America	U.S.A.	700	213
33	Feather	North America	U.S.A.	640	195
34	Maletsunyane	Africa	Lesotho	630	192
35	Bridalveil	North America	U.S.A.	620	189
36	Multnomah	North America	U.S.A.	620	189
37	Panther	North America	Canada	600	183
38	Voringfoss	Europe	Norway	597	182
39	Nevada	North America	U.S.A.	594	181
40	Angel, Lower	South America	Venezuela	564	172
41	Augrabies (Aughrabies)	Africa	South Africa	480	146
42	Tully	Oceania	Australia	450	137
43	Helmcken	North America	Canada	450	137
44	Nachi	Asia	Japan	430	131
45	Tequendama	South America	Colombia	427	130
46	Bridal Veil	North America	U.S.A.	400	122
47	Illilouette	North America	U.S.A.	370	113
48	Yosemite, Lower	North America	U.S.A.	320	98
49	Twin	North America	Canada	260	80

APPENDIX ⊕ L

L ⊕ LAKES OF THE WORLD, BY AREA

All measurements are approximate.

RANK	NAME	CONTINENT	COUNTRY	AREA (SQ MI)	AREA (SQ KM)
1	Caspian Sea	Asia	Azerbaijan, Iran, Kazakhstan, Russia, Turkmenistan	143,000	371,000
2	Superior	North America	Canada, U.S.A.	31,820	82,732
3	Victoria	Africa	Uganda, Tanzania, Kenya	26,828	69,484
4	Aral Sea	Asia	Kazakhstan, Uzbekistan	24,900	64,500
5	Huron	North America	Canada, U.S.A.	23,000	59,570
6	Michigan	North America	U.S.A.	22,400	58,020
7	Tanganyika	Africa	Burundi, Dem. Republic of the Congo, Tanzania, Zambia	12,700	32,020
8	Baikal	Asia	Russia	12,160	31,500
9	Great Bear	North America	Canada	12,095	31,328
10	Great Slave	North America	Canada	11,030	28,570
11	Erie	North America	Canada, U.S.A.	9,920	25,690
12	Winnipeg	North America	Canada	9,420	24,390
13	Malawi	Africa	Malawi, Mozambique, Tanzania,	8,680	22,490
14	Ontario	North America	Canada, U.S.A.	7,440	19,240
15	Balkhash	Asia	Kazakhstan	7,030	18,200
16	Ladoga	Russia	Russia	7,000	18,130
17	Maracaibo	South America	Venezuela	5,020	13,010
18	Chad	Africa	Cameroon, Chad, Niger, Nigeria	4,000–10,000	10,360–25,900
19	Embalse del Río Negro	South America	Uruguay	4,000	10,360
20	Patos	South America	Brazil	3,920	10,153
21	Onega	Europe	Russia	3,750	9,720
22	Eyre	Australia	Australia	3,668	9,500
23	Volta	Africa	Ghana	3,276	8,485
24	Titicaca	South America	Bolivia, Peru	3,200	8,288
25	Nicaragua	South America	Nicaragua	3,150	8,160
26	Athabasca	North America	Canada	3,060	7,940
27	Reindeer	North America	Canada	2,570	6,650

L ⊕ LAKES OF THE WORLD, BY AREA (continued)

All measurements are approximate.

Rank	Name	Continent	Country	Area (sq mi)	Area (sq km)
28	Smallwood Reservoir	North America	Canada	2,500	6,460
29	Turkana (Rudolf)	Africa	Ethiopia, Kenya	2,473	6,405
30	Issyk Kul	Asia	Kyrgyzstan	2,360	6,100
31	Torrens	Australia	Australia	2,230	5,780
32	Albert	Africa	Dem. Republic of the Congo, Uganda	2,160	5,590
33	Vanern	Europe	Sweden	2,160	5,580
34	Netilling	North America	Canada	2,140	5,540
35	Winnipegosis	North America	Canada	2,070	5,370
36	Nasser	Africa	Egypt, Sudan	2,026	5,248
37	Bangweulu	Africa	Zambia	1,930	5,000
38	Chott el Djerid	Africa	Tunisia	1,930	5,000
39	Urmia	Asia	Iran	1,879	4,868
40	Nipigon	North America	Canada	1,870	4,850
41	Gairdner	Australia	Australia	1,840	4,770
42	Manitoba	North America	Canada	1,800	4,660
43	Kyoga	Africa	Uganda	1,710	4,430
44	Khanka	Asia	China, Russia	1,700	4,400
45	Saimaa	Europe	Finland	1,700	4,403
46	Mweru	Africa	Dem. Republic of the Congo	1,680	4,350
47	Great Salt	North America	U.S.A.	1,680	4,350
48	Qinghai (Koko)	Asia	China	1,625	4,209
49	Woods	North America	Canada	1,580	4,100
50	Taymyr	Asia	Russia	1,540	3,990
51	Nasser	Africa	Egypt	1,522	3,942
52	Orumiyeh	Asia	Iran	1,500	3,880
53	Dubawnt	North America	Canada	1,480	3,830
54	Van	Asia	Turkey	1,430	3,710
55	Tana	Africa	Ethiopia	1,390	3,600
56	Peipus	Europe	Estonia, Russia	1,386	3,555
57	Uvs	Asia	Mongolia	1,300	3,366

M ⊕ LAKES OF THE WORLD, BY DEPTH

All measurements are approximate.

RANK	LAKE	CONTINENT	COUNTRY	DEPTH (FT)	DEPTH (M)
1	Baikal	Asia	Russia	5,315	1,621
2	Tanganyika	Africa	Burundi, Tanzania, Dem. Congo (ROC), Zambia	4,825	1,471
3	Caspian Sea	Asia	Azerbaijan, Iran, Kazakhstan, Russia, Turkmenistan	3,363	1,025
4	Malawi	Africa	Malawi, Tanzania, Mozambique	2,316	706
5	Issyk Kul	Asia	Kyrgyzstan	2,303	702
6	Great Slave	North America	Canada	2,015	614
7	Matana	Asia	Indonesia	1,936	590
8	Crater	North America	U.S.A.	1,932	589
9	Toba	Asia	Indonesia	1,736	529
10	Hornindals	Europe	Norway	1,686	514
11	Sarez	Asia	Tajikistan	1,657	505
12	Tahoe	North America	U.S.A.	1,645	501
13	Chelan	North America	U.S.A.	1,605	489
14	Kivu	Africa	Rwanda, Congo (DROC)	1,575	480
15	Quesnel	North America	Canada	1,560	475
16	Sals	Europe	Norway	1,522	464
17	Adams	North America	Canada	1,500	457
18	Mjøsa	Europe	Norway	1,473	449
19	Manapuri	Oceania	New Zealand	1,453	443
20	Poso	Asia	Indonesia	1,444	440
21	Nahuel Huapi	South America	Argentina	1,437	438
22	Dead Sea	Asia	Israel, Jordan	1,421	433
23	Tazawa	Asia	Japan	1,394	425
24	Great Bear	North America	Canada	1,356	413
25	Como	Europe	Italy	1,352	412
26	Superior	North America	Canada, U.S.A.	1,333	406
27	Hawea	Asia	New Zealand	1,286	392
28	Wakatipu	Asia	New Zealand	1,240	378

	M ⊕ LAKES OF THE WORLD, BY DEPTH *(continued)*				
All measurements are approximate.					
RANK	**LAKE**	**CONTINENT**	**COUNTRY**	**DEPTH (FT)**	**DEPTH (M)**
29	Suldals	Europe	Norway	1,234	376
30	Maggiore	Europe	Italy, Switzerland	1,221	372
31	Fyres	Europe	Norway	1,211	369
32	Chilko	North America	Canada	1,200	366
33	Pend Oreille	North America	U.S.A.	1,200	366
34	Shikotsu	Asia	Japan	1,191	363
35	Powell	North America	Canada	1,174	358
36	Llanquihue	South America	Chile	1,148	350
37	Garda	Europe	Italy	1,135	346
38	Towada	Asia	Japan	1,096	334
39	Wanaka	Asia	New Zealand	1,086	325
40	Bandak	Europe	Norway	1,066	325
41	Telestskoya	Asia	Russia	1,066	325
42	Eutsuk	North America	Canada	1,060	323
43	Atitlan	North America	Guatemala	1,050	320
44	Lunde	Europe	Norway	1,030	314
45	Geneva	Europe	France, Switzerland	1,017	310
46	Morar	Europe	Scotland	1,017	310
47	Kurile	Asia	Russia	1,004	306
48	Walker	North America	U.S.A.	1,000	305
49	Titicaca	South America	Bolivia, Peru	997	304
50	Argentino	South America	Argentina	984	300
51	Iliamna	North America	U.S.A.	980	299
52	Tyrifjorden	Europe	Norway	968	295
53	Lugano	Europe	Italy, Switzerland	945	288
54	Takla	North America	Canada	941	287
55	Ohrid	Europe	Albania, Serbia-Montenegro	938	286
56	Atlin	North America	Canada	930	283
57	Nuyakuk	North America	U.S.A.	930	283
58	Michigan	North America	U.S.A.	923	285
59	Harrison	North America	Canada	916	279
60	Te Anau	Oceania	New Zealand	906	276

Seven Wonders of the Ancient World

1 ⊕ The pyramids of Egypt

Constructed between 2700 and 2500 B.C., the pyramids are the last surviving structures of the Seven Wonders of the Ancient World. The largest of the pyramids, which rises over 137 meters (450 feet), was built as a tomb to house the body of Pharaoh Khufu. Historians believe that it must have taken over twenty years to build with over 100,000 slave laborers.

2 ⊕ The gardens of Semiramis at Babylon

The existence of these gardens is reputed, but according to fable they existed around 600 B.C. They are said to have been outside on a brick terrace 23 meters (75 feet) above the ground, encompassing an area of 37 square meters (400 square feet).

3 ⊕ The statue of Zeus at Olympia

Constructed around 450 B.C. by the sculptor Phidias, this 12-meter (40-foot) high statue is of an ivory Zeus wearing a robe of gold, seated atop a throne. In his right hand was Nike, his messenger and a symbol of victory, in his left hand was the scepter signifying his rule over the gods and humankind, and atop his head was a wreathed crown.

4 ⊕ The temple of Artemis at Ephesus

Built around 550 B.C. to celebrate the goddess of the hunt, this temple was one of the largest in ancient times. Beneath its tile-covered roof were rows of columns believed to be more than 12 meters (40 feet) high, leading to a marble sanctuary. The original temple was destroyed by fire in 356 B.C., but another temple was built on the same foundation. This temple was also burned, but the foundation still remains. Remnants of the second temple can be found at London's British Museum.

5 ⊕ The mausoleum at Halicarnassus

Located in southwestern Turkey, this enormous white marble tomb was contructed to house the body of Mausolus, a king of Persian Empire. It was constructed around 350 B.C. by the Greek architects Satuyrus and Pythius and became so well known that the term mausoleum was created to signify any large tomb. An earthquake in the 15th century caused significant damage to the tomb, which was eventually disassembled. Several of its exterior sculptures can be seen in London's British Museum.

6 ⊕ The Colossus at Rhodes

Constructed around 200 B.C. by the Greek sculptor Chares, this 36-meter (120-foot) bronze statue was meant to honor the sun god Helios and celebrate the unity of the city-states of Rhodes. The statue was hollow, supported by stone blocks and iron bars inside its frame. It was destroyed by an earthquake only fifty-six years after its completion.

7 ⊕ The Pharos (lighthouse) of Alexandria or the Walls of Babylon

This lighthouse, completed near 270 B.C., was, at the time, one of the tallest buildings in the known world. Standing over 122 meters (400 feet) high, it guided sailors to the shores of Alexandria, then ruled by King Ptolemy II.

Seven Wonders of the Natural World

1 ⊕ Grand Canyon

Created after millions of years of erosion from the Colorado River and its tributaries, this Arizona landmark is visited by millions of tourists each year.

2 ⊕ Paricutin Volcano

Although it is not one of the largest volcanoes in Mexico, Paricutin has taken a place on the list of natural wonders following its birth in 1943. The eruption spanned ten years and covered about 2.6 square meters (10 square miles). No one was killed from the lava and ash, but it destroyed agricultural land and seriously affected the lives of those living nearby.

3 ⊕ The Harbor at Rio de Janeiro

Located on the east coast of Brazil, the harbor overlooks the Guanabara Bay and the Atlantic Ocean on one side, and mountains on the other. Discovered by Portuguese navigators in 1502, this area houses a huge carnival each year.

4 ⊕ Northern Lights

The northern lights, or aurora borealis, have fascinated people for centuries. Seen as souls, heavenly signs, or even messages from the dead, these shimmering light displays are caused by the interaction of solar winds with Earth's magnetic field. A similar phenomenon occurs in the southern hemisphere as well, but only the northern lights are classified as a natural wonder.

5 ⊕ Mt. Everest

Formed from the collision of Asia and India over 60 million years ago, the Himalayas house Everest, the tallest mountain on Earth. Located in Nepal near the Tibetan border, this snowy peak has fascinated and challenged many climbers and non-climbers alike.

6 ⊕ Victoria Falls

The largest waterfalls in the world, Victoria Falls has a drop of more than 99 meters (325 feet). Flowing from the Zambezi River, the falls were named for Queen Victoria by David Livingstone in 1855, when he became the first European to gaze upon them.

7 ⊕ The Great Barrier Reef

The Great Barrier Reef extends over 1,998 kilometers (1,242 miles) on the northeast coast of Australia. The reef is quite delicate, being comprised of the skeletons of genera-tions of marine life that lived just under the water's surface. The area is home to exotic coral, which is greatly affected by any human or natural interference, and a wide variety of marine life

Selected Sources for Further Study

Books

Arthus-Bertrand, Yann. *Earth from Above for Young Readers.* New York: Harry N. Abrams, 2002.

The Blackbirch Kid's Visual Reference of the World. Woodbridge, CT: Blackbirch Press, 2001.

Brooks, Felicity. *The Usborne First Encyclopedia of Our World.* Tulsa, OK: EDC Publishing, 1999.

Ciovacco, Justine. *The Encyclopedia of Explorers and Adventurers.* New York: Franklin Watts, 2003.

Cunha, Stephen F. *National Geographic Bee Official Study Guide.* Washington, DC: National Geographic, 2002.

Encyclopedia of World Geography. New York: Marshall Cavendish, 2001.

Forina, Rose. *Amazing Hands-on Map Activities.* New York: Scholastic Professional Books, 2001.

Fox, Mary Virginia. *South America.* Chicago, IL: Heinemann Library, 2001.

Furstinger, Nancy. *Get Ready! For Social Studies: Geography.* New York McGraw-Hill, 2002.

Gough, Barry M., editor. *Geography and Exploration: Biographical Portraits.* New York: Scribner, 2001.

Lands and Peoples. Danbury, CT: Grolier Educational, 2003.

Nelson, Robin. *Where Is My Country?* Minneapolis, MN: Lerner Publications, 2002.

O'Brien, Patrick K., editor. *Atlas of World History.* New York: Oxford University Press, 2002.

Oldershaw, Cally. *Atlas of Geology and Landforms.* New York: Franklin Watts, 2001.

Rasmussen, R. Kent, editor. *World Geography.* Pasadena, CA: Salem Press, 2001.

Robson, Pam. *People and Places.* Brookfield, CT: Copper Beech Books, 2001.

Robson, Pam. *Rivers and Seas.* Brookfield, CT: Copper Beech Books, 2001.

Rosenberg, Matthew T. *Geography Bee Complete Preparation Handbook: 1,001 Questions.* Prima Publishing, 2002.

Striveildi, Cheryl. *Continents.* Edina, MN: Abdo Publishing Company, 2003.

Sutcliffe, Andrea. *The New York Public Library Amazing World Geography: A Book of Answers for Kids.* New Jersey: Wiley, 2002.

World Adventure. Chicago, IL: World Book, 2000.

Web Sites

Association of American Geographers. http://www.aag.org/Careers/Intro.html, (accessed May 30, 2003).

"Educational Resources for Cartography, Geography, and Related Disciplines," *U.S. Geological Survey.* http://mapping.usgs.gov/www/html/1educate.html (accessed May 30, 2003).

Geographic.org. http://www.geographic.org/ (accessed May 30, 2003).

"Geography and Map Reading Room," *The Library of Congress.* http://www.loc.gov/rr/geogmap/ (accessed May 30, 2003).

"Marco Polo Xpeditions," *National Geographic.* http://www.nationalgeographic.com/xpeditions/ (accessed May 30, 2003).

National Geographic.com. http://www.nationalgeographic.com/index.html (accessed May 30, 2003).

Postcard Geography. http://pcg.cyberbee.com/ (accessed May 30, 2003).

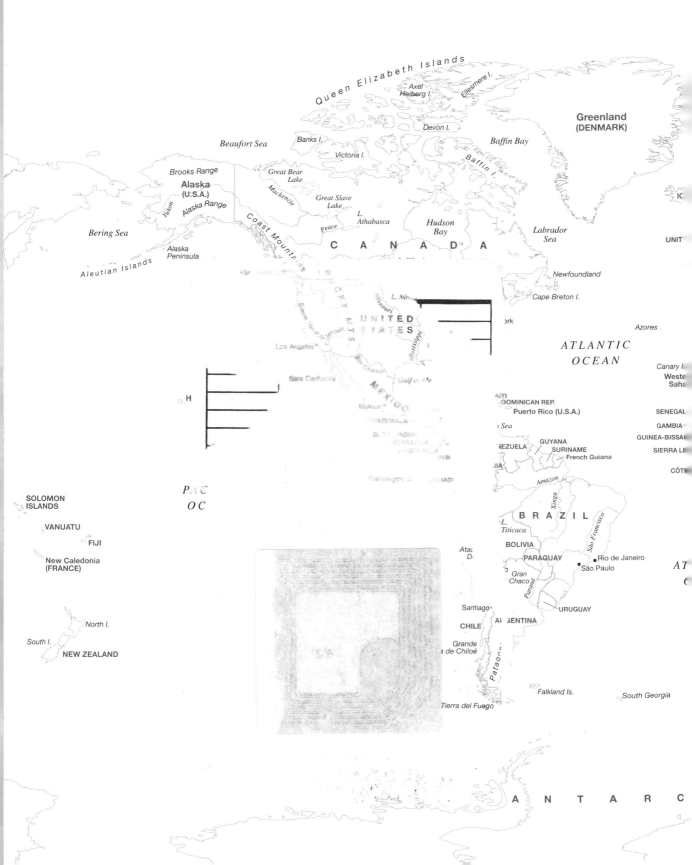